Praise for
Wild Attraction

"Energetics has finally arrived in mainstream Western scientific thought. In *Wild Attraction* it sweeps through the field of relationship science like a tsunami."
— Peter Nelson, PhD, psychologist and social scientist, coeditor of *Transpersonal Knowing: Exploring the Horizon of Consciousness*

"*Wild Attraction* offers insights that mainstream psychology cannot provide. This is an important book with an important message in times when humankind desperately needs to forge new paths to a better future. I place it in the category of 'must read'!"
—Evelin G. Lindner, MD, PhD, author of *Making Enemies* and the forthcoming *Gender and Humiliation*

"I use the Wild Attraction 'facts of life' in my medical practice working with women who report low desire and low arousal—and achieve consistently wonderful results."
—Susan Kay Preslar, MS, FNP, women's sexual health specialist

"Paul and Patty stay true to their scientific/academic base, giving the material a platform of respectability and quality, yet they make it appealing to those of us who are drawn to more esoteric material. This is an important book."
—Don Campbell, president DJ Campbell Advertising

"*Wild Attraction* tells us how to *be* the kind of partner we've always hoped to find. This fascinating book turns every preconception about the nature of relationship topsy-turvy. Get ready to walk around with a new set of eyes!"
—Fayegail Bisaccia, author of *Dancing in My Mother's Slippers*

Wild Attraction

*A Ruthlessly
Practical Guide
to Extraordinary
Relationship*

The Energetic Facts of Life

Paul and Patricia Richards

Ashland, Oregon

Copyright © 2009 by Paul and Patricia Richards.

All rights reserved under International and Pan American copyright conventions. No part of this book may be reproduced or utilized in any form, by electronic, mechanical, or other means, without the prior written permission of the publisher, except for brief quotations embodied in literary articles or reviews.

Wild Attraction and Applied Energetics are registered trademarks of The Senté Center, Inc.

Cover photo by Scott Kurtz
Author photo by Chris Briscoe
Cover and interior design by Confluence Book Services

Library of Congress Cataloging-in-Publication data
Richards, Paul, 1953-
   Wild attraction : the energetic facts of life, a ruthlessly practical guide to extraordinary relationship / by Paul and Patty Richards.
   p. cm.
   ISBN 978-0-9764401-2-3
1. Man-woman relationships. 2. Love. 3. Sex. 4. Mate selection. 5. Sex (Psychology). 6. Sex (Biology). 7. Sex--Social aspects. 8. Spiritual life. 9. Sex--Religious aspects. I. Richards, Patricia Ann. II. Title.

HQ801 .R448 2009
306.7 22--dc22   2008909249

Manufactured in the United States of America
10 9 8 7 6 5 4 3 2 1

For others who shall remain forever nameless
and forever loved…

Contents

Author's Foreword xi

Part I: Head over Heels
1. We Have No Defense 3
2. Energy Is the Realm of Relationship 8
3. Unconscious Telepathy 26
4. Anatomically Incomplete 31
5. The Essence of Attraction 50

Part II: Wrapped in the Wings of Love
6. The Story of All Things 73
7. Being Wild in Ways That Work 86
8. Meeting the Real Needs of the Other Gender 100
9. Necessity Is the Mother of Attention 115
10. There Is No Battle of the Sexes 122

Part III: The Two Sides of the Gender Coin
11. Unsafe, Hobbled, and Aware Males 133
12. Whipped 149
13. Lord, What Fools These Mortals Be 158
14. The Woman in a Bottle 166
15. At a Loss for Words 174
16. Modern Courtly Love and Galadriel 185
17. At the Center of the Universe 190
18. The Aware Female 197
19. The Nature and Inherent Needs of Humans 207

Part IV: Love Is a Wheel
20. The Ultimate Bicycle Built for Two 217
21. The Handlebars: Romantic Power Rituals for
    Extraordinary Relationship 227
22. The Front Wheel: The Six Stages of Relationship 268
23. The Rear Wheel: The Five Steps to
    Extraordinary Relationship 277

Part V: To Have and Have Not
24. Taking Advantage 301
25. Best Friends 309
26. Use It: A Call to Action 316

Afterword by Patricia Richards................................329

Author's Foreword

This book is for singles and couples, for those sexually successful and those who are confused; it is for the young and for the old, and it is for those who are energetically attuned and for those who are not. It is heterosexually based, but it offers much that nonstraight people may find useful.

Wild Attraction is a survey of a previously uncharted, energetics-centered view of romantic love. Its core tenet is this: Even though humans have had eleven million years of male-female experimentation during which to refine the race's skills, our most desperately cherished premises relating to sexuality and attraction are exactly the inverse of what works. From an energetically aware perspective, the relationship behaviors that society most encourages are those that least fulfill the incredible promise of gender. The world is, literally, head over heels.

Great things await us if we can turn things right side up again.

Part I

Head over Heels

CHAPTER 1

We Have No Defense

Energetic Fact of Life #1:
The energetic force of gender and attraction is all around us, and against it we humans have no defense. This is true despite our culture's portrayal of sexuality as a force internal to us and under our control. Your best response to this knowledge: Do not take even the most committed love for granted and work diligently every day to safeguard your fidelity and that of your mate. Also, learn all you can about Wild Attraction.

Somewhere out there, in the darkness just beyond the orange and red glow of a metaphorical campfire, lurks a real power of gender-based attraction that nobody can resist. Nobody. This force is an interweaving of twin streams of nonordinary Energy that we experience as feminine and masculine. In not being consciously aware of this fact of life, you might also not realize that neither your fidelity, nor your wife's or husband's, is really in your power to guarantee, or in theirs. You won't yet know that any man or woman can be compelled to sleep with, marry, live with, or perhaps lie to any person, against all individual interests. If you believe that superior character, morality, or religiosity allows any person to master these twin streams, you are able to think this way only because the most exotic of all animals, which for the purposes of this book I am calling Wild Attraction, has allowed you to think so.

Sexuality and gender, while obviously fulfilling various functions for the race, including reproduction, must be seen as constituting something entirely different from an internal biological process. Romantic attraction is an external entity that is offering to enhance individual prospects for the most profound growth of consciousness and attention that is given to you to ever possibly achieve. Sexuality and gender are about awakening and then remaining awake. If you do not acknowledge this force and help it meet its nonnegotiable needs, you can be capsized in the silvery wake thrown off by its powerful, purposeful motion. In the worst case, you may slowly drown in a gray sea of loneliness or dysfunctional relationships.

Although I am being straightforward about its dangers, this external agency of love is a positive thing. Those who come to respect the force of Wild Attraction inevitably find themselves taking the mechanics of gender much less for granted. They date more before choosing to have sex or settle down, and tend to screen potential lovers with a different eye. People who gain a Wild Attraction perspective work harder to be viable candidates for long-term love. These men and women learn about and practice the art of keeping a mate, and they stop believing that any promise, contract, or habit will bind two people together for better or for worse.

If you are not yet generating a field of attraction that draws others to you, and are languishing in what I think of as "chronic involuntary singleness," the problem may not be that you are unattractive to others but rather that you have not yet learned how to attract and work with this powerful nonhuman romantic ally. To successfully relate to mates and potential mates, it is arguably wise to focus first on relating to this unacknowledged but huge external force—a process that requires fluency in a more intricate language of gender than most of us have been taught from birth.

Becoming familiar with the rules of Wild Attraction is invaluable, but no degree of familiarity will ever give any human being the upper hand. The reality of love—that it is a wild thing ultimately out of our control—is far more powerful than the illusion of love as something we can tame or master.

Those who have seen the Wild Attraction animal close up know something of gender and love as they are about to be portrayed here. The poetry of Rumi, Shakespeare, and countless others springs from this particular well. Those who have felt the full force of Wild Attraction know that no one can offer guarantees—not about sexuality, love, attraction, or fidelity. They know of the existence of a call that, once it comes, must be obeyed. Not everyone hears this signal in its full and compelling fury—and thus society perpetuates the myth that our sexuality is a function of biologically based internal drives alone.

But deep down, almost everyone both yearns to hear that call and fears it in the cells of the body. Those who want to face the prospect of this summons with intelligence and compassion—to own and celebrate their essential wildness but somehow make it *work* as it might actually have been designed to work—are my intended audience.

This force I am portraying can throw you together with an incompatible mate while perpetuating the illusion of free choice. With equal ease, it can isolate you over the course of an entire lifetime. Although this animate force has hopes for you, it often seems to have no mercy. And as long as it is unacknowledged, it is no more reliable than Puck in Shakespeare's *Midsummer Night's Dream* and no less manically zany than the Marx Brothers.

This book is in some respects an account of the sighting of a rare animal previously unknown to human science, not unlike the first reports of the discovery of gorillas in dense green rain forests scarcely a century ago. People scoffed at the idea of man-sized apes in a world that, even at that relatively quaint time, seemed to have been thoroughly explored. The assertion that a Wild Attraction creature exists is more revolutionary; nobody will be bringing back a body part to back up this claim, as someone eventually did to resolve the gorilla controversy.

For most people back then, the existence of gorillas was a purely theoretical question, since few of these large herbivores were foraging in people's bedrooms and backyards. But the question of Wild Attraction is of immediate and practical concern. This creature speaks and acts through us and has the power to inspire within us the obsessive and compulsive reactions that we experience as romantic love and attraction. In describing Wild Attraction in this way, I have no wish to marginalize the roles that our biology and psychology play but rather want to radically expand the sense of what sexuality is. The Wild Attraction model meets this need equally well whether adopted as a metaphor or accepted literally as the description of an actual sentience roaming somewhere in an expanded coexistent universe.

For my part, I see it as the latter.

Whichever way you may choose to frame it to yourself, this thing I am calling Wild Attraction makes a fabulous, potent ally on a road leading to powerful intimacy with the mystery from which we all spring. If you learn to understand it and collaborate with it, Wild Attraction will awaken you, carry you to places you cannot imagine in advance of your arrival, and give you the means to safeguard your love and your mate, to the degree allowed by fate, throughout your life. Wild Attraction can never be domesticated, but it *wants* to be harnessed. And, suggestively, it wants to harness you.

Progressing further into this book, you may be amazed at the rich and complex nature of this remarkable animal, and also find yourself a bit aghast at how little its nature is understood in our culture.

People ignore Wild Attraction at their peril, as most of the human race rediscovers and immediately forgets, every day. But this living amalgam of the male and female gender essences is probably our most powerful friend in the struggle to create ever greater, more capable human beings. This book may in a small way serve as an ongoing reminder of its omnipresence. I hope it will also serve as your guide to the wonders that Wild Attraction wants to bestow upon you and those you love.

Chapter 2
Energy Is the Realm of Relationship

Energetic Fact of Life #2:
Western culture's entire arsenal of relationship skills deals only with physical and psychological factors associated with sex and romance, failing to equip us with the knowledge we need the most, which is this: Relationship is largely created or destroyed in the realm of Energy. Your needed action: Learn about the basic Energy aspects of your nature and acquire fundamental energetic relationship skills. Practice three energetic relationship skills, which usually involve simple physical actions, every day.

In constructing Wild Attraction's recipe for romantic love, two indispensable ingredients, when mixed together, form a base to which many other elements must gradually be added. One is a working model of subtle Energy and its associated realm. The other is a gut-level, real-world understanding of what in this book is called *extraordinary relationship*—who it is for, what it is like, when it is applicable, where the concept comes from, and why it is something you may want to cultivate in your own life.

The most powerful way to prepare this base is to briefly present the relevant aspects of my past and that of my wife, Patty, including the story of how we came together. Everything about this story is unlikely, including the fact that a person with my professional background would eventually write this book on relationship and nonordinary Energy.

My profile is that of an aerospace executive with experience working on some of the world's most interesting technical and scientific programs, including the Space Shuttle, the International Space Station, the Keck Telescope, the now-defunct supercollider, the development of detectors for radio telescopes that could see to the outer edges of the universe, various shadowy defense programs, manned space missions, and instrumentation for measuring environmental conditions deep inside the Earth.

After graduating as a communications-related special projects major from the usually sun-drenched halls of the University of California at San Diego, I rose through the ranks of engineering and technology companies to eventually become a program manager in an aerospace company and later a corporate vice president. I hold a patent on circuit board interconnection technology. My executive career demanded considerable intellectual precision. A parallel preoccupation with martial arts instilled physical groundedness and pragmatism.

Probably no one I met while visiting the halls of Lockheed or the Jet Propulsion Laboratory saw me as a person who would someday lecture about largely unverifiable perceptions of coexistent nonordinary realities and nonhuman sentience. But while attending to the duties of a high-reliability program manager, I was paying serious attention to an obscure tradition called *nonordinary energetic seeing*.

My personal mix of qualities always included a reasonably high dose of apparently the "right stuff" for the exploration of alternative realities. By this I don't so much mean the raw capacity for energetic perception, which is widespread. I am pointing more toward a frame of mind. This quality might best be described as a willingness to say *yes to the mystery*—enabling me to focus for long periods on existentially challenging phenomena without identifying excessively with being different, or projecting too much fantasy into the torrent of impressions with which I became increasingly flooded.

Memories persist from early childhood of being able to see apparently concrete things that my parents and siblings obviously weren't registering. By the time I reached the teenage years, my anomalous perceptual events had increased in richness and taken on a kind of vast "nonordinariness" as well as a grounded, compelling specificity.

These occurrences were often challenging, and my response was to apply a rigorous skepticism. I began to document all of my anomalous perceptions and to experiment with them. Gradually, I attempted to unscramble and decode them, mostly in the hope of proving that they were rooted in science and technology in some way that was simply misunderstood. To this end, a little spiral notebook resided in the back pocket of my blue jeans from my sixteenth year to about my twenty-second. Its pages preserved written descriptions, complete with maps and diagrams, of things that I should not have been able to see because they were removed from me either physically or in time, whether past or future.

Periodically, I would come upon a unique geographical feature that I had never visited before or heard of, or I would witness a singular event, such as a certain bar fight, an obscure ritual, a plane crash, or the sinking of a particular yellow and gold boat in a very specific way, and then I would pull out that notebook, flipping to the page where I had documented my before-the-fact observations in scrupulous detail, often to find that the event and the description matched perfectly. I remember showing my notes to people standing around me, allowing them to read about one-of-a-kind action sequences in detail while the event being described unfolded in real time before us. I can't imagine what those people might have thought and don't know if they were psychologically or spiritually changed. But, over time, that process of documentation and validation changed me.

Concrete energetic perceptions of this kind carry little large-scale significance for me today, but they were incredibly useful during my early years of calibrating nonordinary senses. Frequent physical validation allowed vitally needed reality checks—continuing evidence of overall sensory acuity—while exploring difficult-to-observe phenomena that had no observable counterparts in the material world. High on the list of these was the unacknowledged gender influence moving in men and women and driving some of their most important behaviors. New allies soon appeared in the search for a rational basis for comprehending extraordinary vision. Somehow during this period I found my way into a small ESP study group that met in the basement of the Neuropsychology Lab at the University of California, Los Angeles, locked away from the Southern California sun—an experience that provided an excellent set of academic tools and a pragmatic sense that I was not alone. Later, after I had established myself in aerospace, my first real mentor in the world of energetics appeared, a powerful, truly amazing woman, and my path was set.

What followed was a decade of intensive education, coaching, experimentation, and training from a series of adepts who could have stepped right out of the best cinematic depictions of larger-than-life nonordinary masters. One of them with whom Patty and I remain very close is a brilliant man, Dr. Peter Nelson, whose scientific work on consciousness and mystical experience is the single best description I have encountered, and whose capacity for direct nonordinary perception has few equals in the world.

I saw, and later myself accomplished, many things that I had not up to that point believed were possible. My mentors lived and loved from an altogether different model than I had seen before, one that included and accounted for the effects of nonordinary Energy. These benefactors were very private exemplars of extraordinary attention and advanced consciousness. The journey toward mastery of seeing took up many hours a week in an already crowded schedule, it challenged me more than anything else in my life, and it encompassed a level of detail, specificity, and subtle rigor unlike anything I could have envisioned. This most serious and purposeful of apprenticeships burned a mark onto me and into me that I live with every day and can never forget.

Long after those training years, but also long before I would have assessed myself as ready for the role, I found myself in the mentor position, having recognized Patty as possessing the perfect mix of qualities and capacities to become my protégé. When I first met her, she was a nurse practitioner/nurse midwife and women's health care specialist at the local university student clinic—by no means a pushover for off-the-wall ideas. For her I tried hard to reproduce the rigor and depth that had been the hallmarks of my own training. I had not been married to or sexually involved with any of my own mentors. But Patty and I fell in love. Both in and out of bed our relationship as lovers and mates became one of the cornerstones of our shared nonordinary experience. Her training and development as a master of seeing included phenomena of both sexual and nonsexual energetic travel, merging, and blending that are off the ordinary charts. Her experience in this area is not described in this book. But her sense of what gender is and can be, what it offers, and the full scope and scale of the phenomenon of gender-based love and attraction has become vast as a result of her hard-won periods of contact with a greatly expanded reality. All of this does color Wild Attraction. She lived through these alternate-realm events in the company of another person, me, with whom she could exchange written, precise validating accounts after the fact—an advantage that comes to people all too rarely.

Patty is no longer my protégé. She has attained mastery in her own right.

I feel that everyone can and should access the innate, universal human sense of Energy, but I have a huge regard for rigor, effort, and developed skill. When it is time for me to listen to other people share their nonordinary or mystical experiences, I listen most closely to those few who bear the marks of a long, intelligently supervised effort to sort out fact from fantasy.

Unusual and extreme talent for the nonordinary exists, though it is not common. When it is accompanied by a serious intelligence, the combination confers on those who possess it a special status—they come to have what I think of as a *reason to know*. A person with such a reason to know differs in an important way from another person who may be worth listening to but who speaks from an acquired knowledge of a subject but little or no direct experience. For example, an airline crash survivor can tell you things about living through extreme circumstances that no observing scholar can. Even if that survivor is not a particularly good writer, I will read his or her book with interest because of that person's reason to know. An author's reason to know is not a justification for uncritical acceptance of his or her work, but when that reason is compelling it does provide motivation for paying special attention and asking good questions.

I embarked on this path long ago, solely as an expression of personal interest with no thought of ever playing the role of spokesperson or teacher, as I am doing here. Yet this initially private interest and skill of mine has now been my life's work, and also Patty's, for almost two decades. Our path concerns itself with applying rigorous scientific and academic principles to the development of expanded states of consciousness and unusual attention skills. Its purpose is to develop ways to create better, one might say greater, human beings, people who are capable of making ever more outstanding contributions to today's culture. Obviously, gender-based relationship is a huge part of that.

One way to create better people is to increase awareness of a small set of general principles of Energy. These principles are significant in everyone's life but have yet to receive their due emphasis in Western culture, mainly because most descriptions of them too closely resemble superstitious or religious ideas, or psychological projections.

If you are reasonably comfortable with the idea that acupuncture, martial arts, and craniosacral care are based on real phenomena, the approach to energetics presented here will not be foreign. You need to harbor no deeper level of acceptance or enthusiasm than such fields demand in order to process Wild Attraction's models. A lot of energetic ground is covered in this book (as much as is necessary to discuss extraordinary relationship effectively), but it in fact constitutes only an entry-level introduction to energetic techniques for personal empowerment.

Energetic seeing is not widely known. Members of my small tradition have been around for generations without ever developing a need for, or any interest in, establishing a public presence. The term *energetic seer* is perhaps not a perfect one for use in the modern world. But it captures what we experience better than more widely circulated terms like *psychic* or *shaman*. Much of seeing is informed secular mysticism in the highest sense of the word.

My small oral tradition is not in any sense a religion, nor is it at all cultlike. In many ways, it more closely resembles a philosophy. We have never sought public influence; there is no tithing, no ordering people around or weird sex (which, alas, may disappoint some readers), and no midnight rituals. Seers don't seek to control the weather or tilt the fate of mankind. We live comfortable, ordinary lives without a hierarchy. We tend to answer honestly whenever interested people ask us to relate our experiences and discuss our worldview, but we don't ask to be believed and we avoid imposing our framework onto others.

Seers tend to see negative insights as stepping-stones to positive realizations. The most positive qualities we see in the nature of any given thing tend to define that thing for us. Hence, despite the many disclosures in this book of widespread misunderstandings and mistakes about sex and love, our sense of relationship is hopeful: Humans can do something great with relationship that as a species we may not yet be doing. A true buried treasure, perhaps the ultimate one, is lying somewhere incredibly close by, as if waiting patiently in an unlocked chest at a spot marked by an enormous, luminous red X and covered only by a few inches of sod in our own backyards.

I can offer no better description of the treasure of extraordinary relationship than this: My relationship with Patty is, and always has been, a sizzling and wild commingling of two powerful people, one that has forced me to put her in the very center of my universe and keep her there. It is a constant ritualized playing out of the merging of feminine and masculine power, with her job being to entice, goad, challenge, and inspire me, to demand my attention, to give me a *job*, while mine is to claim, cherish, and indulge her, to lavish her with attention, give her a powerful and elemental force to ride, and in all things to do my job well, while taking care never to be run by her. Our version of Wild Attraction is like alternating electrical current. In this interlocked, fully alive state, one that can only be sustained when true safety, availability, and mutual respect are just as present as love and passion, power over each other passes back and forth as though we dwell in an eternal dynamic wave that is always breaking upon itself. We are caught in a dance in which it is impossible to tell when or if either partner ever truly gains the upper hand; each ensnares the other. This dynamic honoring of the wildness and tenderness in both the male and female actually moves both of us forward in a process of awakening and reawakening, gradually becoming more of what is possible for us as individuals and as a couple to become.

The connection Patty and I share is a testimonial to just how incredibly good a gender relationship can be when mixed with healthy energetics. It is also a "how to" blueprint that spells out the mechanics of Wild Attraction as we experience it. Patty is a born genius at the art of relationship, a person with a *reason to*

know, and I have learned a huge amount by reverse engineering and analyzing things that come naturally to her. We are fortunate to be living out a great union that works well in every significant way, and has changed us hugely.

The most obvious telltale mark of this special connection is "energetic responsiveness," a back-and-forth exchange of subtle signals, touches, and field interactions. Patty often points out that this nuanced, near-constant motion is one of the keys to creating gender magic. Stillness and nonreactivity, the preferred social stance of millions of people, rarely seem to ignite any real gender fire.

Energetic Fact of Life #3:
Although people almost universally think of Energy (if they think of it at all) as being somehow more spiritual than planet Earth, energetics is not spirituality. The needed action: When you think of your energy body, see it as no more spiritual than your physical body; don't try to mimic your spiritual sense of allness by visualizing yourself dissolving out into the universe and becoming one with everyone and everything. Your energy body is like your physical one. It needs to stay bounded and stay home, which means, to keep its power focused internally, where it is most needed. Trust your innate spirituality to take care of itself.

From the perspective of a seer, Energy is not of the physical universe we humans most easily perceive, nor is it divine in the sense of being closer to God or more spiritual than the physical world. It is simply *other*, a coexisting place and medium that will remain impossible to detect directly through any conceivable physical measuring device, no matter how far into the cosmos or deep into the subatomic world we ever penetrate.

In a layperson's simplification, four attractive forces are known to modern physics: electromagnetism, gravity, and the large and small subatomic forces. Energy as I describe it here is not one of these forces, nor is it directly related to them. It represents an unmapped force and uncharted realm that is best visualized as existing within a parallel reality that touches upon our physical and psychological experience and shapes it, but is entirely distinct.

The relationship between the shimmering realm of Energy and the other realms of human experience is similar to the relationship between different layers of an onion. An ant could crawl all across the surface of an onion, could explore it completely, and never discover or get to the next layer down—or, if it was crawling on an inner layer, to the one above. Applying this to your own life, it could be said that there is no way to explore the physical world or the world of your imagination and discover a hatch leading to a nonordinary one. But that doesn't mean a nonordinary world isn't there or that it doesn't affect you.

How can we know whether it exists if we can't see it or reach it?

Imagine that a person is holding that onion, the one with an ant crawling across the surface, in one hand, and with the other hand is pushing a long needle into the onion at a spot exactly opposite the present position of the ant. Imagine that the needle tip penetrates right through the center of the onion and comes almost all the way to the other side, touching the layer just below the layer where the ant crawls but stopping short of penetrating through it.

Now imagine that the person pushes the needle just a tiny bit more, enough to deform the layer just beneath the ant's layer of onion without breaking through. The needle merely pushes that layer outward, creating a bump.

Here is the crucial point. The bending of that deeper layer would naturally also deform the layer upon which the ant is crawling, not unlike the way forces inside the Earth create mountains. The ant would never see the needle, it would never see the underlying layer of onion, but it would see the bend in its own surface layer.

In this metaphor, the needle represents a force called Intent, a force that has the power to deform or move Energy. The onion layer below the ant's layer represents Energy itself. The ant's layer stands for the physical universe.

This thought experiment represents, quite well, the prevailing human condition as seen from my perspective. We all see or otherwise experience many bends in our physical reality onion layer. People get sick, for reasons not entirely clear, and they will sometimes inexplicably get well. One athlete performs better than another in ways that strength and technique don't entirely account for. One singer's voice sells millions of records while another, technically better voice does not. Why?

Sometimes, the causes *are* mostly energetic.

If a person changes something in the world of Energy, that action can deform or alter a thing or condition in the physical world. Sometimes the resultant physical changes are immediate, and sometimes they can take years to happen. The slipperiness of time in this process is one reason why people in general have not yet put the pieces together and come up with a good model for understanding this vital process.

This mechanism also works in reverse. If someone changes something in the physical layer, that action changes the imprint of that physical thing in the world of Energy. A seer can observe these changes as they occur.

If you have ever had a precognitive experience, in which you get an accurate flash of insight about something that hasn't happened yet, you are not really seeing that future physical event even if you get a clear visual impression of it. You are seeing its imprint in another realm. Any image of a physical event that you generate in your head as a result of energetic perception is like a footprint on a white sand beach. It is comparable to the fistlike shape a piece of paper retains after that paper has been pressed down over your closed hand and then lifted away.

When inferring concrete events by means of energetic senses, you are looking at the sand, not ever seeing the foot. You are observing the molded paper, not the actual hand. The image that you visualize is an inference. Your energetic senses are not designed to view the physical world. You have eyes and ears for that.

You as a human being—or rather, the combination of your attention and your capacity for perception—offer the most significant bridge between these realms. You are like a tunnel through all the layers of that onion mentioned a moment ago, a creature designed to live in and on many layers at the same time. I see you, man or woman, as a moving hole in a larger fabric of reality that allows light from the various layers, or realms, to shine through into one another, creating new beauty all the time. From that perspective, you are indeed a marvelous thing, a hole punched in the boundary between what is and what might come to be.

Your consciousness can, with attention, coordinate actions on the different layers of the onion and thus make magic.

If you make love with a partner physically, while at the same time your *energy body* and your partner's energy body are connecting in a complementary form of lovemaking in the realm of Energy, the effect is a kind of gorgeous radiance that changes you and those around you. You are engaging figuratively in the creation of your own personal shimmering Northern Lights.

However big you imagine the potential of human relationship to be, it is bigger than you think.

You need to know a few more things. Energy is like silver oxide photographic film or brown magnetic recording tape. It records human experience with holographic clarity. It captures emotions and stores them for playback at any moment. It is the ideal medium for writing down the assumptions and models that make up a human being. From a memory standpoint, the personal Energy of your energy body, or *energy field*, is your second brain, and it remembers things that your physical brain is also recording constantly, as if you have a backup hard drive. What gets written into that drive—remembered within your energy field—is available in particular to your subconscious mind. Your energetic memory system is shaping very strongly your subconscious sense of what a human is, what life is, the nature of the universe, and, of great importance in terms of relationship, what you think you are as a man or woman.

People unconsciously mess with the models stored in other people's Energy all the time, often for purposes of seduction, power, or control, and almost never for the good.

I have a name for any Energy that contains a record of human experience and associated emotion. That name is *content*. Although content is just Energy, it is special because it has been saturated with a particular memory, model, or message. We all need to get rid of content to be healthy and happy because we produce more of it than we need. Content is constantly being formed as a result of each new moment of experience. It is generated somewhere in the white center of our energy body, and resembles vapor from evaporating morning dew in a meadow. It builds up like carbon dioxide in our lungs and must be vented or it becomes poisonous. So humans need to breathe content, the excess record of their experience, out of their energetic selves all the time.

With each in-breath, humans need to take in new Energy from the external environment also. This is because Energy, in addition to being a realm, a medium, and a recording device, is also our main nonordinary fuel. The more pure raw Energy you take in and retain, the better your nonordinary support for healing, energetic perception, personal timing, and transformational learning and change—and, more to the point of this book, the more potent and remarkable your relationships are likely to be.

A lot of people leak Energy these days, and a lot of them can be seen unknowingly stealing Energy from others in order to get by.

Interestingly, the worst and most predatory energetic habits can feel pleasurable and can play into what might be called the dark side of Wild Attraction. For example, if a male person were to energetically reach around behind a female, tap into her at the small of her back, and draw her vital life Energy out of her for his own use, the woman might feel a sensuous, floating sensation. She might feel especially seen, valued, and loved. She might think that this male person is the man of her dreams. She might sleep with him or marry him.

Disturbing, yes, but it happens every day.

Energy is formed into specific densities and actual shapes by a force I have already mentioned called Intent, a fundamental attribute of human beings that is closely associated with attention. Intent is the force that can create Energy flows such as the one from the woman to the man just described. For now, given that Intent is a lifetime study and almost impossible to discuss in brief, nothing more need be said about it.

This, boiled down to its most rudimentary essence, is the environment we will be looking at in this book, and it is a first glance at the nature of humans as they appear in that world. Energy, content, and Intent are the building block ideas with which I can now briefly describe how and why all human relationships, but especially gender-based relationships, are mostly the province of very real but nonordinary events in an unseen realm.

Picture humans as Energy creatures sailing through an etheric universe. Like the covert flashing of blinking spotlights, called semaphore signals, passing between ships steaming in parallel across a gray sea, humans communicate in languages that most people don't suspect exist. Some of this is virtual subconscious telepathy, caused by the exchange of content. Some takes the form of actions that we can only see with our energetic eyes. People might call it *energy body language.* For example, we pack Energy into our shoulders, breasts, or thighs as signals of interest or availability. We grope with nonphysical hands, we whisper with an energetically conducted voice. We pass secret nonphysical notes, again, in the form of content. Most important, our most fundamental gender responses and needs are determined more powerfully by features of our energetic selves than by our physical bodies or our minds.

Your energy body has a kind of genitalia to match your physical characteristics, and it has its own predisposition toward the masculine or the feminine that you would feel, and that would drive your behavior, even if you were somehow deprived of your physical body. By this I refer to your *energetic gender essences*, which are described in more detail in upcoming chapters.

Energetic Fact of Life #4:
The culture encourages people to believe that, deep down, they instinctively know all that they really need to know about love. In fact, no single human endeavor demands more attention, study, and insight than romantic relationship. The needed action: Start asking serious and well-intended questions of members of the other gender. Ask about what works for them in relationship, and think seriously about the answers you receive. Modify your behaviors based on what you hear and conclude. Not many people actually do this, which is quite amazing, considering the degree of relationship pain in the world.

Probably no human activity offers greater rewards to those willing to apply themselves to serious study and skill development than sexual relationship. The conscious combination of energetic sexuality with physical sexuality is more than explosive. Even a rudimentary working knowledge of Energy and Intent can transform an ordinary love into an extraordinary one, or can bring a person from romantic dysfunction to delightful functionality. Fortunately, nobody has to become an Energy expert in order to accomplish this. A certain basic literacy is all that is required, just as we need a working knowledge of diet and exercise. Unlike some animals on this blue Earth, we are not born knowing all we need to know to maximize our potential, or even to survive. Although some humans in my experience (more men than women) show signs that they think there is a special free pass relating to sex and relationship and they know from birth all that they need to know about love, in the case of romance, sex, and attraction, ignorance is definitely not bliss.

CHAPTER 3

Unconscious Telepathy

Energetic Fact of Life #5:
Despite what modern culture tells us, our most powerful interpersonal communications, the ones that shape our life, are not taking place under our control or even in our daily awareness. They are taking place subconsciously by means of exchanges of nonordinary Energy. The needed actions: Question your own attraction responses (aloud or in writing), avoid impulsive sexual encounters with new people, and rely on friends for much-needed reality checks.

The most life-changing conversations flash between ourselves and others around us with the speed and detail of a computer download, and it is entirely possible that even as you read these words you are exchanging your deepest secrets with total strangers in naked frankness. You do this as constantly and easily as you breathe, often against your own best interests, and usually in pursuit of an irrational agenda that you would never consciously embrace. As you might imagine, nowhere is this unmonitored process more capriciously destructive, or more potentially rewarding, than in your love life.

To really do justice to this observation calls for a portrayal of human relationship as a seer experiences it on a daily basis. A particular thought exercise is useful for this purpose. Whenever

I present this exercise during a lecture, I ask people to close their eyes to the marbled walls of our regular lecture hall and to gently imagine that they have suddenly developed the ability to float above their own bodies, as though their mind could split somehow and allow them to be in two places at once.

I ask you to consider doing this now. Flip through the files in your memory and pick out some reasonably crowded cocktail party scene from your past experience to use as a model. From a position drifting above that cocktail party, look down at your conventional self standing there surrounded by a crowd of well-dressed and well-mannered friends and strangers.

Once you are comfortably visualizing this, grant that the observing you floating up against the ceiling is able to see sudden little flashes, like nearly instantaneous bullets of glowing gray smoke, that spark around your physical body down at the party, zipping to and from other people nearby—flashes that nobody at floor level seems to be acknowledging.

As you pay attention, you realize with surprise that you are aware of the conscious part of your mind that is attending the party, the one resident in your physical matter. Even more unusual, you are also aware of processes going on in the subconscious aspect of that mind. You slowly notice that the obviously telepathic bursts from deeply buried mental regions seem to arise for a purpose: some deeply subconscious part of the physical you that is down there sipping a glass of sparkling nonalcoholic punch is using these flashes to negotiate and draw up relationship contracts between yourself and other people. Neither of the two aspects of mind that are down there attending the party seems to be paying attention to the other. As you survey the festive burgundy and black decor of the party from above, you realize that an out-of-awareness aspect of the day-to-day you is, and has always been, using this capacity invisibly to set the tone and course of entire love affairs, marriages, and other sexual collisions.

This happens long before you speak your first word to the person you are contracting with; often it happens before you consciously notice him or her at all.

Essentially, you are watching yourself make stupid decisions and map out possible romantic entanglements in vivid detail, complete with disastrous endings. And you are doing this interactively in collusion with others present in the room, individuals with whom you would never expect to be considering such racy alternatives. The people with whom your hidden dialog is the most intense are the ones who are physically most studiously ignoring you.

As the observing you floats around up there on the ceiling and watches this scene unfold, it occurs to you that if a person were lucky enough to be exposed to effective, creative models for getting along with others, the supercommunication process you are watching could be a positive force, actively smoothing out that person's life path and paving the way for future successes and awakenings.

You also realize, probably to your horror, that the opposite is also the case. If the physical, partying you has been exposed to models of relationship that are poor or mixed, your unconscious energetic communication is likely to set you up to fail right from the start of each new relationship. This set-up, of course, is also the product of unresolved psychological issues that are largely outside of your conscious awareness. Your subconscious mind uses your energy field quite freely to act them out, as you, and others, are doing with remarkable, almost prescient accuracy.

From your drifting vantage point, you continue to study everyone at the party, from firelight-splashed extroverts to those lingering in darker shadows. You can see that the unconscious telepathy is also the source of an uncanny ability to attract new versions of the same dysfunctional type of mate over and over again. If your psychology is looking for ways to create dysfunctional relationships, your telepathy and energy field will happily arrange it.

How does this happen? Energetic telepathy allows your subconscious to identify and attract that special individual who will in fact be a tragic mismatch but who appears to your conscious mind as someone who is safe to choose and appropriate to go to bed with, perhaps even to marry.

As to what can be done to turn energetic communication into an asset, that is coming a little later on. But right from the beginning of this discussion of Wild Attraction it is important to start asking yourself what you might be communicating to others unconsciously. Once you begin to see what is happening on that more subtle level, you can decide, consciously, what to do about impulses that in the past you took as genuine readouts from your heart about your next romantic moves.

Most of the time, after reading this book, you will smile to yourself and ignore them, as though they were advice urged upon you by your four-year-old son or daughter. The source of the advice is sweet, enthusiastic, well-meaning, often clever, and it is definitely and intimately *yours*. But it is not exactly your best source of relationship wisdom.

To close out this chapter, imagine that the observing you at the cocktail party, floating up beside the chandelier, suddenly picks up one half of a two-way energetic exchange, the way a person might overhear the local half of a two-way phone conversation:

"Are you safe?" a young woman is energetically asking a man who is standing in the blackness of a deep shadow across the room. "If not, that could be all right." Silence.

She continues, "Do you like to rush too quickly into bed?"

Yet another period of silence passes during which the woman picks up an hors d'oeuvre from a tray. "Oh, by the way, have you been abused, or, are you by any chance an emotional abuser?" Her lips pucker as she takes a bite. "Me too." Another pause.

Then she asks, "How do you treat people you have power over?" Another pause.

"It's okay. Tell the conscious me that you're a very nice guy. We'll keep it between us that you will eventually turn out to be a jerk."

As the observing you watches from directly overhead, she slips into a sleek black coat and walks sinuously across the room on a course that will take her very close to the silhouetted man standing beside the room's entrance. Without looking toward him, she asks another silent question. "Do you want to work out your past issues involving a mother who deserted you?" Silence. "Great, I'd like to punish you as a proxy for a father who hit me."

She passes through the doorway with the slightest physical pause and then is gone from sight. The shadowy man quickly puts his drink down and hurries through the doorway after her, calling verbally, "Excuse me, don't I know you?"

Fade to black.

Chapter 4
Anatomically Incomplete

Energetic Fact of Life #6:
Almost all human beings in Western culture believe that they have only one body. In fact, we have at least two. The second one is under the sole control of the subconscious mind and is hidden from our day-to-day experience. It is the gender of this energy body, not the attributes of physical anatomy, that principally defines a person as being consciously male or female. The needed actions: Learn a martial art, a mind-body skill, or a disciplined form of dance to help train both of your bodies to do the same thing at the same time (most of the time, they don't). Invoke this mindset while engaged in dating and sex.

I magine making love with the person of your dreams in golden and pink subdued light in an idealized bedroom, with the benefit of four bodies that are under your and your partner's conscious control—two each, instead of just the physical one that most people are stuck with. Imagine the combinations, the sensations, the nuanced language that become possible, and the multiplication of sensation that would be inevitable.

Energy bodies actually exist. In fact, each person has more than one energy field, and the one that you have most likely heard about is not the one you need to engage for Wild Attraction purposes.

We know that energy bodies exist because some people see and feel them directly, and they can compare accounts of their experiences with a high degree of correlation under controlled circumstances.

As to why they exist, for me the starting point is an observation that is ongoing with my every breath: every physical thing appears to be suffused with nonordinary Energy. When I look at a pencil with my physical eyes, I see its various features—the gleaming yellow wood and the dark gray lead point and the pinkish-brown eraser—but I also see a silvery shimmering glow that extends about a quarter of an inch around that pencil in all directions. I see this phenomenon optically, again apparently with my physical eyes, around everything in the environment. The glow around the pencil is steady, although it occasionally moves independently of the object and regardless of shifts in the surrounding light. It is as tangible as a laser in a dark room, and it throbs, almost the way the light of a fluorescent bulb flickers nearly imperceptibly. Other people may describe this visual phenomenon as an "aura."

With a sudden shift of state of being, in effect turning off my physical senses, I can see the pencil in a different kind of space, unaccompanied by the yellow wood and the gray lead. I would emphasize that I am looking at the very same glow but entirely with energetic senses and in a different realm. The pencil appears in nonordinary space as a beautiful silvery-white cylinder composed of thousands of particles of beautiful dancing motes so small that the Energy pencil looks like a gracefully floating field. What I am detailing here is my actual experience of observing the Energy suffusing the physical mass that, in our normal world, comprises the pencil. The Energy of the mass of the pencil resembles a cloud of gas or a weightless liquid contained by an invisible boundary that endows it with its own dimensionality, a shape that is similar but not identical to that of the physical pencil with which it is associated.

If I could look at your arm with these same "other eyes" at this moment, its Energy would exhibit similar general qualities. I would see a cloudlike field, lovely, in the general shape of your fingers, palm, wrist, and arm. Unlike the pencil's energy field, the field of your hand and arm would be moving, the Energy gently flowing up and down the long axis defined by your bone structure. In other words, because of the presence of your attention and Intent as a living conscious being, I would see purposeful motion in the Energy of your hand and arm that is typically not visible in the Energy associated with a pencil.

Within my frame of reference, it is this Energy, the Energy associated with the physical matter of your body, that is mostly being addressed in acupuncture or other healing arts. I should probably assign a name to it, because there are other energies for us to consider. For the purposes of this book, I will call this visible glowing attribute of your physical body *alpha Energy*.

When you run your fingertips down your partner's arm, this physically linked Energy can cause a delicious tingling sensation as it flashes from person to person. And Energy is in part responsible for the delights you might feel when your partner administers a gentle back rub.

This alpha Energy is associated permanently with the matter of your arm, and it will still be there when you are no longer alive. I have been to archaeological sites and witnessed the opening of ancient graves and seen the same energetic shimmer on long-dead bones that I always see on living body parts, except that it is not moving; the alpha Energy suffusing dead matter looks like the Energy around the pencil instead of the flowing Energy around your living arm.

When your flesh has dissolved into whatever your body's physical matter is next destined to become on Earth, that alpha Energy will follow each particle of matter to its next location, probably into the ground as dirt and dust. I know this because I have watched living matter decompose many times. The floor of redwood forests, for instance, is thick with bark and detritus from fallen trees that are slowly dissolving and returning to the Earth, both physically and energetically. So too will we.

People often express surprise when I tell them that this alpha Energy (which, again, may show up as auras and chakras) is for the most part not the Energy that captures the attention of seers. It is not the Energy with which we will be concerning ourselves throughout this book.

There is another class of energy field associated with human beings, one that is composed of something that, for ease of distinction, I will call *beta Energy*—although it is really the same Energy in both cases; alpha Energy is simply Energy that is bound to physical matter and cannot be separated, as in the case of your arm and the pencil, and beta Energy is free-form, unbound, and independent of physical matter. This second phenomenon is what yields a functional and independent energy body, or human energy field. You can take your energy body out for a spin like a car out of a garage, because although it is normally intertwined intimately with the alpha Energy of your physical body, it can be completely separated from your physical form and is entirely functional without it.

This second body is the body of love, the body capable of a sexuality that is beyond your wildest ordinary dreams. You want this body working for you.

Seers are seers because they live continuously in both the physical universe and the Energy universe, and they do this because they can access, perceive from, and move with this second body consciously, in parallel with their physical-body experience. To develop this capacity is, of course, a huge undertaking requiring a lifetime.

Seers are ardent students of the human energy field because the benefits are perhaps indescribably vast. Yet the advantages of having a second body, one that is uniquely adapted to relationship and love, become accessible from the moment you start paying attention to the possibility that it is so.

This second body gives you access to the realm of Energy exactly as your physical body gives you access to the physical universe. It uses Intent instead of muscles to move and to engage and grasp, push, and reshape other things. It also has senses, an array of at least five that roughly correspond to the five physical senses. These give you the ability to observe and navigate in an entirely different and coexistent universe. These senses also give you an enhanced ability to find, attract, seduce, and keep or form a lasting relationship with a mate.

Your physical body seems to be directly under the interactive control of the conscious, awake, aware you. You probably think the physical universe is the primary, and maybe the only, reality because your conscious mind is virtually enslaved to your physical body and normally sees and hears only what it perceives.

The energy body, on the other hand, answers mostly to what in common language (not in any scientific sense) people call the subconscious mind. To some deep subconscious aspect of you—an ordinarily inaccessible yet actually far bigger portion of your total experience than your conscious experience—the most real world is the world of Energy. For this reason, seers see the average human as being literally "two-minded."

For the most part, the conscious mind can directly speak

and act only through the physical body, while the subconscious, what we might call the greater awareness, can only speak and act directly through the second body, the human energy field. This second mind has the same ease of expression through the energy field that the first mind, the conscious mind, enjoys via the physical body.

Seers do everything they can to change this relationship, to make both bodies equally available to both minds. This blurs the boundary between the two minds and changes their relationship. Instead of fighting for control of the life (and love life) of the individual, each becomes aware of the other's unique and necessary role and the two minds begin to function as a team.

To put it plainly, if you learn to see the motion and expressions of your human energy field, and can learn to speak through it consciously, you are learning to *indirectly* perceive and work with your subconscious mind.

Obviously, then, you have a compelling reason to investigate, and to try to objectively validate, any ability you might innately possess to see Energy and observe your own energy field. You may never experience it as directly as you register the sensation and movements of your physical body, but you can still become literate and skillful in the field of Wild Attraction. You just have to acquire a working knowledge of what might be called simple "nonordinary mechanics" and find someone to show you what to do, both of which this book provides in a basic way.

Whether you stick with this book or explore Energy in other, more direct ways, your increased energetic empowerment is an attainable goal worth pursuing. Mostly, if you approach this within our particular model, the steps you take will involve things you will do with your physical body, rather than things you imagine, such as visualization processes, meditations, or affirmations.

If I could look at you with my nonordinary senses, I would see your energy body, a much larger field of Energy around you than the one flowing through your physical form. If you are a man, I would probably feel impressed by your mysterious translucency and vibrancy as a nonordinary being. If you happen to be a woman, your energy field would flow with a grace and shimmering radiance that you can scarcely imagine. This expanded field would not take on the shape of your physical body and it wouldn't look at all "human." It would extend out from your physical body in all directions, about an arm's length away from the skin of your torso. I observe a great number of these energy bodies every day, and each one looks much like an amoeba, although of great, fluid loveliness, standing up vertically on its long axis.

Normally, through my nonordinary eyes, the human energy field is translucent. Sometimes it can appear strikingly white, and at other times it seems to take on pastel hues. The first time I remember ever really focusing on one, it looked like a glowing ivory white, inverted flat-topped cone, narrower at the top than at the midpoint. (The shape reminded me of a Day-Glo traffic control cone.) I was surprised because it was quite different, much more solid-looking, than I had imagined.

Everyone's field is different, and each one changes so frequently that it is impossible to make a drawing that really represents the phenomenon. The shape of your individual energy field, if I could see it now, would not be fixed but rather would flow and float, much like the giant elongated soap bubbles I used to make as a child with a wonderful toy called Mister Bubble. I would dip the eighteen-inch plastic bubble-making ring in a tray of soapy water and then waft it through the air to create a monster bubble that would float in front of me. I can recommend that ring and tray set as an excellent discovery tool if you want to get a sense of what your energetic self looks like and how it moves.

Imagine two huge, silvery, languid soap bubbles able to call to each other, to sinuously interweave and merge. That is what human love looks like at its most elegantly, energetically engaged.

The amoeba analogy is appropriate because the human energy field has other characteristics in common with single-celled organisms. Like a cell, your field has a wall that functions as a semipermeable membrane: it lets content (energetic records of your thoughts, emotions, and experiences) out of your field, while hopefully not letting content from the outside in. This ability to selectively release content is hugely useful in courting and love.

On the other hand, your *field edge* can allow Energy from the outside to come into and be captured within your field without allowing the vital personal Energy already stored inside your field to dissipate out or otherwise escape.

This semipermeable function is so crucial to seers that the development of a healthy field edge is the central focus of the study of energetic empowerment. If you can become sensitized to your field edge, you can feel your state of health, and you can also feel the interactions between yourself and others in ways that add greatly to your performance and personal presence. You can then be taught to speak and understand a whole language of give-and-take with other people, and of separation and merging, that will allow you to do great things in the area of relationship and attraction and in many other worthy pursuits.

The other vital function of the field edge is to serve as your main energetic sensing tool. Ideally, you would both listen to and kinesthetically feel the Energy universe around you with your field edge, very much as an amoeba must sense the liquid suspension medium through which it moves. Your field edge should be the radar dish that receives impressions from the world around you, and it should function as a powerful microphone through which you can pick up what is being said to you through the equivalent of sound waves in the medium of Energy. Your field edge is the skin that brushes up against things and people and tells you the texture and temperature of what you are contacting. It also transfers a kind of direct knowing from person to person.

It is your most powerful transmitter of love and affection to and from another person.

The field edge receives the ultraquick telepathic bursts from other people that I discussed in the last chapter and translates these raw signals into impressions you can understand.

If your field edge doesn't fulfill these functions, you are in as much trouble as if you were to lose your physical skin. However when your field edge stops working, you don't feel the kind of pain experienced with the loss of physical skin because although the energy body can feel intense pleasure, it normally has no capacity to register pain. This means that you usually don't know when something is going radically wrong with your energy body. When your field edge doesn't do its job, content from the outside world will pass directly into your field and you will read it with another portion of your energy anatomy, your *energetic center*. This is usually unfortunate.

Telepathic communication between human beings without the benefit of a functioning field edge is one of the ways that early-stage love goes wrong. Mainly this is because lovers and other people around you often tell you things energetically about the way you manifest being a male or female person that can injure you, sometimes permanently. They do this by transferring negatives about the gender essences into your system. Hatred, dislike, fear of, or contempt for the male or female is something you can't afford, even subliminally.

Taking energetic messages directly into your energy body

center is like eating food in order to tell whether or not it is poison.

Your energetic center is remarkably similar to a cell nucleus in appearance, and it may function in similar ways. If I were looking at your personal *energy field center*, and if your center were healthy, I would see it as a softball-sized sphere, maybe rusty or light green but more probably silvery white in color, floating gently somewhere in the approximate center of your energy field. It would be composed of a specialized Energy that is directly associated with your capacity for experience itself. It is literally the seat of your awareness.

Content from the world around you making its way to your energy field center and being read and translated there, instead of on the outer skin of your field edge, is a bit like a virus getting to a cell nucleus. The record of experience carried within the invading content becomes indistinguishable from the record of your own experience. You have no choice but to play back and fully experience whatever is stored in that record. That experience, though never part of your own history, will be entirely real to you, at least subconsciously.

The biggest resulting problem is that you have no corresponding conscious memory through which to understand or process the experience you just internalized; you have only the emotional responses and the subconscious issues and difficult agendas to deal with. This is hugely entangling, disempowering, and injurious. Most people have no idea that this mechanism exists, so they waste huge amounts of time, effort, and money, and also endure a great deal of unnecessary suffering, trying to cope with impulses, feelings, fears, inhibitions, and drives that are not their own.

It is possible to be anxious throughout your lifetime because of internalizing another person's experience in this way.

Imagine spending your life with the traumas of a sexual abuse victim running in your system, but without a means to process the originating experience because it was never yours. Healthy love lives are not built on other people's traumas.

The memory machinery of your energy body is not a problem that has been inflicted on human beings, despite these pitfalls. Once you develop a healthy field edge, your energy body presents the greatest of all opportunities.

In the later stages of attraction and romantic relationship this mechanism of sharing content between two people, communicating from energetic center to center and bypassing the field edges, combined with the deliberate blending, overlapping, and merging of energy fields (by crossing through the field edges), provides an incredible vehicle for transmitting the most sublime messages and for the most intimate kind of sharing that two people can ever achieve.

You can see that many of these forms of field edge interaction can be either appropriate or destructive, depending on the circumstances. This is why true civilized behavior requires at least a modest acknowledgment that the human energy field exists.

If you could watch yourself go through a typical afternoon and optically see both your physical body and your energy field, you would most likely see your energy field sometimes engaging in the energetic equivalent of flashing forbidden body parts, necking, invading other people's space, or just plain groping. Sometimes its behavior would be even worse.

People use their subconscious telepathy skills to pick out a person to attract—often making the worst possible choice—and then they use the acting-out power of the energy body to entangle with that target, usually by engaging in energetic behaviors that are psychosexually charged and provocative.

The realm of Energy is a remarkably free world and has no police. Unless you are made consciously aware of what you are doing, you may behave like a teenager suddenly and delightfully rendered invisible and able to tour the locker rooms and shower rooms of the other gender (or the same gender, if that is your preference). If you were to do the exact same things in the physical world that your energy body is doing in the energetic one, you would probably find yourself jailed, shunned, chastised, or divorced pretty quickly and not necessarily in that order.

You don't get a free pass in the energetic world. If you have found yourself in bed with the wrong person, or married to someone you shouldn't be, or engaged in an affair that threatens to cause chaos in your life, you most likely arrived there because of something that you did, or didn't do, originally in the nonordinary realm.

Circle back for a brief moment to the hypothetical cocktail party in the previous chapter, the one in which you imagined two distinct yous: one down among the guests having a good time and the other watching from above. You see an unsavory man reach out with a wisp of Energy and grope or fondle an attractive woman as she passes. She grimaces momentarily and subtly increases her pace, but says nothing and just walks by.

If that same behavior had been physical, you might have seen somebody get slapped or arrested. At the very least, something would almost surely have been said.

People often tell me, "Every woman knows this feeling." Many women have proclaimed indignantly, when presented with this description of energetic behavior in classes and lectures, that they are all too aware that something unpleasant is happening, that the feeling is distinctive, and that it definitely does affect their self-esteem and their views of men, even if they don't know the exact mechanics.

Unfortunately, there is no accepted social context within which a woman can effectively respond. Concerned males in the environment tend to be equally helpless when it comes to objecting. Until something changes in the societal level of awareness of Energy, and our sense of civil rights extends the same sovereignty to our energy fields that we have so painfully and gradually acquired over our physical bodies, women will have to vote with their feet to avoid males who act out in this way.

I would think that since many women are already sensing it directly, this behavior should become as socially questionable as the obnoxious wolf whistling and bottom pinching that never cease to amaze me; these behaviors, moreover, cannot be of much use in getting dates.

Obviously, it is crucial that we learn as a group to open our eyes. Now would be a good time to grab hold of the wonderful energetic tools that have been running amok up to this point and use them to create great relationships, great people, and other great things. It is also time to start objecting to bad energetic behavior, at the very least in ourselves. This is something any person reading this book can start doing immediately. A language already exists for it. "Stop sliming her."

The party is over.

Energetic Fact of Life #7:
Most people think that few, if any, human beings can clearly see Energy or energetic misbehavior. They might also think that we have no everyday language for energetics. But these things aren't so. You can already see well in certain circumstances, such as in the presence of rudeness, and you already have a vivid metaphorical language for talking about Energy. The needed actions: Learn to watch for Energy-related metaphors that may be hidden in common phrases. Learn to name inappropriate behaviors to others using these same phrases, instead of remaining silent.

It might surprise you to hear that, in certain circumstances, what I have been saying about people not seeing Energy is inaccurate. You, and nearly everyone around the globe, can see into the nonmaterial world of Energy almost as clearly as I do. These special circumstances happen all the time, and you can usually be counted on to react strongly to what you perceive.

This sudden clarity about energetic behavior arises, almost unfailingly, whenever you are in the presence of overt rudeness. People who are otherwise insensitive to Energy often show an amazing ability to name Energy abuses as soon as somebody around them behaves obnoxiously in Energy. Because of this "rudeness effect" all human languages are full of phrases that convey "dumped on me," "slimed me," "blasted me," and "screened me out." These specialized expressions give humans a way to hold each other accountable for intolerable energetic behaviors under the protective umbrella of metaphor. Why then, if we have such tools, do we let a woman walk through a room and get slimed without raising a fuss?

The answer is that our deeply ingrained societal conditioning does not allow people to object to negative Energy behaviors that are unaccompanied by corresponding physical ones. The energetic behaviors that do the most damage to our relationships are carried out under the cover of polite physical behaviors that give us no social permission to opt out.

People are energetically blinded in the presence of courtesy. And since most of us are, and of course should be, relatively courteous most of the time, we in this culture are pretty much blind to Energy most of the time.

Obviously, part of the process of opening your eyes to relationship energetics is to start asking yourself questions about what is happening when people are being polite to you. You can start feeling the air around you and wondering what might be going on under the physical surface that you wouldn't have paid any attention to in the past. Your physical body often gives you strong hints of energetic perception: the shudder when a strangers opens a door behind you, the sudden chill at meeting a new and apparently pleasant person. Sometimes these are your subconscious mind's way of telling you something important.

Ask yourself: What is the real intention, or psychological condition, of that good-looking person who is smiling at you from across the room? You don't have to be Nostradamus to start doing this; you just need to ask questions internally, remain open, not ignore your physical discomfort around some people, and then see what happens.

Energetic Fact of Life #8:
Many people, after a brief initial exposure to nonordinary systems or phenomena, believe that they can become self-trained instant Energy experts. This is not the case. The needed action: Refrain from leaping to quick conclusions, and refrain from sharing your opinions relating to what is going on energetically with others.

Here is the moment for a bit of bright sunlight and a necessary aside, one that most readers don't need to hear but if you do need to hear it, is very important. On thankfully rare occasions, people who have listened to my advice to pay attention to the energetic actions of people around them have then gone off the deep end with it, imagining all sorts of bizarre telepathic exchanges, picking fights, throwing tantrums, and causing problems because they wrongly assume that they are accurately reading someone else's Energy or energetic communications.

Although I try never to tell people what to do, in this case I am happy to make an exception. To anyone tempted in this direction, my message is: *Don't do that.* At least not because of anything said in this book. Don't believe that what you think you might pick up by subtly paying attention is factual and accurate. Instead, just give gentle and thoughtful consideration to anything you perceive, and then keep your physical eyes open. Listen internally for direct sensations, but try not to make up detailed, melodramatic stories.

If you undertake this observation process with a humble and open mind, it will leave you with better questions and more curiosity, rather than instant answers. No one becomes an accurate, skilled energetic observer as a result of reading a book. Healthy energetic seeing is fundamentally uncertain, nonintrusive, quiet, and non-self-aggrandizing. Seers, in my tradition, are never self-appointed.

I am writing this volume primarily for people who are reasonably mentally healthy and relatively free of destructive psychological problems or disorders. This is far more a "how to do great things" book than a rehabilitation and repair manual. It is built on the premise that human beings can function well in most or all areas of life most of the time, provided that they are willing to stop trying to validate their own instincts as the sole means for making choices in life and instead rely on a network of friends and allies (including mental and physical health care professionals) to make choices in areas where they have patterns of failure.

High-functioning individuals who are capable of meeting their needs for support and intimacy within a large, open network of interesting, functional friends are the ones who tend to create high-functioning couples. In fact, reasonably high functionality and a healthy network of friends are prerequisites to higher levels of success in the study of Wild Attraction.

I hope that you are mentally healthy and well connected to friends and to a reasonably good support system. Ideally, you have done significant and necessary psychological work at the hands of a compatible and skilled professional, and you have a good foundation in a mind-body practice like yoga, dance, or martial arts. Success in Wild Attraction is most likely if your life includes some sort of grounded and supported spiritual orientation, a high-level technical capability that has taught you real attention to detail, and a personal art or craft through which to express yourself. If you lack many of these elements, then I suggest that you—and your romantic partner if you have one—put this book down, establish some of them in your life, and come back to my work later.

If you are seriously in need of psychological support, then it is vital to go get it. If you have a desire or tendency to abuse or control others, I don't want you reading my book, I want you to seek help. Don't mistake Wild Attraction for a method of avoiding intelligent, modern medical or psychological support, or doing other basic things necessary for health and balance. This book will not allow anyone to skip the necessary steps required for health and still somehow obtain the intimacy everyone rightly wants and realistically needs. I am not a counselor or mental health professional.

Lastly, it is vital that I be explicit about the importance of maintaining personal empowerment. We are dealing in Wild Attraction with the world's most imponderable subject. Your own experience and perception should prevail over anything I, or anyone else, might ever say. This especially applies to material concerning the nonordinary and powers of vision (or claims to them) that are not universally shared. When it comes to things nonordinary, from my point of view, saying anything absolute or definitive is difficult; we are talking about a realm in which perceptions vary and direct physical measurements are impossible. For these and other reasons, everything in this book is best taken as a working model rather than as something to believe in.

Energetic Fact of Life #9:
Nearly everyone believes in love at first sight, and modern films and songs use it as the definition and litmus test of romantic love. But love at first sight is an inversion of the truth of Wild Attraction; it is almost never real. It is more likely a psychological entanglement at first sight, facilitated by hidden energetic negotiations. The suggested action: Take your time in dating and sex and get to know people by getting to know their friends and families and spending long periods of time with them in many environments.

Most people act out energetically, and at least some of their romantic choice-making is being tilted in the wrong direction by their own subconscious Energy-related responses. So what can be done? How do we turn society's model of romantic love right side up again?

A simple defense against making energetically driven, poor people choices is to take your time. Be gently skeptical of sudden powerful feelings for people you don't know well. Energy manipulations, centered in your subconscious mind, never stand the test of time. They can trigger some extremely powerful, almost irresistible attractions in you. These attractions can feel absolutely real, as if they are the universe's indicator that you are meant to be with some given person. But no matter their strength, they are usually false and almost always meaningless in terms of who you are compatible with, or who you love.

Fortunately, these false attractions won't last. So take things slowly. Get to know people gradually. Especially, get to know a new romantic partner's friends and try to see your prospective mate over time in a wide variety of her or his favored environments. This can take months, but that is not a high price to pay for the potential rewards.

This is so important that it is generally my first and last word of advice as a Wild Attraction advisor. It also tends to be the single piece of relationship advice that gets followed the least.

The Energy-based manipulation of your emotions generally results in strong urges that are usually quick, compulsive, and impulsive. Sometimes, so too are the actions that arise from real and lasting love. But until you are good at telling the difference, it is imperative to take your time. If the attraction is genuine, it will still be there in a few weeks or months.

But taking your time usually destroys any dysfunctional Wild Attraction effects. Use this to your advantage.

Chapter 5
The Essence of Attraction

Energetic Fact of Life #10:
Most people firmly believe that human gender qualities such as essential maleness or femaleness and degrees of attractiveness are fixed. This is false; they are fluid and easily influenced. The appropriate course of action: Learn to understand your own gender energetics and make intelligent choices for yourself before other people, or aspects of your own subconscious, make unintelligent choices for you. Do this mainly through simple physical cues using your hands, eyes, and feet.

When Patty and I give talks on Wild Attraction, sooner or later it becomes important to make gender essence real to the audience members experientially. At that point, we ask for volunteers, bringing two men and two women up to the front of whatever hall or conference room we are using. Our usual conference space, the one that has been home to our lectures for many years, is circular, with lightly marbled brown walls, and windows that offer views of a brook and pond outside. I invite you to step into this crucial moment in a prototypical lecture.

From those who raise their hands to volunteer we select a devoted and happy couple and bring them up front. We then choose two singles, one male and one female, who don't know each other at all, to form a second pair.

Once the two pairs are standing onstage, far apart, one on each side of the podium, I ask the audience members if they can tell which pair is the committed couple and which is composed of the two singles. For a variety of reasons, including physical cues, the audience has no trouble identifying which is which.

We ask everyone to take a careful look at the couples, and then to look away from them. I pause and then snap my fingers sharply. Then we ask the audience to look at the couples again.

Usually, we hear a sharp indrawing of breath from the attendees. Suddenly, and surprisingly, the devoted couple no longer "looks" (either to themselves or to the audience) nearly as much like a loving couple. And the two singles have suddenly taken on an appearance much like that of newlyweds. They now radiate the energetic presence that we all identify as "coupleness."

My finger snap was a means of signaling to the audience that I had asked for and cued a small movement of Energy in the individual fields of both couples, a movement that changed their states of being in tangible ways. It was not a magic trick or a Svengali-like hypnotic power. I simply sent a signal that triggered a conditioned reflex, the way a sudden shadow passing overhead will sometimes stimulate an eye blink. This particular instantaneous shift is one that people bring about in each other frequently, though it happens unconsciously. The finger snap was not the signal; it merely marked the moment when an energetic change took place.

None of the four volunteers has moved or changed in any obvious way during the instant it took me to snap my fingers. And yet the sense of connectedness they presented to the group had become entirely different. In the actual lecture that is depicted here, after the passing of a long moment, another snap of the fingers restored the couples to their original state. Again a murmur from the audience signified that the before-and-after comparison had been striking.

How could the snap of someone's fingers change the apparent perception of the state of two couples on the part of an entire audience? Here is an abbreviated answer: When deep mutual safety and availability exist between two members of a couple, their energy fields gradually interlock together. You and all other human beings are able to subconsciously observe this interlock, which we call *energetic completion* and which will be described in detail in a later chapter. Whenever you subconsciously detect this interlock of fields, you consciously register the blended couple as being very much in love and strongly connected, even though you don't consciously see the interwoven Energy. In this demonstration, I cued the two couples to alter their respective levels of energetic completion, and thus brought about a radical and perceptible shift.

This technical explanation leaves unaddressed the broader question of whether one person can actually affect the Energy of another and thus change their experience of genderness and attraction. How could such a thing be so?

Here is the starting point in a multipart answer to this question: *Your degree of femininity or masculinity and your degree of attractiveness are far more variable, and far more under your control, than almost anyone realizes.* This control is available to those who know how to use simple physical movements to radically change certain aspects of the human energy field. This capacity rests on five assertions.

First, within the energy field of each human being are two small structures that convey the qualities of male and female onto that person, quite apart from any influence of physical anatomy. These two *gender essences* are roughly the size of quart or liter milk cartons. They float in the field, cloudlike and slightly luminous.

Second, the gender essences are real, finite, and have *perceived placement*. They are carried in two possible positions within the energy field, either floating just under the left armpit or fixed roughly at the navel.

Third, changing the location of either the male or female gender essence changes a person's *perceived genderness*. Perceived genderness is the degree to which the person experiences male or female patterns of attention, interpretive frameworks, and core gender drives. These changes are so sweeping that they can effectively switch someone from a male person to a female one, or to a gender-neutral being, regardless of his or her physical gender or even sexual preference.

Fourth, by adjusting the precise position of whichever gender essence is at the navel (moving that cloud of Energy either slightly forward or slightly backward toward the spine) a person can radically decrease or increase her or his *perceived attractiveness* to people of the other gender.

Finally, the puzzle piece that brings all this into vivid relevance: *physical acts cue energetic acts*. If a person learns to conceptualize energetic movement, and to trigger it by raising a hand or performing some other gesture, he or she can move the gender essences through simple, intentional physical motions. If you can consciously move your gender essences, you can control your perceived genderness and attractiveness—two huge forces in your life.

These ideas, taken together, represent a radical paradigm shift in relationship science. They give you a level of control almost undreamt of in our culture, and they open the door to a conscious sexual artfulness that is the key to extraordinary relationship. They also help you decode the sexual attraction behaviors that have been going on around you all your life.

To see how physical actions can cue energetic changes and thus affect genderness and attractiveness, step back into our prototypical Wild Attraction lecture.

> After having cued a complete shift in the apparent coupleness of the two pairs of volunteers, I request that the two women volunteers stand close together in the center of the room. I ask the males in the audience to look carefully at them and gently search their inner reactions to each woman's presence—not to compare the women to one another, and certainly not to rate physical good looks, but rather to look at the women as if they were paying attention to close friends who were asking for opinions as to which dress to wear.
>
> The men are being asked to compare the presence of each woman at that moment with that same woman's potential impact if she were suddenly rendered fully confident, available, and relaxed.
>
> After giving the males a moment to calibrate their internal "attraction detectors," I suggest that both women volunteers lift one heel very slightly off the floor, thus shifting the weight and subtly tilting their hips.
>
> As soon as this is accomplished, the body language of the men (and the women) in the audience changes. They lean forward, their eyes widen, and extraneous whispered conversation ceases. The female volunteers have suddenly become much more provocative.
>
> I next ask the two women to look at the luminous green exit sign above the door at the back of the hall. I request that they keep their eyes fixed firmly on this feature while they turn their hips and body slightly to the

right. Each woman's body is now pointing in a slightly different direction than the direction of her gaze.

Individuals in the crowd spontaneously comment, as the women shift into this stance, that they have become even more attractive.

Next, I invite the two females up front to raise their hands high above their heads and keep them there, so they look like dancers clanging tiny golden musical finger cymbals with uparaised arms.

The crowd begins to murmur and exclaim in surprise. The new, even more compelling presence of the women stirs them up.

The changes illustrated in this scene are increases in perceived attractiveness. Even when the volunteers go through these steps while the crowd keeps their eyes shut, the audience reports the same perceptions. According to the Wild Attraction model of human sexuality, this phenomenon occurs because, remember, *physical acts cue energetic acts*. Specific physical actions cued the female volunteers' subconscious minds to change important things in their energy fields; these changes altered the degree to which their feminine gender essences were engaged. The audience could sense these changes even in the absence of visual cues.

Physical actions like those in this illustration change the perceived placement of the gender essences, and thus the genderness, and perceived attractiveness of human beings. This link between the physical and energetic bodies can be used to make progressive changes, so that the control you might have over your sexuality has a dial-up quality like a light dimmer. In our example, the higher each woman raised her hands overhead, the more actively engaged her female gender Energy became. (Incidentally, when a woman uses this raised-hand technique in daily life, she usually does it in disguised forms, such as adjusting glasses, flipping hair, holding the end of a pen or pencil to the lips, or adjusting shoulder straps.)

No one knows exactly why this works the way it does. These energetic changes are simply automatic, mechanical effects caused by simple physical motions. And they operate exactly the same way in all humans everywhere.

Here is what seers see in the energy fields of these women when these changes are happening: The milk-carton-sized feminine gender essence often appears as a glowing, pastel-colored cylinder. When fully engaged and activated, it migrates from the left side of the body to a front-and-center position and comes to rest in an upright alignment directly in front of the woman's navel. The top of the cylinder usually rests at about breastbone level. Each woman's male gender essence remains motionless, tucked under the left armpit. Note that the gender essences look exactly the same in males, except that, of course, the male gender essence is the larger of the two clouds.

It is unnecessary to see gender essence directly in order to use this model. In fact, energy fields themselves shift with such quicksilver liquidity that it is hard to make generalizations about what they look like even if you can see them constantly. It is also unnecessary to believe specifically the Wild Attraction assertion that gender qualities derive from the essences described here. What counts is your willingness to use the specific physical behavioral techniques described in the Wild Attraction model.

The movement of a cloud of gender essence from your left armpit to your belly center is one of two important motions that gender essences can make. It is a change in perceived placement. This movement determines perceived genderness—which of the two gender essences is the dominant filter through which you view the world.

But, as has already been said, a second type of gender essence motion, toward or away from the spine, determines the degree to which gender essence is engaged, which brings about changes in your perceived attractiveness. Without ever realizing it, you, as well as all the people you know, have always had this kind of choice and control over the experience of being male or female.

Most of what you will ever want to accomplish in terms of controlling your genderness and attractiveness can be done with a set of only three physical movements: (1) raising or lowering the hands above or below the nipple line (and forward of or behind the hips); (2) lifting one heel up off the floor or lowering that heel so that you are standing with both feet flat; and (3) shifting the direction of your gaze offline with respect to the direction the body center is facing or swinging it into exact alignment with that direction.

In lectures, Patty and I show people how to use these three physical motion choices to create the dial-up quality of attractiveness and genderness mentioned earlier. Step back in.

> Once again I ask the two female volunteers to fix their eyes on the green luminous exit sign on the back wall and to swivel their hips to the right or the left, so their bodies are pointing in a slightly different direction than their faces and eyes. As they rotate into this position, the glowing cylinders of feminine gender essence that are already resting invisibly against the women's bellies sink gently backward toward their spines. I tell the attendees that this movement of the gender essence looks very much like the motion of a cat snuggling into a deep blanket. It is a settling in. The more this happens, the more fired up each female's gender essence becomes.
>
> Next, I request that the women keep the same off-line alignment and lift their left heels slightly off the floor, and

> *[Handwritten note at top: These movements present curves—parts/features of women's bodies that men don't have]*

> the fired up effect is even further intensified. The act of distributing a woman's weight unevenly, more onto one foot than on the other, causes the gender essence cylinder of that woman to settle even more deeply into the skin towards the backbone. The more this happens, the more intrusively dominant the female gender essence becomes, and the more it magnifies and supercharges that woman's presence and power over the attention of everyone else in the room.

Women are able to compete with each other in exactly this way for the available attention in a space. Not only is this not uncommon, it is typical, and it happens millions of times every day on the planet.

If using physical cues to "settle in" the dominant gender essence increases the women's attractiveness, the physical gestures that cue male genderness diminish their attractiveness, as illustrated in the next section of the prototype lecture.

> Patty then invites the women to relax and tells them that she is about to ask them to do a strange thing: to take on a male gender stance. At her request, the two volunteers drop the lifted heel and put their weight fully and equally down on both feet. She directs them to align their hips straight ahead as though they are gunfighters in a shootout and, lastly, to drop their hands to their belts, cowboy-style. Within a few seconds, all of their powerful allure is gone, snuffed out, at least from the perspective of a heterosexual audience. They take on a noticeably male quality that is not flattering in this setting.
>
> The crowd reaction to this loss is always immediate. Everyone craves the return of that palpable, electric attraction. Wild Attraction is fun.

As the next segment in our prototype lecture shows, the Wild Attraction gestures that increase a woman's genderness and perceived attractiveness work in reverse for males; the gestures that reduce attractiveness in women make men more attractive.

> Next, I ask the two male volunteers to take center stage and make the same changes that the women did, in the same order. It is now the women's turn, from the audience, to provide the attraction meter feedback.
>
> As the audience quickly discovers, the three techniques involving hands up, heel up, and body off-line to line of sight do nothing to enhance the attractiveness of the men. In fact, the more of these behaviors the male volunteers layer on, the less attractive the two men become for the women. By the end of this cycle, the female attendees react to them as though they are a pair of wimps.
>
> I then request that the men drop their hands and heels and relax, and as they do so the unattractive disempoweredness drops away. Next, they step through the second set of body positions. They put their hands at their belts, place equal weight on both feet, and keep their bodies aligned straight ahead with eyes looking forward. These new postures are greeted with approval by the women in the audience. In fact, the audience is now as enthusiastic about the intense masculine appeal of the two male volunteers as they had been a few minutes earlier about the allure of the women when they were at their most powerful.

Power poses

It is remarkable that such simple physical posturing can have such consistent effects on observers. It is even more remarkable that they are palpable even when the attendees close their eyes.

Wild Attraction genderness and perceived attraction effects run deeper than physical body language. While you need physical action to change your genderness consciously (through the principle: *physical acts cue energetic acts*), your subconscious mind can and does manipulate your essence engagement without the use of any physical motion at all.

To repeat: Your subconscious mind is already exercising this control. And unlike your conscious mind, your subconscious does not need the help of your physical body. (This should be a daunting thought, because your subconscious mind probably has no greater degree of strategic awareness than does a four-year-old child.) The subconscious also is entirely capable of moving your energy body without the use of visualization, exactly the way your conscious mind exercises control of your hands.

Energetic Fact of Life #11:
Even though we live in a culture of denial about Energy, most people have been trained to believe that they can control nonordinary, energetic aspects of their own nature through the use of imagination, visualization, and will power. This is most emphatically not the case. The imagination is nearly useless as a vehicle for creating energetic motion or change. It is the most physically engaged people who are the best at manipulating their energy fields, not those who are the most cerebral. You would do well to develop a strong sense of physicality if you do not have one already. The necessary action: Suggest to yourself that your energy field mimic your physical body, and then actually do something physical that is the equivalent of the energetic action you wish to accomplish—for example, put your arms around your mate when you want to enfold him or her within your energy field.

The alliance between the conscious mind and the physical body is so vital as the only way to intentionally bring about effective energetic changes in your system that an entire chapter later in this book is devoted to it. People persist in thinking that they can use their imaginations, usually in the form of visualization processes, to control their personal Energy. Nothing could be further from the truth. Moving things around in our imaginary worlds does not move things around in the energetic one, and those who default to this approach usually lack interpersonal power and influence with the other gender.

The next phase in the prototypical lecture addresses the issue of male and female relative power, and answers the question: What is your most effective stance in dealing with members of the other gender?

> I ask the volunteers to face their partners, the two women on one side of the stage and the two men on the other. I then ask the audience to estimate the height of the males relative to the females standing across from them.
>
> Next, at my request, the four men and women on stage simultaneously adopt the physical postures that engage their male gender essences. These postures are: hands at the belt, feet flat with weight equal on both legs, and pelvis and shoulders lined up with the eye's line of focus. Once this is accomplished, the audience members generally agree that the men appear taller and far more powerful than the women. I tell the attendees that however good the women become at engaging male essence, it is very hard for any woman to out-male a male.
>
> I suggest that the volunteers switch roles. When both genders perform the motions that heighten feminine essence engagement—hands above collarbone, one heel lifted, and body alignment different from the eye line—the women actually seem to grow taller relative to the men, and this time the females are almost universally seen as clearly in charge, outgunning the males. Once again, this

demonstrates an important truth, one that is by no means universally acknowledged: no man can out-woman a woman.

Questions relating to the energetics of same sex couples arise naturally among the audience at this point. Later in this chapter I discuss the applicability of the Wild Attraction model to the interests of this sizable percentage of our population. Even for those whose only experience of these exercises will be in the pages of this book, physically testing these concepts for themselves is essential. Don't keep them inside your head. Have some fun and experiment with them using your own body, perhaps with the help of a reasonably open and curious friend.

In addition, it is useful to watch actors on television and in films with these Wild Attraction gestures in mind. It can also be instructive to watch men and women as they move around in malls and nightclubs. Perhaps most persuasive of all, the next time you pass by the local high school, pause and take a look at the kids on break or at lunch. Really pay attention to what is happening within that swirl of young people. Just by observing them, politely and with sympathy and discretion, you can learn a great deal about the energetics of human sexuality. The hand, eye, and foot gestures that engage the essences are likely to be on display at peak intensity in the schoolyard. The students are merely doing the same things that all the rest of us are doing, albeit more discretely. High schools are showcases of Wild Attraction signals running amok, including a great many that have not yet been discussed.

Here is something that you most likely never learned in high school:

Energetic Fact of Life #12:
Although physical beauty gives people confidence and thus is almost universally seen as the cause of attraction, in fact physical beauty is a relatively minor player. Your personal confidence and willingness to engage the full machinery of energetic sexual attraction are the key factors in sexual allure. The needed actions: Don't worry too much about elements of beauty you can't change. Instead, actively seek out experiences that build your confidence in the energetics of attraction and your ability to engage it successfully.

Give compliments to other people to encourage their confidence, and ask for compliments and similar reinforcing messages from people you respect.

One of the many benefits of attending a demonstration like the ones Patty and I conduct is that the near irrelevance of a person's physical shape and appearance in real attraction may finally become clear once and for all. The attitude and Energy of another human being, man or woman, influences you far more (after the first few seconds of contact) than their physical looks. This is true unless physical beauty or plainness is very pronounced—and even then, physical good looks take a distant second to Energy in terms of determining who you end up being attracted to.

I have rarely met a man or woman who is not physically good-looking enough to find a satisfying match. Usually, chronic involuntary singleness stems from an innate lack of self-worth that damages the responses of the gender essences and either mutes their signals or distorts them such that their natural attractive force is shut off. (One of the many ways in which attraction is switched off is disengagement of the gender essences. In this state, both essences remain in the neutral position under the left armpit, and the man or woman radiates a tangible genderlessness.)

Many of the world's greatest lovers, including, according to most accounts, the dark-haired Cleopatra herself, were regarded as physically relatively plain. In terms of beauty and attraction, the playing field is more equal than you could ever have imagined.

Those who believe themselves more strikingly handsome or lovely feel more confidence and give themselves more permission to ratchet up the power of their gender essences. This is not to say that physical shape doesn't affect the observer. Obviously it does. But our attractiveness is mainly a matter of unleashing our gender essence.

How do you relate to gender essence with the greatest success? Step back into the lecture.

> Patty and I now invite the entire audience to participate. We request that the group divide itself along gender lines, with all the females on one side of the hall and all the males on the other.
>
> I ask everybody to take two car keys, or two pens, and position them under their left armpit. I suggest that they casually imagine that these objects represent their male and female gender essences.
>
> I then suggest that the attendees on both sides of the hall move the object that represents their primary gender essence to their midline, right up against their belt buckle or navel, and then assume the physical postures that go with that essence. If they identify themselves mostly as male, they line up their midlines and their eyes so both directly face the opposite wall and place their hands at the belt buckle position and both feet flat on the floor.

Those who identify themselves mostly as female raise one heel, raise their free hand above their collarbone, and align their body off-axis as compared to their line of sight. As everyone expects by now, the men will be masculine and the women will be feminine. The audience members get the knack of this very quickly.

At this point I tell them that every human being needs to be gender-bilingual—willing and able to use both the male and female approach to language.

Energetic Fact of Life #13:
The common perception is that we should be able to speak to the other gender in our own gender's preferred style of language and get away with it. We are even taught to stubbornly insist on it. This is far from effective as a strategy for extraordinary relationship. You must be willing and able to speak and listen in the language of the other gender. The needed action: Speak to your woman in terms of "we," "they," and "us," inclusively and subtly, knowing that she will take the most general statement personally. Speak to your man directly and bluntly, specifying "you," with the realization that a male will not inherently personalize from a generalized comment; you have to tell him straight out.

I request that the men and women face each other across the open space and give voice to a simple phrase, while establishing eye contact with someone across the room. This phrase is: "You are not doing a very good job." This is a mild criticism—too soft to be effective at changing behavior when directed at a male but too harsh for comfortable use with women.

I ask the men to speak this phrase, as a group, to the women, as we all watch their responses. Then I ask the women to say the exact same thing to the men.

The difference in responses is remarkable. The phrase has no noticeable effect on the men. Males' reaction to criticism in general, as long as their male gender essence is engaged, is to start wondering if something is wrong with the critic.

The reverse is true for the females. When they hear this same phrase, they cringe. They shrink. In a few cases, eyes redden involuntarily.

The direct phrase they have all used, while too non-specific to be effective for the males (because it doesn't mention the man by name or specify what's wrong with the job) is overly potent for the females.

We reverse the roles. I ask the group to shift their gender identity to their nondominant essence. They move their objects representing their dominant gender essence back to the neutral position under their left armpits, and they bring the other object, the one representing their nondominant essence, to the center body position. Everyone also assumes the three physical postures that reinforce their nondominant gender essence. Now that the females are coming from their maleness, and the males are experiencing their femininity, we repeat the exercise, this time using more distinctly male, very direct language: "You are doing a terrible job."

When the males deliver this message to the females, the females gasp in amazement and then burst out laughing. Many report an almost overwhelming feeling of relief. Now, with their male essence engaged, the women don't care what the men are saying. They don't internalize the criticism. For some, it is an entirely new experience.

Next it is the women's turn to speak this somewhat more direct reproach. They say to the men, "You are doing a terrible job."

> And the men, now in feminine essence, blanch, flinch, and some even take a half step backward. One tall, brown-bearded man once commented, "No wonder my girlfriend would look so hurt whenever I tried to tell her what was going on with me, or express a negative. She felt like *this*." He locked eyes with her across the room apologetically. To me he said, "I was speaking to her much too directly."
>
> Most of the men at this point in our lectures look at the women with new sympathy.

In this part of the exercise, both sides come to understand: the innate languages of the gender essences are fundamentally different. The language approach that is necessary to get through to a man is much too strong for a woman. A woman can be overwhelmed by a phrase that barely convinces a man that a problem exists.

On the other hand, a subtle comment might be all a woman needs to understand a particular point. But it could sail over a man's head entirely unnoticed. This effect is purely mechanical, and it happens this way for reasons still unknown.

At this stage in every lecture, I comment on the inestimable amount of pain that has been inflicted in the world because we as a race have not yet realized that the genders differ innately in their communication patterns. Step back into the lecture once again.

> Normally, Patty and I continue this exercise for one more round. We ask that everyone move themselves back to their dominant gender essences, the women in female and the men in male. This time, the critical phrase is in unmistakably indirect, female language: "Some of us, occasionally, could do things a little better than we are doing them."

As before, each side of the room speaks this phrase to the other, one side at a time, as we all watch for reactions. The women, while in feminine essence, deal perfectly well with this phrase. It is exactly calibrated for them. A woman assumes that the phrase is meant to convey something to her and about her, but it doesn't overwhelm her.

To the men, in male gender essence, this phrase is so mild as to be nearly meaningless.

Then, as a group, we undertake one last switch, and move back to the nondominant essence. The men now listen from the feminine, and the women from the masculine.

The phrase is the same as before, "Some of us, occasionally, could do things a little better than we are doing them."

The men, hearing the phrase in feminine essence, understand perhaps for the first time that women hear a request for change most accurately when it is delivered in inclusive, nonspecific, supportive language that a man would shrug off.

The women, hearing this phrase for the first time in male essence, suddenly realize why their men have appeared to ignore them. Some burst into tears. Others laugh. One says, "When I try to speak in my own way to the men, it just doesn't do any good. And now I know why. But I can talk to them their way. I just don't want to have to do it all the time. I want some give and take."

I tell her that I think she is exactly right.

When talking to a person whose male gender essence is strongly engaged, you have to be specific and personal in a way that would shock a feminine person. Even saying "You are doing a bad job" can sometimes be too mild. You might have to speak bluntly and directly, almost in slow motion: "You! Dave! You

... are ... screwing ... this ... up. You used the wrong gaskets. You. Fix it."

To which Dave might reply, "Oh? Thanks, I didn't realize." And he will walk away and fix the problem, probably without any sign of ego damage or antagonism. Really.

The surprise for men is that they can trust women to personalize very general statements. They don't have to be specific, direct, and personal. The women will do that for them. They will make the leap.

The central concept here might appear fairly simple: It's important to talk to people in the gender language they understand, or listen to them in the gender language they speak, if we want to communicate successfully. It's simple, but it's big.

Use this. It works. It can eliminate eighty or ninety percent of your relationship pain and can help you nourish your mate. This approach is the equivalent of a miracle drug in the world of Wild Attraction.

Part II

Wrapped in the Wings of Love

Chapter 6

The Story of All Things

Energetic Fact of Life #14:
The universal specialty of the mind is to take amazing and extraordinary things and reduce them to the commonplace. For this reason, people tend to think they know what human beings are. The fact is, humans are much more than they seem. In fact, everything is unimaginably more than it seems. Sex isn't ordinary and casual; it is life and death and overwhelmingly extraordinary. Your best approach: Start looking for the unexpected in everyone and everything around you, and be sure to voice aloud the best of what you see, regularly. Also, stop talking about sex in the culture's ordinary terms (for example, as existing only for fun or having little meaning) and start talking about it in terms of mystery, magic, and awakening.

Three centuries ago, the surge of material and psychological insights known as the Enlightenment swept across much of the world, washing away many hardened and (up till then) unyielding irrational beliefs. As a direct result of these rising floodwaters, the United States of America was born, as were other wonders. In the freedom that followed, thousands of scientists, engineers, explorers, and educators debunked many destructive tenets of superstition and fundamentalist religion.

Unfortunately, the rising wave of scientific thought (not always truly enlightened) also tossed aside important and subtle notions about the nature of reality we could not afford to lose. Among these are the classical observations that, in a completely secular sense, we are not alone in the universe; that humans are much more than we realize or appreciate; and that reality is incalculably more expansive and intricate than we can perceive through our five physical senses, no matter how sophisticated science becomes. Another insight that has largely been lost along the way is the concept of gender as an external sentient force, which is the key subject of this work.

Modern, science-based culture has defined people, places, and things in greater detail and measured them more precisely than the culture of any prior age. But from a seer's perspective, it has not taught us to perceive the world any better than people did at the time of Aristotle. On the contrary, because we think we know more about the world than we used to, we are actually observing things less clearly.

Along the way, nothing has been more trivialized than our concept of *Homo sapiens*. Although we now understand the nature of human beings much better in physical, psychological, and anthropological terms, most of us are unaware of the grandeur that actually lies resident within each human heart. None of us know the true nature of the sentient beings we argue with, hold hands with, and make love to. In fact, it is a mistake to think we know our lovers, and a mistake to believe that the loving touch of any other person is anything short of a miracle.

There is no such thing as an ordinary person, and no human being has ever fully seen or appreciated another. We are too vast.

In the Wild Attraction worldview, we humans are intricate, lovely, and mysterious. We are indigenous to magnificent non-ordinary realms we seldom consciously see but in which we are as powerful and mobile as elephants on an African plain. A few extraordinarily gifted people are occasionally able to pass wakefully into such worlds, which are as kinesthetically real as the physical one to which most people so fervently cling. The most credible of these travelers have reported that other beings—neither angels, devils, gods, or goddesses, just *others* in endless and unimaginable variety—exist and can at times be related to successfully.

What can and should you do with such reports? Perhaps the best response is to experiment with any potentially useful ideas that arise from them, without rushing to believe or disbelieve, and then see what happens. This is what most people are doing anyway, most of the time. Including you.

Each day, you subconsciously infer your personal reality by subjecting your own perceptions to a simple practical test: if an idea drawn from an experience works, the experience itself *may* be real. Similarly, you can submit other people's perceptions, even of nonordinary observations, to the same kind of testing. You won't get a true/false answer about an extrasensory or mystical perception. But you may be able to form a working model that offers you food for thought, and you might discover a better approach to the process of living a good life.

If someone you respect discloses a nonordinary event and you listen to this tale with curiosity and without judgment, the odds increase that you may someday experience something similar yourself and be able to draw your own conclusions. Sex and gender represent a wild card in this game. Their real promise is transformation. When you are burning in the fire of an enhanced romantic love, you may find that everything you once knew to be true about yourself and the world has suddenly changed.

You have a personal *story of all things*, whether you know it consciously or not, and it plays a huge role in your life. The more thoughtfully examined your story of all things becomes, the richer your life will be. From a seer's viewpoint, your story of all things, and all the smaller stories you tell yourself and others, are a necessary personal art, meant to be taken seriously but not believed. Your story can never be a correct description of reality, nor can it be inherently better than a story created by anyone else.

Your personal story of all things need not be a grand religious or mythological composition. It can simply be a gut-level, honest assessment of what you think is going on in reality. Look around. What do you think is happening, and why?

You may have no better answer than: "Nobody knows what life is really about, and we all must simply make the best of it." Or you may perceive the human world as evolving toward some intended fulfillment and see yourself as a part of this.

Your entire personal instruction book for sexual relationship is but a small chapter in your story of all things, closely interwoven with all the other chapters. Obviously, that chapter must be expanded if you are to meaningfully enhance your prospects for extraordinary intimacy. The Wild Attraction worldview is not being presented here to replace your individual story; it is here to inspire you to expand your own, on your terms. The Wild Attraction story of all things offers far more beauty and wonder, when it comes to relationship, than does that of the prevailing culture. Simply put, in matters of intimacy it is more inspiring. It is also more frank about the dark side of sex and love.

I would find it unconscionable to write a book about something as important as your sex life that did not at least briefly consider some of the more sobering aspects of male-female love. Although it is more often presented as a recreational activity, sex is a life-and-death matter. Throughout history, sex has killed large numbers of people through death in childbirth and the transmission of disease—including HIV, which now infects millions. Huge denial surrounds this issue in today's culture, just as huge denial surrounds the fact that, from a certain point of view, irresistible sexual attraction is imposed on us genetically for the good of the species but not necessarily with our individual interests in mind. Think about it: every day people are driven to potentially ruinous or fatal sexual acts because of the imperative for propagation of the species. This means that you can't run on instinct or autopilot and expect to maximize your love life.

Other serious consequences arise from sexuality, including the production of children outside of the social support network of a pair bond, issues of inheritance and lineage, and other problems tied to proof of parentage (recent genetic tests show that an astonishing percentage of children are not the offspring of the husband and father in the family).

Of equal importance is the awesome destructive power of rape and other forms of sexual abuse. Western culture's disregard for the absolute urgency of dealing proactively with this form of crime is astonishing. Sexual abuse damages the ability of human beings to relate positively to both genders, it reduces our ability to create great human beings, and it causes incalculable harm that extends for generations.

When you consider long-term sociological and individual injury, sexual abuse rivals murder in its seriousness. With murder, the effects are instantaneous and easy to see. With sexual abuse, the damage is spread out over time and much easier to deny.

In addition to these "ordinary world" considerations, sexuality is a minefield from an energetic viewpoint. In Energy terms, casual sexuality can be very destructive to human development. Many energetic changes occur during sexual intercourse and other kinds of sexual connection, mainly in the form of exchanges of content, life models, and worldview. If you could see from an energetic perspective, you would naturally refrain from sexual activity with people you don't know extremely well. And you would refrain from sexual activities that might undermine your self-esteem, or your esteem for gender itself.

On the other hand, it is perilous to ignore or systematically repress your sexuality. A life lived alone presents another list of risks. People in healthy sexual relationships live substantially longer. They enjoy, on the average, more productive lives, higher reported satisfaction and happiness levels, and a lower incidence of major illnesses that reduce quality of life.

This duality—the fact that sex is both necessary and profoundly hazardous—gives rise to the "wild" in Wild Attraction. Wild does not exist without danger. To take the wild out of anything is to tame that thing. Tame Attraction is almost always swept away and overturned by Wild Attraction. The latter is simply more powerful. It runs the world.

You need the "wild" in Wild Attraction. You need to break rules and court risk and try new things. You need to be what you really are sexually and not what is convenient or conforming. Yet wild, in the end, is too big to master. So you also need intelligence. You need to be wild, but in ways that work for you, and in ways that make you a better human being. This calls for education. This book is intended to inspire you to consciously modify your own story of all things. It is also a how-to guide for those who would like to stop bouncing between being tame and being recklessly wild in sex and relationship, and start being wild in ways that work.

Growing up, most of us deserved and needed an exponentially greater exposure to relationship education than we received—certainly we needed much more information on the energetics of intimacy than we received. We needed, in addition, greater protection from sexuality and relationship choice models that destroy our ability to make intelligent sexual choices.

Sexual relationship is next only to life and death as the most awe-inspiring and overwhelming set of choice challenges human beings face. Legislation and moral stricture will never be up to the tasks of regulating this force and guiding you effectively because, ultimately, the scope and scale of gender is simply beyond the human race's collective intellectual grasp. The fundamental premise of Wild Attraction is precisely this: attraction arises from within the human breast, but it is also imposed by an external sentient intelligence whose intent is ruthlessly bent to the task of moving those who ally with it toward union with the mystery of existence itself. Wild Attraction both beckons and threatens, hoping for symbiotic partnership, but ultimately it can sweep into the ancient savannah firelight and carry a person off into the darkness, regardless of his or her trust in the fire's circle of safety. Wild Attraction is actually and truly dangerous.

In other words, your overprotective parents were right.

The attempt throughout history to define and dominate human sexual activity by dogmatic authority may in part be a subconscious recognition and fear response to the overwhelming strength of the force of Wild Attraction and an attempt to keep it in check by fiat and dread of punishment. As destructive as the repressive approach has been, the other side of the coin is equally misguided. I speak of the widespread modern denial that sexuality is anything but a recreational indulgence, and the accompanying pretense that it has no meaning beyond pleasure or reproductive choice.

Neither of these worldviews makes sense from a Wild Attraction perspective or fits into its story of all things. You could say that Wild Attraction as a model for human behavior represents a daring third alternative to fear and denial.

This assertion brings us out of the shadow of a frankly darker side of human sexual relationship and into the radiance of gender's endless capacity to inspire selfless love.

> **Energetic Fact of Life #15:**
> Our culture hypes a self-centered vision of sex and relationship, focused on what we can get out of sexuality and what relationship offers to us as individuals. This is a fatal inversion. Relationship works best when you think of it as a vehicle of giving and contributing and as a secular spiritual practice, keeping your own interests present but not predominant in your choice processes. What can you give to your mate? What can you do for gender itself? The required actions: Catch yourself when you are fretting about your own needs and satisfactions. Ask your mate what he or she really needs from you every day. Perform at least one action daily that contributes something to the gender essences in both you and your partner—or, if you are single, for a person of the other gender in your environment.

Wild Attraction is about intelligence, an attitude of moving *toward* things we don't entirely understand that might be called *yes to the mystery*. It is about the profound awakenings described by our greatest mystics and in our most revered traditions. Its story of all things is a celebration of the unearthly magnificence of love and of the human capacity to relate successfully to powers greater than our own.

Rather than fighting the Wild Attraction force or denying its existence, this book offers a blueprint for artful and loving alliance with it. What do we as individuals have to offer to gender itself? What does it need from us that we can freely give? How can we extract ourselves from the culture's self-interest-based model, the one that keeps most people wondering what sex and love have to offer to them?

You might ask yourself other questions: How can you increase your curiosity about what you can offer your mate, or prospective mate, as a lover and appreciate of gender itself? Can you play the male or female role, and use its powers with grace and enthusiasm? Can you carry the torch of a tradition of respectful and unselfish gender-based love?

Wild Attraction is a model about giving—not only to your mate but to a thing you can't directly see whose existence and nature you nevertheless can infer from what you observe and feel. If you are really honest about your experience in sex and love, you can sense that giving is what *works* in love.

The idea that it is possible to discover what works is the keystone in the foundational tale of reality that supports Wild Attraction.

Energetic Fact of Life #16:

Society tells us subliminally through nonordinary Energy that no one's life works completely in all areas. Therefore, the process of choosing a mate is reduced to an effort to pick someone whose life doesn't work in the ways we can best tolerate. This is a tragic misconception. People and their lives can work in all the important ways. Extraordinary relationship thrives only when both partners believe in total functionality and pursue it effectively. Your needed actions: Examine every major area of your life: money, spirituality, physical health, rest, friendship, and many more. Make a list of what you produce in all areas, and mark those in which either too much or too little of what is needed has become a negative factor. Seek the help you need to bring yourself to at least a minimum functionality. Don't stop, and don't lose faith. Don't listen to the negative voice of your culture or to your own sabotaging subconscious mind. Your life can work. And you can work in every significant way.

When one of my daughters reached adulthood, she was kind enough to submit to a luncheon during which I, in the dwindling role of father, offered her some last parental advice. Looking across the table into her remarkably open and positive eyes, I recalled a story about Brigadier General Jimmy Stewart, the famous actor and war hero. When facing a similar moment with his own recently engaged daughter, he avoided any "birds and bees" talk and came up with just one brief sentence: "Treat people well, and people will treat you well."

Like Jimmy, I talked about relationship while staying away from the birds and bees. My line was: "Surround yourself with people whose lives work in every important way, and you will become one of them."

Amazingly, and delightfully, our individual potential as humans to function adequately in all important areas of life is far greater than most people realize. The cultural depiction of humans is a lie: we are not permanently cursed with fatal flaws. We can be as completely functional as we expect a new car or TV set to be when we bring it home from the dealer. People, just out of the box, can successfully figure out what works in most contexts. We can also remake ourselves, repair ourselves, and supplement our own instincts and capabilities effectively enough to live largely free of long-term patterns of dysfunction. Huge resources exist in our society to help us accomplish this.

Anything can be said to work if it helps you to actualize a latent capability or to achieve a higher level of functionality or insight. What works is what makes you and those around you palpably greater people—more able to produce beauty, reduce chaos, make powerful and constructive choices, and pass these capacities along to others. In addition, what works is what allows you to produce *just enough* of what is needed in each area of your life so as to maximize your overall quality of life. What works is what produces not too much and not too little of everything, including hard living, bad luck, and misfortune, of which everyone actually needs a certain amount to be at his or her best.

The notion of "what works" applies to sexual intimacy as well. Why would you want to sleep with anyone who doesn't work? Once you and your partner work as individuals, you can be wild in ways that work. The gender essences within you will then be able to work for you, (and you for them). So too will the external force of gender itself.

For most people, living a life that works is not difficult. What is sometimes difficult, in a world that seems to be doing its best to convince us that being flawed is normal, is to believe that it can be done.

When you work, and your partner works, you have time to focus effectively on the things that gender needs from you in order to do what it does best.

Energetic Fact of Life #17:
People think that romantic love is about duos.
This isn't true. An extraordinary relationship is really a trio, a three-way connection between you, your partner, and the intelligent external force of gender. Your needed response: Perform small actions, Energy practices done through physical motion, that acknowledge the nature and needs of gender essence at least a few times every day, such as opening the door for your female mate, or waiting for someone to open a door for you if you are female. Also, speak occasionally to the gender essence in your partner, for instance, "I love men" or "Women are the most wonderful phenomenon on the planet."

Your story of all things will never be complete unless it includes a thoughtful model of how the gender essences work and how you can give them what they need to operate at their optimum.

The male and female gender essences are not finished and complete as entities, and they don't work well if you see them that way. They are separated components of something that was once whole and which is waiting to be reassembled. They are literally small broken-away pieces of a single larger gender force, the one lurking just outside the glow of the ancient campfire. When your gender essences are merged—combined fully with the gender essences of someone else—a small version of the unified genders' immense energy field and intelligence is formed near to you and your mate.

Patty and I call this local Wild Attraction field the *supergender* because it is different from, and more than, either the male or female. It is the result of their merging, and it bestows onto the couple a profound, relaxed wisdom and grace that is palpable to others.

There are several amazing propositions in the Wild Attraction story of all things, and this is one of them: something in you and a part of you that nevertheless isn't you has needs, loves, and wants. In this sense, lovers are not couples; in fact they are communities.

I do all I can to treat Patty as well as possible, both as a person and as a woman, because I love her to a maximum conceivable degree. I also treat her with as much gallantry as I can muster because of that love.

In parallel with my vast love of Patty herself, I am also moved to love, respect, and appreciate the femininity that helps to animate her, which I see as a separate and equal being and as a specific, accessible embodiment of a universal principle of love and union with all things. Every time I open a door for Patty, or pay loving attention, or speak to her in the language of the feminine, or perform any of a thousand other actions in a week that derive from my appreciation of her as a woman, I am nourishing and thanking a wonderful presence within her that is bigger than any individual woman. *[marginalia: Makes sense]*

My interest in honoring and serving her womanhood does not arise from self-interest, not even from the species form of genetic self-interest described beautifully in evolutionary psychology. It would be there if I had no physical body at all. The impulse arises naturally within me as a part of my energetic inheritance. In seeing to the innate needs and wants of Patty's femininity as well as of Patty as a total person, I am making it possible for gender to give something to me and to her—which it is always trying to do.

To relate to Patty is to discover that I am more than just part of a couple. I am a part of a wonderful love triangle, consisting of Patty, me, and gender itself, which is a direct representation of the incredible mystery of life.

CHAPTER 7

Being Wild in Ways That Work

Energetic Fact of Life #18:
Western cultures promote the idea that men and women learn about gender and relationship through obsessive examination of their own thoughts and feelings. This is not the case. Gender suffuses all things in your field of view. You best learn about sex and gender by looking at the natural world and by exposing yourself to the high-level creative expressions of other humans. The needed actions: Spend time in nature. Seek out high-level art. Ponder the shape, feel, aesthetics, and motion of inanimate things with an eye to gender and sexual symbolism. Especially, look for places and things that radiate a sensation of genderness similar to that surrounding markedly masculine or feminine people. Bask in these experiences.

One of the messages of this book is that gender is not just a human state of mind; it is a constant energetic quality that pervades all of nature. One way to increase consciousness of this fact is to look around and consider the many things around us that seem to partake of genderness. Watch for the way that <u>complementary</u> dualities unify themselves naturally (stars and black sky, water and land, shade and sparkle, mountain and river, life and death).

My community boasts a wonderful green jewel at its center. Lithia Park is a winding wooded preserve, right in the heart of town, wrapped around a crystalline river that serves as a grand water feature gracing Ashland's central plaza.

The watercourse is (as women tend to be) habitually peaceful and frequently serene. It is a tree-shaded, curved backbone of water that streams over huge gray rocks, overlaid with a series of picture-book bridges, decks, ponds, and children's playgrounds. Lithia is one of the most delightful parks I have ever seen, and it played a huge role in my decision to live where I live. It is an incredible attraction.

I have been told that this park exists today only because, a little over a hundred years ago, the women of the town undertook a campaign to give birth to it. They did this in the face of opposition from the local men. Had the women not taken up the cause, most likely this glorious wonderland would have long since given way to pavement and buildings. Women often see value in different ways than men, and in different places.

Many people over the years have mentioned to me that something about Ashland, and the park especially, strikes them as strongly feminine. They describe this as a tangible sensation.

You may find it worthwhile to seek out such a place in your own community, because exploring a landscape that is strongly male or female offers insight into the nature of gender and provides a kind of access to femininity or masculinity outside the human body.

Both Patty and I lived in the park's shadow during our courtship period, in separate but nearby homes, and even today we live only a few miles away from it. Its ambience is soothing, healing, contemplative, mysterious, inclusive, and very beauty-oriented. Everything about it is sinuous and curved. Lithia seems to me to be essentially feminine, and if the park were a person and if I were single, I would probably date it. It is smart and aesthetic and safe and available and it has no major flaws. The park is very much like Patty. It gets wild at times, but only in ways that work in the long run.

That phrase, "wild but in ways that work," is of vast importance in the Wild Attraction model. The "wild" in Wild

Attraction is the secret of its potency, and of ours. The wild is not inhibited and should not be. A person in full possession of his or her share of this "wild" could and would do any crazy thing.

Our job as human beings is to embrace that wildness and somehow make it work. This requires constant curiosity and an ever-increasing understanding of both gender and human nature. For this reason, as you start paying attention to nature itself and begin seeing gender elements moving around out there in the broader universe, keep your eyes open for the wild, the dangerous, the unpredictable. You can see this in very simple things, such as the process of clouds colliding, merging, and parting. You can see it in ocean waves.

People have been ascribing gender to nonhuman elements in the environment since as far back in time as records have existed, including references to the Earth itself as "mother," to the land and sea as male and female, and to stars and constellations as representing lovers of both genders, and the tendency to refer to ships as "she."

While many of these ascriptions may be projections arising from human psychology and imagination, at least a few are very likely the result of subconscious glimpses of the genderness inherent in all things.

The more you pay attention to gender outside yourself, the greater the chance that you will respect the needs and interests of gender within yourself and potential or actual mates. In addition, you are likely to more easily put aside your sense of individual entitlement and do those things that support the union of the genders so they can give you what they very much wish to provide: a ticket to awakening and a journey into the mystery behind all life.

Lithia Park is part of the landscape of this book for another reason. The people-watching prospects offered by the park are excellent. Also, for whatever reason, people find it is easy to *see* Energy there.

Whenever Patty and I watch people who are walking through the park alone, we mentally sort them into two general categories: alone and *available*, and alone and *unavailable*. We also watch for cues that they are either *safe* or *unsafe*, because candidates for the sort of relationship experience we share must be both available and safe, in a specific sense that I discuss in detail in part III.

Single people often scope out other single people in Lithia's forested preserve, and occasionally they actually connect, or try to. If you could observe the nonordinary aspects of this process through Patty's eyes, or mine, you might see frequent bursts of energetic dialog flashing between individuals who are physically pretending to ignore each other.

Strangely, people are frequently attracted to other men or women who seem obviously of the closed-off or unavailable variety. People are also oddly attracted to others who (to Patty and me, anyway) seem clearly unsafe. Perhaps you, like most people, have directly experienced this unnerving tendency, which is part of the human condition and perhaps always will be. Human beings often try harder to connect with unsafe and unavailable people than to cultivate relationships with those who are open, healthy, high-functioning, and available. This is, among other things, the result of the fact that we need the wild. We need risk and danger in our lives. It wakes us up, to name but one of its many benefits. But following the urge to mate with unsafe or unavailable people is seldom the best means to access wildness. It amounts to being wild in ways that *don't* work.

While Patty and I observe these kinds of bad choices in all settings, we find it especially surprising to see them unfolding blatantly in the park. For whatever reason, the energetics in that setting are so clear that we are inclined to assume that everyone is more sensitive to them, only to realize that this isn't the case. The feeling is very much like watching a horror movie in which the heroine walks down the steps of an old mansion alone by the flickering light of a yellow candle, as if oblivious to danger, when it is obvious to everyone in the theater that she knows the monster is right there.

Energetic Fact of Life #19:

Our culture often asserts that unavailable or unsafe people are especially exciting and desirable candidates for relationship, perhaps only waiting for love, acceptance, understanding, patience, example, or compassion to convert them. The actuality is quite different: Sustained intimacy or extraordinary relationship is never possible with an unsafe or unavailable person, and you cannot find relationship success if you are one yourself. The needed actions: Disconnect from unsafe or unavailable people as soon as these qualities become evident (usually after a three-time test). Examine your own behavior and do whatever it takes to become safe and available to others while sustaining full personal and energetic empowerment.

Up to now, we have been looking at single people strolling alongside Lithia Creek. Couples are entirely different. Watching couples move around the park is more of a zoolike experience. They form energetic microcosms much as animals in the zoo often ignore their human visitors and live in an artificial stucco world of their own. Like creatures in a zoo, couples often find that their insular Energy removes them from the wild. This is one reason why most love songs are about single people struggling to become couples, and why marriage is usually the end, not the substance, of the fairy tale. People rightly observe that coupleness as practiced in our culture can lack wildness—and many of them sense that wildness is essential in a successful human life.

Many of the people Patty and I see walking in pairs appear to be happy couples, yet a consistently high number show various energetic signs of being unhappy in their relationships. Most notably, unhappy couples show gaps or depressions in their energy fields. These gaps, or *docks*, as we call them, send out "I am romantically available" signals to singles who happen to be in the neighborhood. Usually, the partners who look like this to us are also engaged in considerably more energetic dialog with other people around them than are members of apparently contented couples. Not surprisingly, they are using these energetic channels to signal subliminal interest in extramarital affairs.

Apart from any consideration of love or compatibility, unhappiness in couples often has its source in issues related to wildness: either too much of it, in ways that don't work, or too little.

Every once in a while, Patty and I see someone strolling alone through the park who looks like a good candidate for extraordinary relationship. If that person happened to be you, this is how you would appear to us:

You would look as though you had positive feelings about your own gender and that of potential partners. You might radiate a relaxed personal availability without looking needy, and a sense of being engaged in some strong personal interests: arts, sports, or other life-affirming pursuits.

You might also project a sense of "what you see is what you get"—a palpable field telling others that you have no hidden sides and that you are willing to talk openly about your experiences and feelings.

If you were our candidate for extraordinary love, walking at ease through Lithia Park, you would be a *yes*-based person—positive, welcoming, and open in most circumstances—who is comfortable both saying and hearing the word *no*. You would radiate awareness that being wild in ways that work means taking risks only with people who will respond to the word *no*. (Failure to take no for an answer is a warning sign of power and control issues that can extend even to violence. An excellent resource on this issue is the book *The Gift of Fear* by Gavin de Becker.)

You would be flexible and accepting in a way that says you are looking for friends more directly than for lovers—in fact, that you expect to become friends long before any gender relationship might develop.

As you contemplate this idealized rendering of yourself, you may feel that you could never be this good a relationship candidate. Consider this: Although candidates for extraordinary love need to be functional all around, they do not need to be perfect. No one is. Flaws don't exclude you from extraordinary relationship as long as you are willing to address them.

In the Wild Attraction model we discriminate between human foibles and fatal flaws. Flaws (such as unaddressed addictions, patterns of dishonesty, or inability to control aggression) reduce intimacy and make real relationship impossible. Foibles (such as crazy passions for pizza, mild forgetfulness, or occasional perfectionism) don't interfere with love and may even enhance it. They are humanizing qualities—constantly subject to improvement without needing to be cured or solved. Good relationship candidates have reworked their fatal flaws and brought them up to the level of interesting and tolerable foibles, usually with the help of others.

Many people see their own principle flaw as a pattern of being fatally attracted to other flawed people, yet this flaw too can be turned into a foible that no longer runs their lives. The issue of flaws and foibles is a nonnegotiable in Wild Attraction; good candidates do whatever it takes to turn the one into the other because it is the only way to move forward.

Sitting at ease in the park and watching people from our perspective, your perception of the nature of men and women might broaden. Every person you viewed might seem to be partly female and partly male, regardless of physical gender. This is because (as described in chapter 5), everyone, whether man or woman, carries both the male and female gender essences internally. Whichever gender essence appears in a person's energy field in greater volume is usually the source of his or her primary gender identification.

It is common for a person to carry a great amount of one gender essence and a small amount of its complement. If you could see this visually, a person might appear to bear within them a quart of feminine and a pint of masculine, for example. These ratios differ from person to person and seem to be largely fixed over a person's lifetime. The majority of human beings carry significantly more of one gender than they do of the other and tend to show up as more masculine or feminine accordingly. The sizable minority who are born with equal or nearly equal volumes of male and female essence tend to present themselves to the world more as blends of the genders, or with qualities of motion and appearance that tend to soften the intensity of masculine or feminine qualities. Both ends of this spectrum are populated by aesthetically pleasing people, and every mix of male and female works fine in the world of Wild Attraction. The key is to discover your unique blend, to own it, and to be honest with yourself and others.

As you sit by the bank of Lithia Creek and look for illustrations of these principles, as Patty and I often do, you might notice that a few of the single women walking around in the park display particularly "girlish" qualities. They tend to move in exaggerated curves, they carry notebooks or bags up against their chests the way some girls carry their books in junior high. But, as even the most cursory examination of the visitors to the park will show, not all women are in this category. On any given day, the women walking amid the park's greenery are all over the map in terms of degree of femininity, from very feminine to an understated or hidden girlishness, to women with mature or more "get the job done" femininity to those with relatively masculine movements and attire.

You might notice a comparably wide range of genderness among the men in the park. Some walk, move, and focus in a straight-ahead, "manly" way. At the other end of the spectrum are those whose motions, manners, and dress are curved, flowing, rotational, soft, and inclusive—more feminine.

This variability is something everybody learns to accept in childhood. What we do not learn in childhood is the concept that variations in genderness are not just the result of physical genetics or psychosocial conditioning but are energetic in origin. Issues of sexual orientation naturally come to mind as you ponder the gender ratio concept, which makes this a good moment to explore issues of alternative sexual preference and gay or lesbian orientation from the viewpoint of Wild Attraction and gender essence.

According to the Wild Attraction model, sexuality is diverse across the population from birth. Humans can arrive on the planet equipped with any conceivable inborn ratio of male and female gender essences. While it does seem to be true that those with male-female ratios closer to 50:50 tend to be less strikingly masculine or feminine in personal sexual affect, the ratio by itself does not seem to be the driving energetic factor that might lead a person to a nonheterosexual lifestyle. The fact of being gay, lesbian, bisexual, or straight seems to relate instead to the difference between an individual's physical gender and her or his dominant energetic gender essence. A person carrying a predominance of feminine gender essence while living in a male body may be moved toward homosexual preferences, to cite one obvious example. Having an energy body of one gender and a physical body of the other is quite different from possessing a relatively equal allotment of gender essences. The latter simply mutes genderness.

Viewed energetically, gay and lesbian unions can clearly produce gender-based relationships that are as powerful, effective, and fulfilling, and as successful in producing great people, as straight unions. In my job as a lecturer I focus frequently on heterosexual examples because that is my personal orientation and it is what the majority of people experience. But as a trainer—and especially as a seer—I have had the opportunity to work with people of gay and lesbian sexual orientation on a regular basis. It is my experience that nonstraight people confront the same basic dynamics of male and female gender essence that straight people do, albeit with more complications but also more opportunities.

Wide variations in sexual tastes occur in people of all preferences; indeed, the huge variation in sexuality is part of the wildness that permeates the human relationship environment. That said, great extremes of sexual impulse are not the province of this book, and no effort is made here to account for them. Putting aside the variations that might be outside the framework of the Wild Attraction model, it is fair to say that most of the time and in nearly every successful couple, including nonstraight couples, one person engages more of one gender essence and the other partner takes on more of the other.

In this sense, sexual engagement in Wild Attraction does not so much involve "being yourself" as it requires each partner to play either the polarized female or male role, completely and exclusively, in a ritual of sexual merging, regardless of the inherent proportions of the two essences each carries. Another, inverted way of saying this is: if you offer your partner an active blend of the gender essences, male and female mixed into one, you miss the effect that comes from merging one partner's feminine with the other partner's masculine essence.

When you are learning to merge your gender essence with that of someone else, you will probably find the process works best when the two of you pick complementary gender roles, like taking the male and female leads in a play. You can trade these roles back and forth as often as you like. This method of sexual polarization builds energetic charge. It is a way of being wild, and keeping the wild in relationship, that works extremely well.

In nonstraight unions, I have noticed more flexibility and more opportunity than in straight couples to pass these roles back and forth, switching from male to female essence within a single encounter. This strikes me as a huge advantage, since all people need to honor both genders within themselves.

Hopefully, it is obvious that my own and other seers' energetic observations support the view that a single universal truth underlies both heterosexual and alternative lifestyles. Throughout this book, I encourage you to take the words *male* and *female* as referring to a person's dominant energetic gender essence and also to the particular role he or she is playing in a couple, regardless of his or her physical anatomy.

I also take this opportunity to frankly apologize to readers of nonstraight sexual orientation if the language in this book or its assumptions, due to ignorance or lack of insight into gay or lesbian sensibility or experience, offends in any way. It is not my wish to do so.

Wild Attraction contains an innate tension that is especially relevant for gay and lesbian people: You are invited to understand your own gendered nature and express it in a genuine way. You are also asked to divine the mechanics of gender essence in universal terms and perform its rituals, regardless of who or what you think you are. As if this were not hard enough, you are saddled with the task of determining the gender mix of any prospective mate. This whole process requires both unjudging acceptance and relaxed honesty, qualities that are not universally evident even in a place as serene as the wooded preserve at the heart of my home town.

As you sit in Lithia Park, look closely once again at the women walking by. Some women seem to be aware of, and comfortable with, the particular degree of femininity they are projecting. Others seem to be projecting an intensity of femininity, or lack of intensity, that is different from their actual nature or desire—that is, they are actively working against their own fulfillment and happiness. Why would anyone do this?

Unfortunately, people will misrepresent themselves in order to be predatory or for other dysfunctional reasons. Women will do it to attract men who might not have found them attractive if they were being honest about themselves. They will also manipulate gender essence engagement to underrepresent femininity and thus dodge unwanted male attention. This is an understandable but ill-advised strategy: people walk unknowingly past their own perfect love matches every day, without recognition. This happens because one or both potential lovers are not portraying themselves honestly.

Men misrepresent their innate genderness just as often as women. I recall watching a man in his early twenties as he spent an entire Saturday morning looking for love amid the tawny rusts of the fall season in Lithia Park. He walked up and down the trail, passing Patty and me many times, striking up conversations with women and obviously attempting to make a connection.

He amazed us because he was very adept, subconsciously, at manipulating his apparent proportion of gender essences by varying his degree of gender engagement. If he met a woman on the trail who we saw as an 80:20 mix of feminine to male, he would present himself as the complementary inverse of 20:80, female to male. If a half hour later we saw him walking with a woman who looked to be a 90:10, he would have morphed into an apparent 10:90.

Unconsciously, he had figured out how human gender essences can be moved around and was manipulating them for seduction purposes. And it worked. He *did* get the attention of a lot of women that morning. Of course, any woman he might have seduced as a result would very likely have a ratio that didn't complement his own actual nature, making a successful long-term relationship unlikely. He was being wild in ways that don't work.

Whether you are a woman or a man, it is a sure bet that this kind of seduction technique has been tried on you. It is one of hundreds of energetic manipulations that happen every day and trigger attractions in all of us, although even people who do this very well aren't consciously aware of what they are doing.

If you have ever awakened beside someone in an unfamiliar, dimly lit bedroom and realized with shock that you made a dreadful mistake, it might well have been for this reason. You would have been tricked through the innate needs of the gender essences within you. They will never stop asking you to find people with a matching but inverse gender ratio. Once you know this, and if you take your time in the courtship process, you can see through this mechanical effect and learn to ignore knee-jerk, ultimately meaningless attractions that arise from gender essence tricks that create only the appearance of a good match.

You have your best shot at extraordinary relationship when you can ignore false or mixed signals, turn away from those who offer wildness only in ways that can never work, and seek out safe and available people who are good risks as partners in Wild Attraction.

But these concepts represent only a small fraction of the needs of the gender essences. The more clearly you understand all of them, the better your chances of being wild in ways that take you to the real treasure of extraordinary relationship.

CHAPTER 8

Meeting the Real Needs of the Other Gender

Energetic Fact of Life #20:
People assume that they should be able to speak to their dates or their mates in the same terms they use to talk to themselves internally or to speak to others of the same gender. This is a road to relationship hell. The genders speak radically different languages and have different sensitivities. The dominant gender essence in you and in your mate will wilt if forced to speak and hear only the language of the other gender. Your required approach:
If you want your man to feel happy, to feel seen, and to do things cheerfully for you, tell him "Good job!" as often as you can. If you want your woman to feel happy, to feel seen, and to bring joy to both your lives, tell her "I love being with you." Mix these up and no one will be happy.

[handwritten: Like a child?]

[handwritten: Would be amazing to hear?]

Do you know what your mate, or your prospective mate, really needs from you? Alternatively, if you were asked by a mate to express your needs, in terms of gender, are you confident that you know what they are? Odds are, you may understand your personal preferences and psychological issues, but you probably don't understand the needs that are imposed upon you and on any prospective partner by your energetic gender essences. These needs, which are nonnegotiable, are the subject of this section of *Wild Attraction*.

Need is a thorny issue in male-female dynamics. Extraordinary relationship depends on moving past need to a place where creative expression and mutual exploration of the Mystery becomes the predominant intent. Need-based relationships, which are codependent and entangling arrangements, seldom or never provide even average levels of intimacy and fulfillment. But in order to move beyond need-centered love, real needs must be clearly understood and accepted. For the most part, the gender essence needs are among those that must be met to whatever degree the day-to-day conditions of your life allow.

This means, of course, that you have to understand what these needs are.

The starting point for the exploration of the contrasting needs of the male and female gender essences is the idea of affirming messages. Voicing this concept in talks and lectures over the years has had a major impact on many women in particular, and resulted in a high volume of grateful feedback.

Women need to hear that they are valued for themselves alone rather than for what they accomplish. The want appreciation for their intelligence, as well as for their feminine gender essence and their physicality. They want to hear: "You are gorgeous," "That was gracefully done," "I love watching you move," "Your eyes are incredibly deep, mysterious, and hypnotic," "You are the most intriguing and incredible woman," "It is wonderful being with you."

Women need to receive this input for free. However independent and capable women are, the gender essence in them can cause them to secretly dream of living in a world in which, in order to receive this core message, they need to do nothing other than be here, now, in all their splendor. They need to live someplace where the males of the world will cherish and protect and celebrate them because being a woman and carrying feminine essence is *enough*.

Most women seem to me to be secretly tired in a way that is so constant that they never even think about it. They are tired of being valued and rewarded only for working hard, for doing their part. The femininity in them is generally willing to do this, yet for them the message "Good job" is somehow never really enough.

For reasons unknown, to feel deeply met and ultimately satisfied every woman must receive a positive, affirming, and personal message from the males in her life—and from the females too—telling her that she is valued and cherished, seen and respected, for herself alone and not for anything she might do, accomplish, or supply. I could never overstate the importance of this: *valued for herself and her gender alone*.

Men, in glaring contrast, care almost nothing for hearing that they are valued for who they are—that they are nice guys or sweet or pleasant to have around. Here is a "secret of the masters": men love to be valued for what they do. If you tell men "Good job!" or some equivalent, they will instantly brighten up, love you for it, and work forever. Men are designed to do. Knowing that they are accomplishing and producing effectively in the eyes of women is deeply satisfying to them.

In one of the first ever Wild Attraction talks, in the early 1990s, Patty and I described this language element, and a woman raised her hand to ask, "If I tell my partner 'good job,' will he do more work around the house?" To general laughter, I assured her that yes, very likely he would.

It can be fun to try this out. It works, even if the man knows you are doing it deliberately. As a prelude, tell him how sweet he is and how much you appreciate him. My prediction is that he will not really care about this message. It may even slightly deflate him. Then simply tell him "Good job!" See which message gets to him.

These two messages, "Good job" for men and "You are precious for yourself alone" for women, have been among the most commented upon, and appreciated, ideas in Wild Attraction lectures over the years.

The next pin to be pushed into our developing map of gender needs is the concept, alluded to in the previous chapter, that both gender essences are driven by one overwhelming demand: to experience the other as deeply and completely as possible, the ultimate expression of this being the complete merging of the male and female essences of two people.

What do I mean by "experience"?

At one level, I am talking about physical and psychological contact. Picture yourself standing close to your first "true love" and register the sort of white-light glow that probably surrounds that memory. Perhaps you can remember the sensation of your hands moving forward to touch that person, as though of their own accord. At another level, I am talking about the effect of Energy on your responses. Try to separate into layers the sensation you recall of the compulsion to touch your partner. See if you can sort out the purely physical lust from the generic fascination of gender unleashed.

When I speak of each gender essence experiencing the other as directly as possible, this includes, over and above all genetic and cultural influences, a drive within each of us to strive to *watch* the other gender. We must deeply internalize the shapes and motions of members of the other gender's physical bodies. We are driven to secretly track them while they are planting yellow sunflowers or walking down the street, or, especially, to observe them as they perform high-level actions that glaringly reveal the nature of that complementary gender. We listen for the voices of the other gender, we want to breathe in their scents.

If you are a woman, think of that buff, shirtless guy with the tool belt. If you are a man, think of the girl on the beach in the bikini. These are images we can't help but track and fixate on, even if we are self-consciously looking away because we are not supposed to show that we are captivated.

To a woman, the mere sight of a male person going through the processes of daily life can be satisfying. Women will yearn to see the simplest expression arising from the other gender and take delight and comfort in it without any need to possess that person or to do anything beyond enjoying the male's presence and gender honesty.

This yearning for the deepest possible experience of the male gender essence can take many forms: Women may want to hear the way males use language and to watch how they move. They may be fascinated by the way males make choices and solve problems. They may hunger for male touch and be fascinated by the male perception of the feminine, by a male's desire for them, and by the ways men want to relate to women. Women often enjoy watching men work. They will sometimes want to provoke men and watch how they respond. They want to be the center of their man's attention, to know that they can generate appreciation and interest.

Men have their own versions of these same yearnings. They need to see women and hear their voices, to observe how they make choices and know their touch. Most of all, men need to touch into the very *world* of women, to enter it and find solace there in the softer, more sensitive and delicate side of life itself.

Go back to that gauzy scene of you and your first love. When Wild Attraction kicks in, and the chemistry of gender is strong, the yearning to merge with another person is not a gentle sense of appreciation. It becomes a strong physical, sexual compulsion. It becomes about total, all-body touch, about rhythmic blending, and about the exchange of body fluids and core intimate responses. If you have any life experience at all, you must know experientially that at times each gender yearns to know the other at the highest possible level of intimacy, not just as a casual appreciate. This drive is fundamentally energetic. It comes from the gender essences you carry, which are themselves linked to that external universal force I am calling Wild Attraction. Through these essences, the yearning and fascination that are part of a profound and sentient outside force are transferred to your individual psyche.

I have a stack of books in my office that constitute a sampling of human literature going back thirty-five hundred years. Sometimes I pull examples out as I talk with visitors about my experience of Wild Attraction as an external sentient force. I never begrudge the search for other ways people through history have said the same thing: we partake in the lovely, merging dance of an actual gender creature, something that is far bigger and more powerful than we ourselves can ever be as individuals, every time we experience authentic romantic love.

Literature and art are filled with overt descriptions of this phenomenon, from Cupid to Puck to Venus and beyond.

Most people I know experience this gender-based hunger to merge and think that it is simply another physical need, like hunger. They may feel the presence of Wild Attraction and interpret the accompanying sensation in terms of conventional attraction and lust without appreciating gender's true grandeur.

Discovering the source of gender is like the discovery that the matter of our physical bodies is not just dirt, it is, literally, stardust. The matter of our physical bodies was originally made inside a star.

Your energetic gender essences have a comparable cosmic origin, described here as a sentience that bestows some of its own vital Energy into each of us as male and female essences. The force of their conjoined form as it exists somewhere around us has more on its mind than our sensual pleasure or mutual personal delight. Gender gives us strength beyond our individual natures, resources with which to undertake the creation of new, ever more fulfilled human beings in a process that only begins with conception and birth; it is lifelong.

This gender hunger moves us to seek sexual play, intercourse, nonsexual closeness and tenderness, partnership, cohabitation, and the sharing of burdens even as it confers differences in language, use of power, and personal aesthetics that make the other gender at times all but unintelligible to us. It gives us strength to meet the challenge of parenting.

Think about yourself, once again, standing in the white light of your first love. Turn the prospect over in your mind that the physical body, which is obviously important and can appear to be the sole source of attraction chemistry and sexual drive, might in fact have been only one component in your sexuality. Perhaps instead it was just one player in an ensemble cast. Did your mind connect a nonphysical, fundamental male or female gender essence's innate, almost spiritual yearning directly to your physical sexual anatomy? I would answer yes to that question.

Wasn't that experience of first love really much bigger than mere sexual genital contact? Wasn't it like the discovery of a whole new world, a whole new understanding of reality? Wasn't it an amazing revelation in which you were shocked to realize that virtually everything is more than anyone had ever told you?

It probably was so remarkable to you, so extraordinary, that, as with all nonordinary experience, your mind retreated from the realization; you normalized to it and have forgotten the enormity of that moment's impact. Right then, though, you knew that the universe was more than anyone had ever suggested.

If you did not have an experience like that, you might consider trying again.

What about those of us with no memory of a first sexual love? Humans without overt sexual drive or who have experienced injuries that bury their sexuality often still manifest a gender essence yearning in the form of an attraction to the aesthetics of the male and female in art, creative expression, and intricate uses of power, all of which are direct embodiments of the gender essences.

It is very likely, judging from my most profound exploratory seeing experiences, that we would still have our fundamental genderness, our love of things masculine and feminine and our yearning to merge, even if we did not have sexualized physical bodies at all.

Think for a moment about the days before your first love. Recall the way you noticed men and women, and boys and girls, when you were a young child. I would bet that prior to hormonal sexuality, you still responded to gender differences and were drawn to each of them in different ways. You discovered them and pondered them and wondered at your place within them. This claim on your attention obviously can be attributed to many sources, but I would ask whether one important source of your feelings was never physical, was with you then, and is still with you now. Search your experience with subtle curiosity.

Energetic Fact of Life #21:

As often depicted in modern entertainment, a woman is expected to leave her world when she is courted or becomes mated and enter the man's world, where she either lives happily ever after or is forever diminished, marginalized, or repressed. (Think Archie and Edith Bunker.) This is yet another destructive inversion of what actually works. In energetic terms, it is the role of the male to enter into the woman's world, bringing with him something exciting and exotic from his own realm. Your best approach: If you are a man, visit her place. Meet her friends. Bring her gifts that grace her space. Take her to the events she loves. Ask questions. Be present as an appreciative force in the processes and moments already underway in her life. Maintain an independent, vibrant life and world of your own so your presence in her world is meaningful. If you are a woman: Make him come to you, and make your world an exciting, inviting feminine place for him to explore, one that is positive about the presence of men. Dodge the tendency to abandon your own world and become an ornament in his.

Patty and I tell couples that, ideally, men enter the world of women and not the reverse. We have an answer to the classic question, "Your place or mine?" The answer is "the woman's place." The man goes to her place as a symbolic statement that he is interested in bringing amazing, high-functioning male elements into her world, and that he doesn't see her only as a nice addition to his. Men who fail to bring something new and exciting into a woman's world, and to join her in it, seldom make good candidates for extraordinary relationship.

Males need to be seen as capable in the eyes of women. Men want women to admire them, they need to be wanted by them, and they want women to want to surrender in a particular way to them. Underneath their fascination with feminine choices and approaches to life, most men feel a desire to possess the woman of their choice. This may not be a politically correct thing to say, but it is true. The form of possession I am speaking of, however, is not the horrifying and unhealthy dominance, control, or ownership that the word *possession* so often conjures up. Rather, it has elements of power and promise and excitement that are irresistible without crossing the line into being brutal or diminishing. It calls for intelligence and nuance, and when done well it embodies the concept "wild in ways that work." Almost every woman, if she is honest, wants to be claimed by a powerful force that is both wild and cherishing. Healthy possession is more like romantic claiming, in which the male makes clear to the woman, and to his social group, that she is his first choice, that he will do what it takes to captivate her, and that he is committed to the mated relationship. I can't stress enough that this type of claiming is of a positive and affirming variety, not a "can't take no for an answer" psychological obsession. And it is an important one.

More subtly, women claim men by arranging to be claimed by them.

Energetic Fact of Life #22:
The rules of political correctness, and the very real problem of rampant emotional, physical, and sexual abuse, demand that we refrain from aggressive dominance-submission language and brutish behaviors and anything that encourages them. Despite this, and perhaps inconveniently, it is a fact that men need to possess their women and women need to be claimed by their men, both energetically and sociologically. Your jobs: If you are a man, make sure your woman feels claimed by you. Do this by stating

> that she is yours and developing the energetic "feel" that she is chosen and that you will attentively support this choice. If you are a woman, invite energetic claiming on a regular basis and reward it by allowing your enjoyment of the process to show. Also, visualize yourself binding and claiming him as you cue him to claim you.

Patty often tells me that the number one complaint among her circle of female friends and clients is that they do not feel adequately claimed by their mates. This is a telling point. Many women want to feel that their male partners strongly want them, will make an effort to protect and defend the relationship, and will be forthright in designating them as chosen and spoken for. Claiming is not just a physical and psychological issue. A man can and regularly should energetically claim a female mate.

While a woman may want to be possessed in a very particular way by the person who treasures her, a man might yearn to possess and claim the woman he longs for with a depth of feeling he can't explain. Most men have no language for energetic claiming and no way to frame it, so they do what they can without understanding how to complete the energetic process that is being asked of them. They pursue, have sex with, cohabit with, hold, watch, perhaps they marry. But without energetic total merging and claiming, all those conventional attempts at male-female union may never be quite enough. The yearning remains.

The next key stopping point on the gender essence map has to do with differences in language again. The language of the feminine gender essence is inclusive and beyond thought. It is empathetic and presumes connection and responsibility.

The rules of feminine language require that women speak and listen in multiple channels or modes at once. Women are designed to communicate with greater nuance than men. For this reason it is wise to speak to a feminine person with greater subtlety than when speaking to a man. When making important remarks, accompany them with body language, such as eye contact and facial expression, that line up and say the same thing. If possible, offer a woman the same statement using the language of physical touch, and give her reinforcing gifts, or the identical message in written language. Functional women insist and thrive on rich and genuine communication. Here is some good advice for men: Hold her hand and look into her eyes while you tell her you love her. Give her a gift with an accompanying card that says "I love you." Later that night, surprise her with a massive bouquet and another card saying "I *really* love you." Involve her eyes, ears, nose, and the skin's capacity for registering loving touch. This is how the feminine works, and there is nothing condescending or manipulative about communicating this way. You have to speak in the language of the person you are speaking to. Keep sending these signals; they are important.

The language of the male essence, on the other hand, is a language of action, and it highlights single-channel communication. Male-speak presumes neither connection nor responsibility. It is insular and linear. Words alone will often do. Action alone will often do, which is why so many men try to speak to their women through loyalty, earning a living, and simply showing up. In male language, this would be enough. As we have seen, effective communication between men often requires extreme directness and an unemotional, relatively slow and readily deniable approach. Between men, a slow run-up to an important emotional disclosure is usually followed by a return to less emotional topics before the end of any communication that includes the sharing of deep feelings. For instance, men will typically talk about football, slip in the important emotional revelation (often while facing away from each other), and finish up with a few comments about cars.

If I am talking to a group of women about these things, I often pause at this point and say, "I have more to say. But before I go on I would be interested in hearing what you have to say." And then I listen to them carefully. For one thing, the feminine essence in them gives them perspectives I don't have, and I am, after all, half the time a man talking about what it is like to be a woman. I stop not because I doubt that the women are keeping up with the flow of ideas. My real reason for stopping and asking for the women's comments is that I want to model listening to what the female portion of our population has to say. This is a change of pattern that needs to happen on the planet.

The women usually offer something useful, poetic, or intelligent that I would not have seen for myself.

Over and above all the considerations named so far, in terms of gender essence needs, is the issue of beauty and its role in our lives. If you are a woman, you carry a particular torch through the wilderness, a consciousness of beauty that is nothing less than the entire human aesthetic.

Although males, with their tendency toward outward expressions of power, may co-opt the roles of author, painter, and writer, it is the females who embody the capacity in humans to recognize, generate, and value beauty.

All the things that males work to create—the curves and depths of texture, color, and form—derive directly from the essential feminine. Often, male creative expression is mainly the artist's innate motion to get as close to the feminine as he can, and to express the feminine within himself. But he will always need women. He can seek an aesthetic, but women are the aesthetic.

While men *do* art, women are asked by the gender essence within them to *be* a work of art in body, mind, and spirit. Every male creature, and every feminine one, wants each woman to be this, although this yearning is seldom accurately voiced in our society. A woman is a statue, a painting, a costume, an epic film, and a sunset all rolled into a single amazing phenomenon. And even though all women share a single, uniform feminine essence, the individual work of art that is a woman is always unique; no two can ever be alike, even if they are twin sisters.

Perhaps the most important thing I have learned as a male seer about gender and relationship is this: Women are the most miraculous and precious creatures that walk upon the Earth. We as men should pay the deepest possible attention to them.

This is not to say that men are not equal. In a curious way that is common in energetics, two apparently mutually exclusive facts can be true. The gender essences are balanced in grace and in every other way. At the same time, the center of Wild Attraction, the beginning of the trail, is the exaltation of the feminine; the feminine is a first among equals and, in a sense, is more fundamental than the male. Any thing or process has to have a center, the pressure point at which to direct force to bring about change. When it comes to escaping from the "head over heels" world of modern romance, the feminine essence is that center. Once both men and women learn to better appreciate the feminine, our collective respect for males will also increase. Celebrating the feminine is thus the first stepping stone on the relationship Yellow Brick Road.

Given the depth to which these words are true, it is incredible the degree to which women are perceived as workhorses, or all-purpose burden bearers, or sources of inspiration for effort or attention, or utilitarian objects. A woman can achieve great things, take on huge challenges, and be the most serious of persons. But anyone in whom the feminine essence is dominant needs first and foremost to be a work of art.

Most women want to create beauty and either consciously or covertly want to move and speak and think in beautiful ways. Most women yearn for beauty the way a starving person hungers for bread. Women can see it everywhere, in places men will miss. I am completely serious. I have seen my wife, Patty, physically trembling while standing in front of Monet's painted blue water lilies in the twilight of Paris. If it is possible, I loved her even more after witnessing this incredible feminine capacity to appreciate beauty with all the cells of her body.

The women I know need and deserve to be appreciated and enjoyed, to transfix me and other men by means of their presence alone, in the manner of a sculpted Rodin lover or a Venus de Milo. And why not? The aesthetic force that created those artworks is resident within them.

You may by now have noticed a common element underlying the needs described up to this point. To understand the gender essence needs as deeply as they truly require calls for *attention*, which is the central ingredient in Wild Attraction and the next topic for us to explore.

Chapter 9
Necessity Is the Mother of Attention

Energetic Fact of Life #23:
Most people in our world expect romance to decline after the honeymoon period. Lovers subconsciously assume that they will be able to get away with simply being themselves, without the burdens of artifice and sex that courtship demanded. This deeply rooted model is entirely misleading. Each gender must forever wield the fire that most fascinates the other. Women need men who will provide sophisticated and positive attention, and men want women who will provide sexuality and charge. Your job: If you are a male, pay attention to your woman as though your life and relationship depend on it. They do. If you are a woman, make sexuality and seduction a hypnotizing art and an irresistible binding force, and never let it become either a demand to which you reluctantly submit or a selfish personal indulgence.

It is the single overwhelming role of the male to pay loving, appreciative attention on an almost constant basis to the female. It is the role of each female person to carry, keep alive, and embody the flame of sexuality within a couple. When both genders do these things, they bind their mates with gentle but nearly unbreakable bonds of love.

Even more than being honored with rituals of power and language, women need one preeminent food, and that food is attention. Without it, no matter what other sustenance is provided, they will wither and starve. The admiring attention of powerful and aware males is the clay that women sculpt into great works of art, if given the chance. Male attention, offered with real appreciation and respect, is the paramount source of nourishment for the feminine essence. It is the key to all healthy gender-based loves and to truly meaningful sex.

Failure to remember to pay attention is the number one shortcoming of men in relationships.

When a woman walks through the dining room and her man is sitting at the dining table reading a paper, the field of his attention must register her, as though his zone of focus is water in a swimming pool and she is swimming through it, leaving a wake.

The female person *must* feel this attention or she will feel unseen and unloved. She is designed to live in a world of energetic nuance, and her nature requires that her man converse with her verbally and energetically at least a part of every day.

My advice to males: Never let a female partner undress in your presence without a graceful and appreciative gesture, comment, or other acknowledgment of her beauty.

Never let a woman cry wordlessly without asking what is wrong.

And always take the time to listen carefully to what females have to say, especially your mate. Women often refrain from insisting or fighting to be heard. Instead, they will quietly and perhaps bitterly withdraw from you. When this happens, it is a great loss to men; a positive and irreplaceable light goes out. This is happening right now in the world on a huge scale. Remember that our culture conditions men subliminally to interrupt women or to discount their remarks. Men are even trained to appropriate females' suggestions as their own. Women are bombarded with this discounting treatment.

Pay attention to them and show them that you are always interested. Watch for subtle cues as to what women like and then surprise them by getting it for them.

Give them flowers every week, but not at predictable times. Do things to show that you are paying attention.

Women are naturally creatures of Energy. They are intrinsically attuned to it and can read and transmit subtle cues in the environment. They are looking for partners who can speak this language, who display a nuanced, almost-female capacity to detect and respond to the subtle cues that women send.

Extraordinary relationship presumes a comfortable relationship with individual power. The power that counts the most is the power to signal and respond in a language of almost imperceptible cues on an ongoing basis. This process builds charge and mutual fascination, and a playground of explosive mutuality and sexuality is created and sustained. It requires, however, both partners to be awake, actively engaged, and interested in the language of the other.

Later in this book I devote some pages to what Patty and I have observed to be one of the biggest hurdles in jumping from conventional thinking to extraordinary relationship thinking. It is so relevant to the subject matter of this chapter, however, that it's worth touching upon here: People are trained to think that they have a license to be who they think they are and still get love. No such license exists in the worldview of Wild Attraction. Instead, people appear to have been given a mandate to do what actually enables the gender essences to bestow their most priceless gift.

Energetic Fact of Life #24:
Nothing is more celebrated in Western culture than the idea of self and the right of each individual to be who and what that person believes himself or herself to be. Proving that it's possible to follow their own instincts and still make life work is the main activity of most men and women. But you are not your instincts or inclinations. They are much more random and much less fixed than you have been led to believe. And they tell you little or nothing about what is actually needed in your life behaviorally or what actually works. They are mainly habits. Your task: Abandon your fixed sense of self. Refrain from defending it or using it as an excuse to indulge yourself or to not pay attention. Avoid expecting special dispensation that frees you from the facts and rules of life and love. Figure out what works, every day, and do it.

One of the main premises of Wild Attraction is that a person is not a stable, fixed personality. A person is not even a single entity. A human being is actually a collective, like a village, a fusion of many aspects of role and character gathered together. This being so, we are far more fluid creatures than most of us realize, and there is no justification for clinging to a fixed idea of self as an excuse not to do what actually works.

Even though you may see yourself as painfully shy, you cannot expect to have intimacy if you stay in the background. If you dislike conversation or paying attention or sending positive messages, the laws of the universe won't bend for you. You will have limited relationships if you act on the basis of your perceived nature, whatever it is, merely because you think it is you.

Very intelligent people I have known have fallen into this trap. My advice, which I wish I could skywrite across the

Northern Hemisphere (and Southern Hemisphere, too), is to do what actually works and put what you think is your fixed nature aside. This is an almost sure way to find out that you are more than you thought you were.

Nowhere is the human desire to ascribe fixed self more evident than when it comes to habits and preferences involving attention. I am beyond amazed at how difficult it has been for me to persuade men to really take this advice about paying attention to heart. If you are a man, save yourself a lot of time and heartache and dedicate yourself entirely to this pursuit; it will change your relationship world and hugely increase the quality of life of your mate. To speak in the language of men: You ... need ... to ... do ... this. You.

Paying attention to the degree that actually works is not necessarily easy, but it is much simpler than divorce, single-parenting, or the anguish of repeated failure in relationship.

I am almost equally amazed at how hard it is for women to realize that they are the keepers of sexuality in relationship, not the men. It is ultimately up to women to signal interest and to provoke, inspire, and create sexual charge. The men will take on this role if they have to, but this division of labor really isn't the way gender essence works best. The female is designed to start sexual motion through subtle and deniable cues. The male partner is set up to carry out the physical direct work of sexual initiation, ideally in response to signals that originate from the woman.

Speaking to the women now: If women take sexuality on board, not just as an answer to their own needs for sexual expression, or as an obligation, but as a kind of sorcery through which to bind (not as in bondage) their mates, and see it as a major relationship art and tool, their men will love them for it and be unable to think of ever leaving or straying.

In a very real sense, we are not solely responsible for our own loyalty and fidelity. In terms of the nature of the gender essences, it is more real to take responsibility for the fidelity and loyalty of our mates, as well as our own, and let them take responsibility for ours, as well as their own. We don't have to slavishly satisfy the personality and psychological needs of our mates. That's what they have friends and therapists for, and that's why they need personal interests and pursuits of their own. But to keep a truly good candidate for great relationship, we do have to satisfy the needs of their gender essence—and in fact we are the only ones who can.

This means that you can and should expect to carry the fire of gender for your mate, either through extraordinary attention or sexual charge, and you have a right to expect and demand that your mate will play his or her gender role for you, as two dancers might move together onstage.

Women have a right to demand attention far more than males will spontaneously give. And they have a right to leave if they don't get it. They have no choice in the long run.

In the same way, men have a right to expect sexual sorcery from women, and sooner or later most of them will leave, in one way or another, if they don't get it. Ultimately they are probably right to do so. That is the nature of the gender essences.

I have heard innumerable excuses from men to justify their not paying enough attention and from women who drop the ball on sex. Misconceptions about these issues are so serious and deeply embedded in our culture, and so mired in issues of political correctness that I am going to keep this chapter short and sweet as a way of underscoring the dire simplicity of what I am saying.

Given the complex social issues and long history of repression of women, it is understandable that women have trouble comprehending that healthy sexuality is what they have to offer in most relationships. Sexuality in the context of Wild Attraction is not an obligation, but it is a necessary and beguiling art that can't be negotiated away in the presence of an empowered and fully engaged male.

The general failure of males to pay attention is much less excusable. The fact is that after eleven million years of human history on the Earth over ninety percent of all living males don't know this, or won't choose to act on it. This is not the fault of the feminine essence within women.

If women are ever granted the attention they need in order to fully embody the feminine nature they carry, there is no limit to the joy and great works they will bestow upon the world.

Chapter 10
There Is No Battle of the Sexes

Energetic Fact of Life #25:
Modern culture's language for sexuality starts with the idea that the sexes are opposite, that one is superior to the other, and that ultimately one of them can and should "win." This gender warfare model is, along with the chimera of love at first sight, widely promoted in comedy, romance, and drama alike. These depictions are wildly destructive and utterly false. The genders are complements, not opposites, and there is no battle of the sexes other than what we as cultural automatons bring to the process. Your job: Don't listen to negatives about the feminine or the masculine or how they relate to one another. Don't voice them yourself. Object to their depiction in the media. When interpersonal problems arise, point to the lack of awareness in the humans involved instead of blaming masculinity or femininity or stereotyping men and women. Celebrate gender and speak for its mystery and grandeur. Tell your date or your mate that you approve of, and take delight in, his or her genderness.

For a decade and a half I have sat in my office across from people of both sexes who had been deeply hurt, sexually or romantically, by the other gender. Men are incredibly vulnerable to critical judgment from women and to the withholding of access, energetically, sexually, or psychologically, by women as a way of gaining power or punishing. This is sad. No relationship in which these elements are present ever really works, at least not as seen from my chair.

Women, on the other hand, are deeply vulnerable to the contempt, scorn, or inattention of men. This vulnerability is inherent in the feminine essence. Because the feminine gender essence prompts humans to universalize from any particular, if a person playing a male role in any woman's life causes her pain, she is almost forced to see cruelty as a flaw in masculinity as a whole. And she is very likely to feel diminished, maybe even destroyed, by it.

Perhaps the most important single bit of wisdom Wild Attraction has to offer both men and women is this: anything that damages any person's innate ability to love and appreciate both gender essences is a grave and terrible injury. My nonordinary experience leads me to a passionate conviction that we as humans would be wise to avoid this at all costs. Instilling negatives into men or women about either gender can have terrible long-term consequences in the lives of our mates, descendents, and friends. It constitutes a source of incredible pain and loss of human potential.

The measure of any culture is the way its women are treated. I have been to places on Earth where the treatment of women is immeasurably worse than it is in the West, yet with all the knowledge at the disposal of people in Western societies, our gender-treatment gap is arguably less excusable than that in less-developed areas on the planet.

Patty and I spent time in New Guinea and saw a culture in which, in some areas at least, the men spent all their time becoming beautiful. They adorned themselves with feathers, sticks, and even irregular red stars cut out of aluminum Coke cans. They invested years of effort in making wigs out of their own hair. They prized the women mainly for their ability to farm. No valuing of feminine beauty was built into that culture at all, according to the men and women I spoke to.

We never saw a woman indulge in aesthetics. The women's dress and motion were always entirely utilitarian. They appeared drab and listless as they moved through our parts of the rain forest. We were told that women's fingers were regularly cut off by the men when their children were stillborn or died young. They were not deemed worthy of medical attention, in many cases. Nearly all women were beaten at the discretion of their husbands, acquiring telltale tattoos to mark and heal the bruises. Rape was apparently all but routine. Men were expected to have multiple wives for status reasons, and those wives slept with the pigs, which were about equally valued. Murder in the parts of New Guinea we visited was the leading cause of death and was legal as long as the murderer paid a penalty, called *compensation*, in terms of pigs. Males were worth three hundred pigs, at the time we were there. Women were worth thirty.

That culture is in serious trouble as I write these words; international observers fear it will collapse entirely.

I am not completely down on New Guinea, despite its treatment of women. Like any place on Earth, many compassionate and interesting people live there. We found them to be aware of life in the United States to a greater level of detail than most Americans are aware of life in New Guinea, and they were as horrified by some of our cultural tenets as we were of theirs. I personally experienced many acts of courage, kindness, and insight, even though we were in their homes at a time of great stress, in the middle of a war. But that culture fails, in my eyes, because it codifies the exact inverse of what Wild Attraction demands.

By comparison, Western culture is obviously worthy of a better report card, but perhaps not better to the degree you would think. The problem of male indulgence in the West is barely discussed within my field of view, yet it is an epidemic. Too often, in my opinion, men get indulged and the women do the work, for less reward. By the principles of Wild Attraction, males should not be indulged, by which I mean they should not put the burden of their needs or their selfish and unreasonable interests onto women. Women should not have to tiptoe around male temperament. A case could be made that it is the women who should be indulged, because, frankly, it is enough to bear and raise children and to carry the human aesthetic. Empowered men who can't be run by women should be cherishing and intelligently valuing them, and doing it with a sense of fun and delight.

I can envision far, far better treatment of females in the Western world than our women are now receiving, and I would suggest to anyone that it is well worth taking a long and serious look at gender issues in America and elsewhere and forming an educated, independent opinion. In many ways it is the most important single set of issues in our lives. Extraordinary relationships create extraordinary cultures and amazing people.

I have taken my own look, both conventionally and through the eyes of a seer. From my perspective, in the West we practice a different mix of brutalization and marginalization than the New Guineans, but our cultural norm still partakes of a barbarity that, although much less, is on the same continuum as New Guinea. It is a continuum that we must get off of entirely.

Alongside the necessary discussion of serious negatives relating to the state of the art of sexual relationship worldwide, it should be said that humans are wonderful creatures. Most people, when given knowledge and a chance to use it, will make compassionate choices and treat each other well. And, significantly, chivalry is alive and well on the streets of America.

A few years ago, two close female friends of Patty's and mine phoned me up at nine o'clock on a weeknight. They were stranded, having turned into a supermarket parking lot with limited visibility and then high-centered their new Volkswagen bug on a poorly designed bit of curbing. The belly of the car was balanced on that curb like a turtle stranded on a rock; its wheels were not touching the pavement.

I drove over to help them out. As I approached, I was bemused to see them, two attractive women in overcoats standing in the cold by the car, which was tilted at a thirty-degree angle and clearly undriveable. From blocks away I could see that they were waiting nonchalantly yet in fact engaged in "leaving gaps," a process I describe in future chapters.

Within a couple of minutes, no fewer than twenty men had coalesced around those women and that car, which was strange because there was very little traffic. They brought with them every needed tool, from tow bars to crowbars to jacks and hammers and canvas towing straps. Finally, a guy showed up who was a professional tow truck operator. He knew exactly what to do.

We all cooperated beautifully and with typical male scarcity of words. We could have been a pit crew, it went that smoothly. Ten minutes later, we had that car up off the curb, ready to drive. We even repaired a few minor broken bits and pieces. With a few nods, the men dispersed. Party over.

It wouldn't have happened quite as quickly if it had been me standing in an overcoat beside that car, although sooner or later it would have happened. Men help. That's what they do. The drive to help that is innate in the male essence has saved me, and many others like me, even in desperate circumstances when helping meant serious risk to lives and to families. That's why I love men so much.

Better models for the roles of women and men are being born every day and their dissemination is a powerful motion on our planet.

So what would I advise?

I would advise men and women to do everything in their power to regard both genders as the wonders they actually are, and to recognize that the gender essences themselves are incapable of harming each other, even though the people who carry them may cause harm.

I also would urge women to seek out and focus on the aware, powerful, and chivalrous men in the world and let those men define for them what males are.

Many men hurt women, obviously and unforgivably. But the male essence itself does not. It exists to serve, honor, and cherish them. The day a woman meets a complete and aware male, she will know this.

I would advise all men (you) to snap out of the indulgence of seeing women as trying to control you or remake you or somehow steal your power. Women raised most of us men and were asked to exert a necessary control over us, while the men in our lives probably weren't around nearly as much. We may have resented this, especially as we realized that our female parent couldn't completely understand us.

It is part of our growing up process to individuate and take control of our own lives and snap out of the infantile fantasy of female aggression toward us. They did their jobs. Now it is time for us to do ours (yours).

We as males have to get behind women and play the only role that works, which is the confident assertion of male power with extreme reverence and chivalrous support for the feminine.

Energetic Fact of Life #26:
The cultural norm is to think that all things are defined by their average quality or level of attainment, or perhaps by their worst moments. This is false. The measure of any person, place, or thing is the most exalted or most profound quality that you observe about it. You are your best moment and greatest talent. So is your mate. The only way of defining your universe that optimizes you and your life is to attribute meaning and value based on the best qualities you can see in everything, everywhere. Your task: Shake off negativism and averagism. See the whole picture relating to any object you perceive, and put the best part of that picture into the center of your field of view, the center of your thoughts. When you speak, begin and end with the best you can say and distribute the less exalted elements here and there in the middle. Most especially, be a mirror that reflects your mate's greatness back as his or her defining quality, while appreciating everything else you see. Look at your own reflection in a mirror and take it in.
You are defined by the highest and best within you.

I sometimes post Wild Attraction axioms on the walls of my office. One of the most prominent posters says this: The three most important elements for relating to gender essence, and to our lovers, are: confidence, confidence, and confidence.

Think Rhett Butler and Scarlett O'Hara. Think Matt Damon or Sandra Bullock or Bogey and Bacall. I used to live and work in Hollywood, and I met a few famous desirables. The energetics of widely admired people are different from those of people out of the spotlight. In most cases, a star's great looks are not directly the source of their power. Rather, their looks give them gender confidence. It was the confidence, and the love and enthusiasm for both genders, in the stars I met that usually struck me the most. Think Cary Grant.

Can you think of any widely desired sex symbol whose most significant feature is not at least the projection if not the reality of confidence?

The need for confidence applies to both genders. Everyone needs confidence in order to successfully participate in a great love. But no one develops confidence alone. We develop it with the support and encouragement of those around us. And we can't have confidence if we are afraid of each other.

Encouraging fearfulness and uncertainty is perhaps more profitable than encouraging confidence. It may induce people to buy more products, for one thing. I have read the words of experts who claim that the culture has a stake in maintaining an undercurrent of uncertainty, especially in women, who are the dominant consumers.

Also, clearly, misogyny (which is rooted in men's fear of women) remains alive and well around the world, even if many places are well above the low-water mark of New Guinea. Many males, either knowingly or subconsciously, are geared to try to keep women subjugated. This desire is obviously institutionalized in a number of religious traditions, where, incredibly, it is held to be sacred.

The world we have ended up with too often and too powerfully encourages uncertainty, fear, and lack of confidence, covered over with an ignorant, dogmatic bravado in men, and in women, a self-destructive promiscuity or a punishing, angry avoidance of all things male. Our society, from my perspective, has become in some ways a showcase of dysfunctional sexuality.

Many men do fear women. This fear can run deep, and it can fuel some of the barbarism that takes place in living rooms and bedrooms, sometimes right next door. I can see this fear, energetically, as I walk down the street. It looks a little like wafting cigar smoke hovering around certain people.

Sometimes it is thick in the air. As a male, I wouldn't encourage any male to fear women. The feminine essence in women does have a tremendous hold on men, but it is also every male's most powerful natural ally.

To men I would say: Use this alliance. Avoid any woman who doesn't know that women are the allies of powerful males. Lavish attention and intelligent indulgence on those who do. Never abuse women in any way. Ever. You can do more damage than you might think, and you can do it more easily than you might think.

The concept of the battle of the sexes is the greatest human tragedy of all time. The digs and insults and sarcastic characterizations of both genders that are prevalent today should become as unmentionable and intolerable as the "n" word. Censorship concerns apart, we would do well to scrap every sitcom that celebrates and glorifies male-female antagonism. That would eliminate a lot of television shows. It also might eliminate a lot of pain that your children and mine may otherwise experience in the future.

If you are living in some sort of dream in which men and women are still out to get each other, or in which it is still okay to insult or abuse or make derogatory jokes about the other gender and then to expect intimacy, this is your wakeup call. It is time to snap out of it.

Part III

The Two Sides of the Gender Coin

Chapter 11

Unsafe, Hobbled, and Aware Males

Energetic Fact of Life #27:
People are conditioned to think they have to bounce back and forth between unsafe but exciting partners and safe but relatively boring ones, and that no alternative exists. In fact there is a third choice. In reality you can select from among three kinds of partners: the dysfunctional wild (unsafe), the tame (hobbled or unavailable), and the intelligent wild (aware). The only choice that will bring you extraordinary relationship is the intelligent wild— wildness that really works, a relentless gender passion combined with compassionate, intelligent functionality. Your needed actions: If you are a woman, you need to find an aware male. If you are a man, you need to find an aware female. If you are not one of these, you need to become one. Look for people who can paint outside the lines, surprise you, take risks, and creatively break patterns, yet whose lives are full of beauty, plenty, and self-expression, and who are held in esteem by those who you, and they, respect. Study them, question them, learn how they do what they do, and write it all down. Imitate them. Then tell your friends what you have discovered, because this knowledge will be truly worth sharing. These people are your key to extraordinary relationship.

When it comes to relationship, all the men and women on Earth can be divided into three types: *unsafe*, *hobbled* or unavailable, and *aware*. Of the three kinds of males, only the *aware males* are viable candidates for successful extraordinary relationships. Less than five percent of all men fall into this group. The good news is, usually a woman who wants one can get one, because most females are looking for the two other kinds and may not even suspect the existence of the third.

In the film *Indiana Jones and the Last Crusade* the hero and the villain confront an ancient Knight Templar, a devoted guardian of a great secret, in a small chamber filled with a hundred ornate cups and chalices, each of which might be the long-sought Holy Grail. The Knight advises Indiana Jones that whoever drinks from the Grail receives the gift of youth, and with it, the gift of very long life. On the other hand, the Knight says, drinking from any of the other, imitation Grails that line the walls of the cave results in instant aging and a terrible death.

The armed villain picks up the flashiest cup, jeweled and golden, and drinks greedily. He almost immediately convulses in front of the fourth person in the scene, the requisite pretty adventuress. She screams as she is forced to witness what might be the world's worst bad hair day: the villain sheds his healthy white locks, shrivels, and dies of advanced old age within thirty seconds.

The Knight turns to Indiana Jones and dryly notes: "He chose unwisely."

Jones, of course, takes his time before making a selection. He chooses the meanest and most modest cup—small, irregular, and made of rough wood. After Indy drinks, he retains his hair and his youth.

The Knight smiles a knowing smile. "He chose wisely."

This scene, depicting an adventurous woman confronting three very different men in the context of a life-or-death choice in many ways parallels the choice process in romantic love that men and women find themselves in every day.

In addition to the obvious analogy, in which Indiana Jones represents the aware male, the villain is the unsafe male, and the Knight is the hobbled one, the aware male also represents the equivalent of a Holy Grail from the viewpoint of women. If a woman drinks from the wrong cup (a unsafe or hobbled male) she could lose the prospect of long and healthy life.

During a typical Wild Attraction lecture, Patty and I open the topic of the three kinds of males by asking for two volunteers, usually a man and a woman, to come up to the front of the room and wait until their role becomes clear. As they come up, I write the three categories of men onto a whiteboard and circle the first one: *unsafe male*.

An unsafe male, we explain, is someone who carries predominantly male essence and does a good job of meeting one of the key demands that male essence makes on its host: making quick and confident choices. Unfortunately, the unsafe male only thinks of his own needs; this is what makes him unsafe.

Patty then explains that male essence is the essence of immediate action. Males embody the capacity to make unilateral decisions and to act on them with full commitment, even if those decisions involve taking unpleasant actions; and even when they mean the risk or certainty of his own death.

This decisiveness, while available to females in equal measure, is actually *required* in males on a daily basis, just as they might need multiple vitamin supplements, to satisfy a demand of the male essence within them. Indecisive males neither look nor feel quite right, in ways that usually don't apply to indecisive females.

Patty points out that most women find something pleasing and reassuring about watching males make powerful choices. Usually, somewhere in this discussion, she mentions Rhett

Butler as played by Clark Gable in the film *Gone with the Wind*.

I generally add that the feminine essence demands something different but complementary from women: a capacity to make deeply considered, harmonious choices that are usually open to consensus and compromise. Women need the opportunity to make this kind of choice on an almost daily basis in order to be completely comfortable and healthy.

Clearly, both choice styles are needed by the human race. In fact, at times both genders need to be able to embrace either style of decision making.

Patty or I point out to our lecture audience that throughout history, both genders have had to make sudden and difficult male-style decisions in order to survive or to ensure the survival of those they care about. We must run from floods and fires, sometimes without hesitating for as much as a heartbeat. When someone is injured or endangered, rescue has to happen without hand-wringing.

Also, we must recognize aggression, and if we cannot run, we must unhesitatingly respond, we have to "do something!" *Indiana Jones* and other action films, superficial as they may be, speak to this very real male attribute.

Men, more often than women, are drawn to these roles, thrive on them, and actually seek them out. I have fought fires, and watched and been a part of daring rescues. Being connected in any way with these manifestations of manhood seems to feed the male soul. It is a way for men to approach Mysterium Tremendum; our decisiveness under pressure is a small counterpart to the awesome awakening power granted to women in childbirth.

But male decisiveness is only a good thing when it is connected to a compassionate intelligence—one that can see clearly the source of its own impulses—and a mind that innately understands that the thoughts, feelings, and experiences of other creatures, especially their pains, are as real as one's own. I want to look in a man's eyes and see strength and a profound ability to act on choice. But I also want to see profound self-knowledge and poignant sympathy when he looks at another person who is suffering. When I don't see these things, I switch quickly to a state of heightened alert.

No one would want their male banker, doctor, or policeman to be making choices without profound compassionate awareness. The inborn male capacity for endless choice, that predisposition to act immediately on impulse, is a horrific loose cannon in human society when it is present in a human being who lacks real depth or empathy.

When I fear people, it is not because of their strengths or even their dispositions; I fear them for their capacity for cruel or capricious choice. This capacity run amok is most in evidence, naturally enough, in males.

I have known murderers and rapists and talked with some of them at length. I have looked into their eyes and seen, at times, an absolute disregard for the pain they cause. Sometimes I have seen unabashed enjoyment, even glee, at the thought of causing human suffering. I have looked down the barrel of guns and felt knives at my throat; never was this at the hands of a woman.

Without seeing such unsafe males close up and unmasked, it is difficult for a person with a conscience to believe that such a powerful capacity for cruel choice exists.

Not all unsafe males are at this extreme end of the spectrum of heartless choice. Most would not necessarily choose to hurt others and are relatively blind to the pain they cause. Yet close encounters with unsafe males can go a long way toward perpetuating long-term negative stereotypes about men, and also about women as victims. And these stereotypes are more poisonous than the unsafe males who inspire them.

It is easy to blame the male gender for the ills of the Earth. But the problem is not the presence of the male gender essence and its capacity for what might be called *wild choice*. Rather, it's the lack of compassionate awareness of the human condition itself within a person carrying male essence. This is an important distinction. Lack of empathetic awareness is not an innate feature of masculinity. But lack of awareness is in some ways humanity's biggest single problem, because it brings about the existence of the most dangerous creature on the planet.

When you combine within any man the uninhibited power to make immediate and creative choices and deep, compassionate intelligence, the result is often a creature of unbelievable strength and kindness. A man with these qualities is an aware male, of whom more will soon be said.

But the machinery of male choice and strength alone, unaccompanied by such wakefulness, is, quite simply, dangerous.

Energetic Fact of Life #28:
Nearly everyone blames the male gender for the presence of cruelty and violence in the world. This is understandable but entirely wrong. Male essence is neither the problem in the world nor your problem in particular. The problem is lack of awareness in the men you choose to be around, or lack of awareness within you, if you are a violent male. Your vital response: Avoid unsafe males and promote compassionate awareness in human beings, including yourself, at every opportunity without demonizing male gender essence. Expect and demand the highest personal character from those around you. Assuming that you are an aware male or female, act decisively, even aggressively if needed, so that unsafe males and females do not dominate the language and system choices in your world. Vote this way. Actively defend females from unsafe males.

At this point in a lecture, I usually produce a serviceable rendition of an unsafe male by manipulating elements in my energy body. As a simulated unsafe male, I stroll close to Patty or take a winding walk around the two volunteers who were invited to come up front with us.

The audience invariably shows signs of discomfort. They fidget and avoid eye contact. People usually comment that a danger zone has formed around me, one that seems unyielding and aggressive. It maintains its shape without giving way to the personal space of other people when I step near them, as though I am cutting through their energy fields as I pass by. My eyes tend to lock onto other people's faces and force eye contact with them as I move.

It's the bad-guy-in-the-Wild-West look, the Hell's-Angel-on-a-rampage look. We sometimes call it the Clint Eastwood look. Someone in the crowd usually comments that this character is someone they have seen many times.

When I create this character I am actually dialing up an old acquaintance. His name was Arnie and at one time he dated a friend of mine in high school. Arnie was smart and had a bit of style, but he was also a brute and my particular crowd avoided him.

Word reached me quickly on the day that he asked my friend, who I will call Marci, out to a school dance. Rumors circulated over the next few days that Marci and Arnie were becoming an item. Most of my male friends were as puzzled as I was. Marci was a delightful person, notably kind and good-hearted.

What was she seeing in Arnie? I seriously considered saying something to Marci, but, uncertain of my role, took a deep breath and let it go.

About two weeks later, friends noticed that Marci had bruises on her forearms and biceps. I asked her about the bruises, and told her that I wondered whether Arnie was responsible. I shared that my friends and I had long regarded Arnie as a bad sort and that we were all concerned when she started dating him. If she was having any sort of problem with Arnie, several of us was available to support her in whatever way she asked.

I won't ever forget her response. She quickly grabbed my forearms, leaned forward with tears glistening in her eyes, and asked, "Why didn't you tell me?"

I never learned the full extent of the abuse Arnie inflicted on my friend. But some of my male friends and I remained alert and protective to make sure he never bothered her again. That sorrowful look in Marci's eyes, and the sound of her voice as she asked me her question, have stayed with me and have had a permanent impact on my worldview.

My answer to her question was this: Arnie's nature was so obvious to me and Marci's other male friends that we could not conceive that she was unaware of it. We had all felt constrained by politeness not to intrude into her private life.

I resolved during that conversation to never make that mistake again.

With Arnie in my mind, I continue to impersonate the unsafe male for the Wild Attraction lecture attendees as I begin to carry on a polite conversation with the audience. Patty points out that my surface politeness does not really change the basic signal of the Clint Eastwood walk, which people can still pick up on if they tune out the words and pay attention.

She asks the attendees to note the danger signal I am sending out, memorize it, and take it seriously whenever it shows up out there "in the wild." Patty has medically treated too many women who didn't.

The unsafe males in the world, whose numbers are reasonably high, lack something, and that lack can make them a hazard.

However, they are still human beings, entitled to consideration, and we have to share the planet with them. Many who can be described in these terms are peaceful and pleasant when it suits them. Arnie is probably out there somewhere, holding down a good job, and maybe with a wife and kids. He is probably also causing pain somehow to someone. Unsafe males can hold jobs and fit in, they can smile and tell jokes. Empowered people can get along fine with them and work toward common interests. But you should never put yourself under their power. And avoid being anyplace with them where no one else is available to witness their actions.

You don't want to be the woman in the car alone with an unsafe male or the employee dependent on that check.

Despite all this, unsafe males are often highly sought after by women.

Why is this so? Is it possible to avoid this trap? The answer that Patty and I always offer when asked the second question is, emphatically, yes. Not only can women escape it, they can establish much better relationship patterns in the space of months or a year.

Patty and I have observed that attraction to unsafe males often works as a chain reaction. Once a woman has been entangled with one unsafe male, she can be internally compelled to seek out more of them. This can be a subconscious effort to replay the distressing situation again and again until she "gets it right"—that is, until she succeeds in turning an unsafe male into someone with whom she can experience real intimacy—a tendency we call *resolution sickness*.

A woman caught up in this pattern might pass right by a safe and available man while she is subconsciously focused on attracting what in fact is the last person on Earth she should ever sleep with. Moreover, the conversion of character she seeks is nearly impossible to accomplish. And even if she were to succeed, it would not change or erase her own sorrowful past.

At this point in our lectures, we see many heads nodding, as well as signs of agitation and sadness. I remember at one lecture seeing a woman raise her hand and tell Patty, "Okay, so we can see ourselves in this model. How about a little *hope* here? What can we actually do about it?"

Patty responded by saying that three things are true: First, high-level, functional potential mates really do exist. Second, men and women can adopt effective behaviors that work, even if those behaviors are not the norm in our culture. Third, simple energetic tools and techniques are at hand; no one has to be an expert to use them. They just have to be willing to do what actually works.

Then she offered some practical advice: Although you can easily be trained to identify unsafe males on the basis of Energy and affect alone, the best way to identify them is to apply a simple test of character. Ask these two questions: "How does this person treat those over whom he has absolute power?" and "How does he act when there is no authority restraining him?"

A man's treatment of women, children, employees, and anyone else over whom he has even momentary unrestrained power is a powerful window into his character. That is why, in Patty's words, if you are a woman, how he treats you, and your children if you have any, in private settings is of utmost importance.

Energetic Fact of Life #29:
Pop culture promotes the idea that people should ignore early signs of psychological or behavioral problems in a prospective partner, in the interest of an almost ditsy commitment to inclusion and tolerance. The truth is that you cannot tolerate long-term patterns of serious dysfunction in a mate, and you can never afford to ignore

early warning signs. A woman's best move: As you get to know a prospective mate, ask yourself two questions: "How does this prospective partner treat those over whom he has absolute power?" and "How does he act when there is no authority restraining him?" If the answer to either of these questions is "badly," it is probably best to break off contact, no matter how attracted to him you may be.

What should a woman look for?

Men who throw temper tantrums, make demands, take advantage, bully, refuse to take no for an answer, or make even small forced sexualized demands are unsafe. Beware of those who show contempt for or cause needless pain to those who are smaller, ill, or poor. This is often done with a trivializing cue or under the guise of humor. Be particularly wary of men who are dismissive or subtly cruel to children or animals. Watch for this kind of behavior, and if you see it, don't ignore it or rationalize it away.

I have seen Patty shake her head at this stage in the lecture and share her experience as a women's health care nurse practitioner. "Women are relational, and they like to give second chances. They don't like to assume the worst, and they aren't being trained to take early warning signs seriously. You can change that in yourself by learning to notice small things and daring to think the worst at times. Don't waste your time trying to change a noncandidate into a candidate."

I usually add: People seldom get better as they move into relationship. They usually start by putting their best foot forward, but if their persona is a façade, things tend to get worse, not better, from that point on. If this is the case, break it off as early as you can. If you don't, you may have much more trouble later, and a lot more healing to do.

Human qualities that are deal-breakers sometimes don't show up until you become "family" to another person, which can take months, or a year, or longer. This can make people who are noncandidates for relationship quite hard to spot in advance. But sometimes, like tiny cracks in a car windshield, small behaviors creep out that could eventually grow to become the equivalent of shattered glass down the road. If you learn to take your time and pay attention to early warning signs, you have an advantage.

If you are female and have trouble reading and responding to early warning signs, consider doing a few things to prepare yourself for screening relationship candidates. First, make a list of five things that functional people in your life always do (for example, they always make and keep promises) and a companion list of five warnings of dysfunction that you have seen but ignored in the past, to your sorrow (such as lying or failing to take no for an answer). When you are in doubt about a potential partner, use these lists as a reference to help you move past your emotional denial and take action in spite of strong feelings of attraction.

Next, write down three statements you can use when you need to break off relationships with dysfunctional people. It is best if these statements don't invite debate, negotiation, completion, making a parting point, being seen, or additional contact or discussion, yet are not insulting, offensive, or dismissive. An example would be: "You are a fine person, but I realize now that the necessary deep chemistry just isn't there for me, for no reason that I can explain. I know it can never be there, and though you are a valuable person, I am clear that I don't want to continue to see you." Remember, you are looking for physical and energetic disconnection and nothing else.

Most women find it much easier to work out what to say to escape a potential unsafe candidate when they are not under the pressure of serious, entangled attraction. Hence our advice that you compose the escape phrases now. This simple writing project is designed to help in a different way too. Many women find they don't really know how to handle the breakup itself. Prepare yourself now, and you will be more likely to act decisively when you have to. If and when a relationship candidate fails your functionality test, use the phrases you create in this exercise, over and over if necessary, and avoid using other phrases that are not similarly well thought through.

Finally, this reflective writing procedure is intended to prepare you to react to small telltale warning signs before you experience serious problems with a mate or potential mate. If you have any doubt about your personal safety, seek professional help to work through the process of disengagement. Patty and I think that if you have a history of attractions to unsafe males, you will probably need the support of friends and mental health professionals to break the cycle and reprogram your attraction responses.

Moving out of habitual relationship patterns is within the reach of everyone, but it requires some effort and attention. The most significant obstacle people encounter seems to be what I call *instinct entitlement*, which was discussed briefly in chapter 9. Men and women can feel tremendous loyalty to their instincts and enormously entitled to do things the way they inherently want to, instead of facing the fact that certain behaviors work in the world while many cherished individual response patterns don't, and never will.

Consider this analogy: You get up each morning and slide into your car. You pull out of the driveway, and head off for work. And each day, regardless of how you turn the steering wheel, instead of taking you safely to your office, the car delivers you to some unpleasant destination—one day the city dump, the next day the neighborhood sanitation plant. Later in the week you find yourself making a rolling stop at an emergency room door. Another day you find yourself driving up an airport runway against the take-off traffic. No matter where you want to go, your car either takes you nowhere at all or to places that you never want to see again.

How long would you keep driving that car? My bet is that you would sell it or scrap it almost immediately. If a car doesn't take you where you want to go, you will stop using it and get another one.

The majority of people keep relying on the same set of instincts over and over again when making romantic choices, believing somehow that the old instincts that have taken them to the relationship equivalent of a reeking canal or a toxic waste site are somehow, this time, going to get them to the "office" of love. Sometimes instincts can lead to fulfillment, but they are a mixed bag of subconscious assumptions, random associations, bits of ESP, buried memories, and the psychological mind's attempt to resolve some old issue. Most of the time they cannot be trusted.

Wild Attraction is about selling that instinctual car and doing what actually works.

Until this instinct issue is named and dealt with, you may not be able to enjoy the benefit that Wild Attraction offers. If you try a new approach out of this book, have some initial success, but soon it just doesn't feel right and genuine for you, your natural tendency may be to abandon it and go back to your usual patterns. This could be a mistake. You may very well have been moving, perhaps for the first time, in the right direction, and instincts, even counterproductive ones, can be very convincing.

My advice is to examine and test the situation for yourself. Study long-term relationships patterns—your own and those of others—to see what works and what doesn't. Create a chart of your relationship history. Trust the advice of people who do well with relationship choices. Replay the "car that takes you nowhere" thought experiment. It is designed to help you change, if you need to.

Patty and I never come away from a lecture feeling that we have done justice to this concept, which can't be overstated, hence its recurrence at various points in this book: Love is not about finding out who we are or what we want or about being ourselves. It is about finding out what works in terms of creating and sustaining great relationship. And doing it.

The concept of doing what works is important across the board in Wild Attraction, but especially so when it comes to unsafe males. Whatever a woman's instinct may tell her, unsafe males are never successful in relationship, and, in my experience, nothing can change this. No amount of love or good sex or repetition of kindness or submission or discussion can be counted on to change an unsafe male into someone you can relate to sexually or have sustained intimacy with. And as long as you are trying to do this, Wild Attraction will not be able to give you what it is innately designed to offer.

Whether an unsafe male is physically or emotionally unsafe, or whether he is more sophisticated in making self-serving but morally blind decisions, the symptoms of unsafety almost always become evident over time.

Over time. That is a key phrase. Although it means that you can no longer afford to rush or skip steps in increasing intimacy, and that you may have to wait at times for gratification, it also means there is hope. Hope lies in taking your time, distrusting your instincts, relying on friends and other support systems, and paying educated, intelligent attention to your nature, and that of any potential mate, with safety and availability in mind.

Although many people find it depressing to acknowledge that unsafe men and women exist in large numbers, my core message is one of optimism. Aware, high-functioning males and females are also out there. When they meet and combine, they and those around them are strengthened. More of what is actually possible becomes real. Humans can touch the figurative fingertip of God through romantic love. Reality is far more than it seems, and one way for all of us to see more of it is to ride the wave of gender as far as it will take us.

Chapter 12

Whipped

Energetic Fact of Life #30:
Women search for a safe, emotionally codependent man as an antidote to the wild male who they are aroused by but can't relate to successfully. They think they can establish a long-term relationship with the safe, "hobbled" male and get what they want and need from him. This is not the case. If you can run him, over the long term you won't want him. The suggested course of action: Learn to identify the hobbled male by his deference and exaggerated emotional caretaking of you. Pass him by in favor of the aware male, an independent, decisive, and compassionate man you can't run.

Once a woman has been sufficiently burned or frustrated by her attempts for intimacy with an unsafe male, she will often bounce to what may seem to be the only other available option, the *hobbled male*, who may supply some relief but in the end won't hold her interest over time. Bouncing back and forth between these two types of males has been the plight of many women, because each offers what the other can't give. The unsafe male offers male essence and an exciting, wild "charge," and the hobbled male offers safety and compassion. But neither offers what her feminine gender essence in fact actually needs, which is reasonably safe, deep access to true male power.

A hobbled male is alive and well inside just about every man I know. Hobbledness seems to be a territory that most of us males pass through at least briefly, much like the teenage years.

A hobbled male is one who has been conditioned to be safe by his society or, specifically, by the women in his life. Hobbled males are usually "nice guys." They are soulful. They are highly attuned to the emotions of others and will often discuss their own feelings and listen closely to those of women. They tend to be hypervigilant about the wants and foibles of the females around them, and can be seen to jump to the service of women, and even other men, under a deceptive banner of chivalry

You will know a hobbled male mostly by his emotional vigilance. He will tend to become entangled with you because he will be sensitized to try to manage the emotional tone of a human duo or group, and he will tend to safeguard relationships and to do whatever is needed to sustain them. If you have a conflict with a hobbled male, trying to fix or preserve his relationship with you will be central to his response. This can, of course, be convenient. But the one thing he can't do is the thing most vitally needed. He can't offer a woman access to the male essence in full power.

Both unsafe and aware males have a huge advantage over hobbled males in terms of creating charge and holding a woman's interest. They are also far more capable of responding to life pressures outside of the frame of relationship and facing issues directly. They can walk away more easily from inappropriate behaviors, they can speak for themselves, and they can name hard truths without managing the other person's feelings or trying to sculpt or control how they are seen.

Hobbled males, on the other hand, usually have trouble with behaviors that require directness or call for unilateral decision-making.

Women can run hobbled males, in ways that they can't run unsafe or aware males. One way is to use scorn and harsh judgment, tempered with occasional praise. Hobbled males have been highly sensitized to criticism, to the degree that they feel physical pain. The other way a woman can run a hobbled male is to selectively grant and withhold physical access to her female body, emotional connection to her female mind, and energetic access to her all-important feminine gender essence.

Turning to a series of relationships with hobbled males is what my high school friend Marci did after the disaster with Arnie. She found these boyfriends safe but ultimately not very satisfying. The first of these was Kurt, a friend of mine.

Kurt was very attentive. He brought Marci flowers and wrote her poems. I have memories of passing the two of them walking along the track field together, discussing feelings and relationship issues. Kurt had tender, glistening eyes that I suppose people would describe as "puppy-dog." I often saw him respond to Marci's remarks as though her every wish or fancy was his command.

From my perspective, it was clear that Kurt needed something fundamental from Marci, and that this need put her in a more powerful position than she had been in with Arnie. Kurt was also clearly incapable of choosing an action that could be threatening to Marci. But he was inhibited, and he struck me as somehow "less of a man" for it. He did not, at all costs, want to be seen as a bad person. Most of his Energy, in fact, seemed to go into proving, to Marci and everyone else, that he was not an Arnie.

At the time, I thought that he had constructed his personality as a statement of how deeply he was horrified by what I am calling unsafe males. But from my perspective today, I think hobbled males are not self-made. They are created by cultures and families that are struggling to make sense of the existence of unsafe males and find a way around this problem. Unfortunately, it isn't a successful solution.

The seeds of the hobbled male mentality are planted when a young male child is saturated with the concept that there is something innately wrong with the masculine, something undefined but so serious that the masculine itself needs to be managed, governed, rejected, and restrained.

When the child is subliminally conditioned to believe that the antidote to this "not-okay" status is the approval of females, he can become addicted to this reassurance and will want it on a daily basis. By maintaining a mix of cues, it is possible to condition boys to become highly responsive to criticism, after which they will respond strongly to the granting or withholding of the access to the feminine that the male in them absolutely needs.

This creates a safe male, but one that in the end a woman will probably not be satisfied with because he cannot give her the access she needs to his male essence. He doesn't have access to it himself.

My personal imitation of the hobbled male, offered in lectures, is an evocation of the essence of Kurt. I suspected even back in high school that he would end up in a suit and tie as a high-level, denatured professional salesman, selling his main product, the feeling of safety.

As I recall him today, Kurt was a master of relationship. He was very "facial," in the sense that he used Energy and body language to call attention to his face more than to his body. Eye contact with him, featuring those artificially soulful and aware eyes, was always significant and reassuring.

The hobbled male is a presence that I can turn on like a switch, and it always causes something in me to reach forward and envelop the first several rows of the audience energetically.

As with the unsafe male, the appearance of the hobbled male in me always draws comment. At first people seem relieved that the unsafe male has vanished from the room. As the relief wears off, I begin to notice sparks of recognition flashing among the attendees. This guy, too, is familiar to them. I usually walk down the rows of seats and pause to kneel down and chat. The codependency of the hobbled male apparently doesn't look very good on me. Within a moment or two, people start asking me to shut that personality down.

At this point in the lecture, Patty reminds the attendees that every person carrying feminine essence is stuck with a real, nonnegotiable need to experience another person carrying the complementary male essence, which means a male person who is capable of making any required decision unilaterally. This is something a hobbled male is inhibited from doing.

People carrying female essence also need to experience a male person who they might challenge in terms of power but in fact cannot run. I can attest that powerful women will do everything possible to cue me to become entangled with their emotional construct. They act as though they really need significant power over men, or at least to not be dependent on them.

But this is in fact a challenge, not an actuality. It certainly appears to me to be true that one of the female's jobs in the dance of the genders is to challenge the male in healthy and provocative ways. Women may send signals to the effect that they will love a man more if they can run him, by which I mean, they can make him do whatever they like by granting access to their bodies or Energy, or by granting or withholding approval and alternating this with criticism. But any cue to a man from a high-functioning and healthy woman that she wants to run him is actually a challenge, not a genuine attempt to control. When this challenge comes from an aware female, that woman secretly wants the man to call her bluff.

The feminine gender essence in women doesn't actually want to run men. On the contrary, and ironically, it compels them to want men who, ultimately, they can meet as equals and try to run but who can't be run.

Ultimately, an aware female will lose interest in a hobbled male who she can run.

Energetic Fact of Life #31:

Hobbled males, and many females, think that women always need to be believed by their partners. But the opposite is true. If you are a powerful, aware woman trying to run a man, you need to be disbelieved by him; he needs to see that something more subtle is going on. Assuming you are psychologically healthy, when you demand to be independent, self-possessed, and in charge, you are, consciously or unconsciously, asking to be doubted. Your best approach: If you are a woman, challenge your man, and see if he can pass this test by not allowing you to run him. If you are a man, believe that your woman is powerful, but don't believe that she is always telling the truth about wanting independence and power over you, however convincingly she sends this message. Make a unilateral decision (tell her what restaurant you are taking her to). Claim her. Never be brutish, but be ritually assertive when she is being defiantly definite, at least once a day.

Marci used to tell me that she craved the day when Kurt would finally decide on his own which movie to see while out on a date. Hearing Marci's sigh of complaint, I realized for the first time the degree to which women are relied upon to make detailed choices for friends, group, and family, and how letting a decisive male person make the choices might be a relief from the feminine decision-making role. Females face an especially huge burden of small and large choices when they have children. I saw the subtle but important difference between being an Arnie who brutishly forces his own choices and living as an empowered male who offers a female partner a chance to revel in the decision-making power of a creature who thrives on immediate unilateral choice.

I am happy to say that Marci, who bounced back and forth between several versions of Arnies and Kurts, eventually broke out of this cycle of relationship with unsafe and hobbled males, and found herself with what we here call an aware male. Hers went by the name of Daniel, and he was what some of my friends called "the real deal." It was hard to find a flaw in him, which is saying a lot because Marci's friends subjected Daniel to a great deal of scrutiny, a fact which perturbed him not at all.

An aware male has threaded the needle. He knows that embodying male essence successfully is a matter of nuance. If he veers a slight bit to one side of the path, he becomes an unsafe male. If he veers just a little too much in the other direction, a hobbled male will stand in his shoes.

There is no easy answer to being male—just as embodying the feminine is hugely complex for women.

An aware male is independent yet also responsive. He understands the feminine and responds to it without trying to become it. (Again, he can never "out-femme" a female, just as a woman can never "out-male" a man.)

Such a man is daring and confident and willing to break rules. He initiates motion and takes risk. And he is almost unfailingly considerate and conscious and altruistic.

The aware male retains full male essence engagement. He doesn't dial his gender back or tone it down to make the women around him feel comfortable. He can decide against the grain. He can be centered in his own judgment. This leaves him free to adore, and serve, the feminine without real concern for losing personal empowerment.

He loves being male as much as he admires those who embody femininity. Even though he cannot be controlled, his compassionate awareness makes him as safe for women as real males ever get. He can see where his own choices are coming from, and he can anticipate the effects of his actions on everyone in his field of view. His choices are thus shaped by his nature but never hobbled.

He is not inhibited and he is not managed. His innate vision can be trusted to restrain the wild in him when it clearly won't work, leaving him with that wildness intact and at any moment capable of providing a needed action.

The Indiana Jones character is a cartoon depiction of such a person. Rhett Butler personified him. Aragorn in *The Lord of the Rings* is a nearly flawless depiction. The aware male is the most celebrated of the male types, but despite this, many females believe that such males are as mythical as unicorns when it comes to ever meeting one themselves.

This disbelief in aware males is a problem. It certainly gets in the way of a female person's ability to attract and choose one. A related disbelief in men—the idea that women should be expected to tolerate less than an aware male because so few are available—probably gets in the way of men's intent to become such a person.

Wild Attraction is intended to be a message of hope. If you are a male and you are unsafe or hobbled, you can change, and it will be worth your time and effort to do so. This book can provide you with realistic models and practices.

If you are a female who has not yet seen her fair share of aware males, you are within reach of new ways of attracting and keeping them. You already have more power and more choice than you may realize.

If you are an aware man or woman in a great relationship, consider the proposition that even more is possible once you are in relationships that really work. You can have a fabulous time discovering what that *more* might be.

CHAPTER 13

Lord, What Fools These Mortals Be

Energetic Fact of Life #32:
People think that relationship skills are the keys to long-term success in intimacy and sex. Wrong. It is the power to make a great choice of partner at the beginning of the relationship that mostly determines success. Your best play: Take your time and choose wisely. Date a wide variety of people. Move slowly. Rely on your friends to help you see things in your prospective mate that you can't. Memorize the qualities that make up a candidate for extraordinary relationship and aggressively weed out potential mates who don't have them. Most important, don't settle for "noncandidate love."

The most angst-ridden questions I am asked by female lecture attendees arise from their involvements with unsafe or hobbled males. Each time a truly heart-wrenching question comes my way, I hear an internal voice that sounds like the Knight Templar in the Grail scene from *Indiana Jones* saying, "She chose unwisely."

These questions are being asked too late. The real answer, which I never voice in public forums and rarely give even in private, is: Get out of your present union, transform yourself into a candidate for extraordinary relationship, and find a partner who is a candidate also.

Most of the work in relationship is in the initial choice of a mate. This is *obviously obvious*, to coin a term for something that is in plain sight but all too frequently overlooked. The relationship skills that Patty and I practice account for only five to ten percent of our success in extraordinary relationship. Most of the heavy lifting was done at the beginning, during the choice process itself.

For this reason, the Wild Attraction model is grounded in the idea of candidacy and the mechanism of choice. Extraordinary relationship involves becoming a great candidate yourself, learning to identify other great candidates, then learning to court and seduce a great candidate, and finally keeping or binding that candidate, to you, over the course of a lifetime. Much more is said about these vital steps in part IV of this book.

In other words, relationship derives from the capacity to choose successfully, and to be chosen, and then to keep making those choices every day. By this I mean the choices that actually work.

The many and capricious energetic forces that I call Wild Attraction act on people by influencing their choices. Sometimes they do this compassionately and in support of your valid individual interests and needs, but often they do it in error or out of caprice. Nowhere is this more successfully illustrated than in Shakespeare's comedy *A Midsummer Night's Dream*.

In that wonderful play, as you may know, the immortal bard presents us with Oberon, a fairy king who is locked in a complex quarrel with his queen, Titania, who has been spurning his amorous advances.

Shakespeare shows us, in the first act, what happens when sexual attraction goes haywire. Hermia, a young woman who is being pursued by an ardent suitor she despises, engages in a classic conversation with her friend Helena, who, as fate would definitely have it, is madly and unrequitedly in love with the very man who is smitten with Hermia. Hermia complains to Helena, "I frown upon him, yet he loves me still."

Helena answers, "O that your frowns would teach my smiles such skill!"

The irritated Hermia marvels, "I give him curses, yet he gives me love"—to be answered yet again by Helena, "O that my prayers could such affection move!"

Hermia says, "The more I hate, the more he follows me."

Helena sadly notes, "The more I love, the more he hateth me."

The key point here is the stark brilliance of Shakespeare's representation of Wild Attraction as an internal force in each person, wreaking havoc in an individual's psychology. I can scarcely imagine an adult member of any audience, dating back to the day that play was first performed, who would not know from personal experience exactly what these characters are talking about.

But *Midsummer Night's Dream* takes the sense of gender compulsion as a wild, sentient force farther, not just portraying it as internal to humans but capturing perfectly the external powers of attraction. Shakespeare portrays these forces very much as I experience them: as having innate intelligence, individual character, and manipulative intent.

For those unfamiliar with the play, the characters of Oberon and Puck are well-meaning, sympathetic, foible-ridden, capricious, driven at times by selfish agenda, bemused by human stupidity, and supernaturally powerful. So is Wild Attraction. While Oberon is king of the fairies, Puck is a kind of night spirit possessing magical quickness and other powers, including invisibility. He attends Oberon and executes his commands. The characters of Oberon and Puck combined come closer to representing the powers, interests, methods, and sympathies of the Wild Attraction creature than anything else I have seen in literature or entertainment.

There is no substitute for seeing the play (the recent film version with Michelle Pfeiffer will do nicely enough), but I will briefly sketch the plot dynamic to make my key point, which is that something is really out there and that it has in some ways a near-human personality, is often sympathetic to us, and is actually tilting our romantic choices. Conceiving of the supergender as having an individuated and fully formed personality gives you a significant advantage; you will be able to relate to it much more deeply and lovingly.

Here is the relevant action:

King Oberon, watching young Helena pursuing the man who hates her, sympathetically dispatches Puck to set things right. Puck is to use the nectar of a magic flower to redirect the woman's passion from the unloving man and enchant her so that she falls in love with a second man, one who actually loves her in return. This plan, of course, goes awry as Puck mistakenly applies the flower juice to her eyes in the presence of the wrong man, thus breaking up another, previously happy couple and causing comic chaos.

The mistakes of Puck, though his actions were well-meant, speak to the nature of the creature Wild Attraction, and also to the mistakes of each person's subconscious mind. Oberon, the fairy king, shows that he is not above bending the rules of attraction for his own purposes, as he seeks to gain the upper hand over his queen and enact some comic vengeance. Oberon accomplishes this with the same flower juice, which, incidentally, is described in the play as deriving from a field where an arrow shot by Cupid (yet another embodiment of the Wild Attraction creature) fell to Earth.

Oberon tells Puck, "Having once this juice, I'll watch Titania when she is asleep, and drop the liquor of it in her eyes. The next thing then she waking looks upon, be it lion, bear, or wolf, or bull, on meddling monkey, or on busy ape, she shall pursue it with the soul of love."

Titania, of course, awakens to see a man who has been transformed by Puck, playfully, into a braying ass.

I have seen people compellingly attracted to people who are no more suitable than Titania's new lover. Her misfortune has most likely also happened to you in all ways except the most literal. The external forces originating from Wild Attraction have surely cast you into a seemingly enchanted state in which your choices were comically or tragically redirected. From this state there is almost always a painful awakening and a human mess that requires cleaning up.

If this sounds too poetical and fanciful, or as though I am just indulging my fascination with this particular play, I suggest that you look again at what is happening around you, or even in your own life. Those who have been overtaken by Wild Attraction in full flood know that extreme attraction feels like an irresistible enchantment that shatters the illusion of free will. They simply do what that attraction demands, even to the destruction of the entire structure of their lives. This full-flood exposure does not come to everyone, but it comes to many.

It is all too easy to become used to love in the most common and ordinary sense, to find oneself saturated and normalized by the fact that most people eventually feel absurd sexual compulsions and pair up, and fail to appreciate the amazing phenomenon that is happening all around us.

Fortunately, it is within our capacity to manage the whims of Wild Attraction somewhat better than the play suggests. We need not be entirely vulnerable to the powerful out-of-awareness forces represented by Oberon, Puck, and the wildness in the minds of the other characters. If Wild Attraction is an external sentient thing, it is possible to relate to it as a friend, despite the lover's chaos it can author, and to learn its ways and work with it to cocreate a better world.

Puck, who also goes by the name of Robin, at the end of the play offers a parting consolation: "Give me your hands, if we be friends, and Robin shall restore amends."

Energetic Fact of Life #33:
People are conditioned to believe that despite the Western world's high divorce rate, most people are moderately successful in love sooner or later and have a reasonable capacity to eventually find their ideal mates. This is not the case. When you compare what is actually possible in relationship to what is currently being achieved, it is clear that most mates are subconsciously selected to avoid extraordinary relationship and to minimize change. Your best course of action: If you are not now in extraordinary relationship, stop running on attraction autopilot. Create, in writing, a detailed word portrait of the person you believe could awaken the truly extraordinary in you. Explore the concept of your ideal lover. Do this based on a review of your romantic history and as an exercise in honesty about the question "What really changes me?" instead of "What presently attracts me?"

Very few people actually pair up with a partner who is their optimal choice. And few seem aware of the underlying forces that move them here and there through the relationship forest, or the ways of alliance that could keep them from acting unknowingly as fools of love. I watch in general aghast, amazed, sometimes delighted, and often in suspense.

It is often the capricious side of Wild Attraction, not the genuine mutual recognition of a deep link between mates, that is responsible for the relationships that Patty and I see around us every day, including many that last a lifetime. The relationships

I am talking about might not be bad, and some may be really good. But what we are not seeing are the relationships that people might have had if they were knowledgeable about the nature of attraction and love. Who might they have been with? Who might they have become that they did not?

Of all the perfect elements of Shakespeare's play, the foremost for me is its implication of an opportunity to relate to the wonderful force of Wild Attraction as a friend and ally, even as, left to its own devices, it can wreak such chaos.

Theatergoers, if they thought such a creature as Puck actually existed, would probably give or do almost anything for the chance to meet him and make friends with him. In the play, one is left, tantalizingly, to wonder what sort of magic it would take to find such a being and forge the kind of bond that Puck is offering. First, you would have to be able to see him, and under normal circumstances he is invisible to mortals. Secondly, you would have to understand his greatly expanded worldview and find a way to relate successfully to a creature far more powerful than you. Shakespeare offers few clues as to how a normal human would do this, but Wild Attraction provides a blueprint for just that process.

Midsummer Night's Dream is useful as a reminder. If you can visualize Oberon and Puck, you can visualize the Wild Attraction creature. If you are one member of a couple, imagine that Puck and Oberon are out there, and maybe you will work a little harder to keep your mate. Don't leave gaps for Puck and Oberon to fill, or they may do things entirely unrelated to the nature and needs of you and your partner. They could break you up.

If you are single and you are out in the world, remember that Puck and Oberon are out there with you, too, and try to take the time to counteract their capricious influences on your passions as a first step to relating to them more successfully, as allies. With this in mind, wait through the night, and another and another, if possible, before you leap into someone's bed. It could be the bed of a braying ass. If you are man, you could wake up beside what I call a *woman in a bottle*, the female version of the hobbled male, which is about to be described in detail.

For my part, I like to visualize Puck and Oberon working with me, not off somewhere on their own trying to figure me out. Like us, they need and want things, most especially to foster the merging of male and female essence and to help foster advanced consciousness in other living things. I try to help them. For me, that mostly looks like paying loving, positive attention to Patty while offering her undiluted male power. Oberon and Puck are not a problem; they are a miracle.

In your life, as well as mine, it simply *works* to think of them as a miracle that is always waiting to happen.

Chapter 14

The Woman in a Bottle

Energetic Fact of Life #34:
No female image is more widely celebrated in the Western world than that of the unbearably attractive woman who is forever out of reach. Any woman can put her feminine self on provocative display behind an impenetrable energetic shell. Yet this model is relationship suicide. If you are a woman and you are energetically walling yourself away, you will find yourself pursued only by hobbled and unsafe men; the aware males will be looking elsewhere. The right thing to do: Keep undesirable men at bay using adult communication skills, not by altering your energy field. Tell those in whom you are not interested that they should seek feminine company elsewhere. Be willing to talk about your life and feelings with increasing candor as you move toward greater intimacy. Remain open, positive, affirming, and ultimately fully available to the man of your choice. Remind yourself that you are not your own treasure. You are the treasure of your extraordinary lover.

Women can, and very often do, put their feminine essence on display and then surround themselves with a transparent barrier of Energy that cannot be breached. They can beckon and promise and tempt and seduce, and then leave the attracted male with nothing at all of what is most enticingly offered: meaningful contact and merging with feminine essence.

The woman in a bottle character appears with surprising regularity in modern entertainment and art. The Star Trek franchise features her in most of its TV episodes and movies, examples being the Vulcan Lt. Saavik, the ex-Borg Seven of Nine, Captain Janeway, and the Vulcan science officer T'Pol. *Lara Croft: Tomb Raider* is another of the many games and films that make use of this device, which is a blatant tap dance on the heads of males. In fact, the woman in a bottle might be one of the most common archetypes in the modern era. I suspect that most males have been strongly attracted to more than one woman in a bottle in their lifetime.

Often the woman in a bottle is depicted in the media as strong, brave, and intelligent. Usually, while her gender essence is intensely engaged, in fact she is self-possessed (self-possession, although not discussed in this book, is an energetic stance of its own). Her sexuality is a treasure locked away for herself alone. The energetic message being sent out to vulnerable males is this: You can see, you can worship, but you can't really have.

While he may not present an ideal model of male empowerment, filmmaker Woody Allen did an outstanding job of depicting energetically unavailable females in his film *Annie Hall*. In one scene, Allen's character is making love to his costar Dianne Keaton, but she is disinterested and detached. An ephemeral version of Keaton's Annie Hall famously sits up, moves out of her physical body, and gets out of bed. This translucent *her* watches from across the room, bored, as Woody Allen's character engages in intercourse with her temporarily uninhabited body. He senses eventually that something is missing, and yearns for more from her.

This scene is a rendering of a literal truth, not just a metaphor for a psychological mechanism. Most people don't "see" the impenetrable Energy veil around an unavailable woman, or her energy body evacuating her physical body, but they can feel their effects and be wounded by the loss of access. As with rudeness, people usually sense the energetic signature of the woman in a bottle very well subconsciously, and they can and do dip into metaphor to describe this unavailability energetic. A male may say, "She just didn't seem to be *there* for me" or "She wouldn't let me *in*."

Since the woman in a bottle is an energetic stance, it is not just a combination of behaviors and body language; it is an actual Energy, which means that it can be put on or taken off, like a blouse, sweater, or skirt. For this reason, amazing changes in individual presence and perception, to the point of virtual changes in personality, are within the grasp of anyone. People are not their behaviors, stances, and preferences. The human personality is in many ways mechanical, determined by accidental energetic models that become stuck in place and are played over and over, like a musical phrase on a scratched phonograph record.

Changing your energy field and thus instantly developing a healthier presence is much like lifting the phonograph needle from the stuck groove on that scratched record and putting it down again a bit closer to the center so it moves on to the next part of the song. Exactly how this is done from a strictly Energy standpoint is beyond the province of this book. But the short and simple approach is to change your Energy by changing your daily physical actions. In the case of the woman in a bottle, this might include: Move toward people physically, rather than away from them. Avoid crossing your arms over your chest. Speak your truth unless there is a compelling reason for silence, rather than guarding it until you are compelled to disclose. Hug people spontaneously.

The woman in a bottle is the direct counterpart of Kurt, the hobbled male, as described in chapter 11. The two may not look alike on the surface, but in both cases what the other gender needs—safety and attention from the man, and sexuality and loving availability from the woman—is promised but never fulfilled.

The woman in a bottle archetype plays an important role in this book because she is the most common female response to abandonment and abuse. She is also the energetically dysfunctional feminine model that is most instantly recognizable in most people's experience. Any person, male or female, can energetically shield or lock away his or her gender essence as the woman in a bottle character epitomizes. And any individual can, at any time, opt out of the motion that is at the heart of gender-based attraction: contacting and blending with the complementary gender essence within a lover's field during sex and in many other moments in daily life.

Another human being can force access to your body or your mind, but rarely or never to your gender essence. This fact, unfortunately, does not dissuade people from aggression. And it does not dissuade men from seeking out collisions and entanglements with unavailable women over and over. In fact, the types of males who become entangled with a woman in a bottle are unsafe males, often looking for victims, and hobbled males, looking to be victimized.

Although she is the most common of the hobbled or unsafe female models, the woman in a bottle is merely one of the many versions of the unavailable woman, who include the *self-possessed woman*; the *workhorse*, who becomes her working role and buries her feminine essence; the *maternal femme*, who accesses and makes available only the managing and nurturing side of the feminine essence; and what we call the *bluff woman*, who accesses and projects only the sister, "one of the guys," or best friend aspects of femininity. (Needless to say, these patterns are reflected in male counterparts, all of which are specialized versions of the unfortunate supersalesman Kurt.)

All of these models deny prospective lovers direct access to the total feminine essence. Women displaying them will attract and mate with men who relate to them as colleagues, sons, or brothers and best friends—not as lovers.

Any woman who repeatedly relates to male mates in these ways can look to her energy field and wonder if she has picked up an energetic model that is not serving her, or alternatively, if some buried trauma is driving the subconscious mind to set up the same bad relationship again and again. If the answer to either inquiry is a possible yes, she need feel no guilt.

As we have seen, both the human energy field and our deep psychological nature are largely out of our conscious control. Furthermore, the two are inextricably linked. Psychological issues drive the subconscious, and the subconscious drives the energy body. Memory and actions on the part of the energy body (energetic memory includes images stored as content) feed back into the psychological self, which again drives the subconscious mind, which again drives the energy body, in a continuous and insidious loop. For this reason, pursuing a parallel process of ongoing psychological inquiry is important when you are seeking energetic perception and empowerment.

Energetic Fact of Life #35:

A great many men, consciously or unconsciously, think that women are the enemy. This concept is the root of much evil in the world. If you are a man seeking intimacy or extraordinary relationship, you have no option but to perceive the women in your life as allies. The thing to do: Study your own remarks. Record yourself in an hour of discussion in a mixed gender group on a typical day in order to track your real choice of words. Look for negative language you may unknowingly use in relation to women. Look at your humor as it relates to feminine people and things. Listen to your tone of voice when you speak to women or about women. Even if you don't view yourself as thinking of women as the enemy, you may at times be unpleasantly surprised by what you hear. Listening to yourself and questioning the hidden beliefs your language reveals is the beginning of changing those beliefs.

Most people are aware that male-female conflict is nearly epidemic, but few really know how it sustains itself. For men, the start of the process may be male resentment of women, perhaps arising in some men from a failure to fully individuate as they grow up—an inability to claim personal power after being controlled during childhood by mother figures who did not intuitively understand them or grasp the nature of their male essence. (Again, women are not to blame for this; the same gap in understanding happens between fathers and daughters, but women are more often the regulating parent in the household.)

An adult male, untrained in the needs of the feminine essence and already perhaps carrying resentment, offends or injures the women in his life either accidentally or deliberately, depending on whether he functions as a hobbled male or an unsafe one.

The women respond with self-destructive entanglements involving unsafe men or frustrating relationships with hobbled men. They engage in criticism, avoidance behaviors, or withholding—including energetic withholding of feminine essence—in order to gain safety and control. It is worth adding that a woman doesn't require her own strongly negative exposure to males in order to develop a woman in a bottle stance. Energetic models can be passed from mother to daughter, and the daughter, with no history of mistreatment, will carry on the chain of resentment.

A man's response to these behaviors most often takes one of three forms: he corrals the woman (the classic hypercontrol of an abusive husband), tries to steal the gender essence Energy (having sex with a woman while in fact treating her hatefully), or actually tries to destroy the feminine essence by debasing the person who carries it through humiliation or other forms of abuse. The extreme form of these behaviors, the horribly high incidence of rape and incest, ensures the continuation of the cycle of dread on the part of women and gives rise to ever more women in a bottle.

To stop this process, both genders must take the strongest possible measures to restrain violence against women and at the same time put aside the negative ascriptions that now lie so heavily on the shoulders of both genders. In practice, the place to start is with the men, because of the depth of misogyny and its vast cultural support. Men need empowering models that offer a far better understanding of the role of the male and female in society and in the broader universe. They need to snap out of the illusion that females want to control them and put aside childish or adolescent resentments.

Just as there are three types of men, energetically speaking, there are also three energetic models that encompass all women. Besides the woman in a bottle, the other two are the *unsafe woman* and the *aware woman*.

The unsafe woman is the equivalent of Arnie, the prototypical unsafe male, except that she is usually emotionally rather than physically aggressive. Unsafe women wield negative judgments, critical feedback, dry and brittle forms of presence, and energetic techniques to exclude males from their social network.

Like Arnie, unsafe women are capable of aggressive energetic and physical choices and lack compassionate awareness of the source of their own impulses and the consequences of their choices in human terms. Also like Arnie, most unsafe women are not only behaviorally unsafe but also energetically dangerous. Their energetic signature ranges from the subtle to the extremely overt and can be identified in the energy field, much as people afflicted with alcoholism may share a common element of presence, an alcoholic "feel," that is sometimes tangible. Unsafe women exist in reasonable abundance, and the destruction they bring about is considerable. But I am devoting less space to describing them than I did to discuss unsafe males because the scale of this problem is different for the two sexes: men tend to turn their negativity outward in dramatically aggressive, often physically violent ways far more than women do. That said, men need to show the same kind of care and caution in screening for unsafe women that female people have to exercise with unsafe men.

The third category of female person is the aware woman. She is the counterpart of Daniel, the aware male with whom Marci eventually found a truly great relationship. To talk about this category of woman, it is necessary to create a definition of the word *chivalry* that takes energetics fully into account.

CHAPTER 15

At a Loss for Words

Energetic Fact of Life #36:
Most people view the English language as a finished work, adequate to our language needs. No greater misconception exists. The language available for understanding ourselves as males and females, especially for expressing the true nature of the gender essences and creating extraordinary relationship, is meager and inadequate. With regard to female nobility of character, language is woefully missing. What to do: Create your own language. In particular, look for ways to talk about greatness in women.

*I*t has already been said in this book that while the genders are equally magnificent, the way out of the topsy-turvy mess that humans have so far made of gender relationship—a tragedy that becomes evident when a typical present-day relationship is measured against its true potential—is the overt celebration of the feminine.

Celebration and empowerment of the feminine is increasingly proving to be the key to a more functional and productive culture. Studies show that corporations with a high percentage of women on the board or in upper management are more profitable than firms where males dominate. The most effective way to improve lives in distressed Third World countries is turning out to be empowering the women. The micro-loan movement is based on this principle. A recent book called *Why Women Should Rule the World* by Dee Dee Myers, former President Clinton's press secretary, is one among a flood of such works on the real role of women in civilization. But despite the current change in the roles of women in the marketplace and leadership, fundamental problems remain in the language of gender itself.

The Western world's vocabulary for describing and passing along strong, positive female models is unfortunately downright poor. Consider that words delivered via the media are the primary source of education today. Look at the images created by the writers of books, songs, commercials, television shows, and films. Flip through the channels on broadcast TV and jot down the gender-related phrases you hear at random. Look at the language that sells. No one could have designed a better system for depicting women as powerless, vapid, uneducated, materially obsessed, codependent, malicious, and sexually objectified if they had set out deliberately to do so.

Today's entertainment and news writers may be professionals, but you, personally, can do much better at framing intelligent sexual language. In fact, you can do better than the culture as a whole, and the time to start is right now.

Perhaps you have never thought of the fact that *you get to invent your own words.*

This is a remarkable idea. Language is not something we are just presented with. We are expected to add to it, and if we are really present, we will find it necessary to do so. The language already in common usage is really about other people's experiences and about the past. The need to express what life is like for each of us *right now*, to ourselves and to those who matter in our lives, invites us to become language creators. You are obliged to find a distinctive way to express what you are uniquely experiencing.

Although language creation is too huge a subject to cover adequately in this chapter, it is important to sketch out a few of the basic methods. These are: (1) altering existing words to create new shades of meaning, (2) redefining existing words either partially or entirely, and (3) creating entirely new words. All three can be of use as you change your language.

The first approach, altering existing words, is the lightest form of language modification, but it can also be the most pleasant. ("Rush Limbaugh? A bit *talky* for me." Or, "Isn't he a bit alpha male–ish?") Inventing something new in self-expression, even if it's whimsical, can change you and those who hear you more than you might suspect.

The process of deliberately inventing language that is then outwardly expressed can feed back into your internal articulation and, in effect, change the nature and quality of the voice in your head. Your imagination, acting only internally, can't accomplish this because thought has difficulty acting upon itself. Changing your inner articulation happens by focusing on forms and content that are physically expressed. This is arguably one of the key purposes of art and literature; they create deeper and more powerful human beings. Even the most frivolous experiment in linguistic creation can at least shake a bit of rust off your mental gears. Truly creative and serious attempts to find new modes of expression can radically change your worldview and increase the power of your attention. As a practical matter, you actually can't afford to neglect language creation if you want to avoid slipping backward into habit and memory and away from presence in thc moment.

The second approach to changing spoken language is to redefine existing words, as is being done rather heavy-handedly in this book. The meaning of the word *gender* itself is redefined in these pages, and specialized definitions are given to dozens of others, including *Intent, Energy, centering, field edge, seer,* and *realm*. This is happening not just to present an argument or expand the reader's knowledge. If your language is expanded, you are expanded.

You are invited to take this prod toward linguistic creativity fully on board and start using language in favor of the genders, not against them. This is why so much space in a book on relationship is devoted to the matter of language.

For example, the noun *honor* needs to be redefined in terms of women so it means something more than sexual abstinence. *Honor* certainly has nobler, richer implications when used in reference to men. Similarly, when you hear the word *endurance*, the first images that come to mind, whether you are male or female, are probably male-related. The same is true with the words *pilot, doctor,* and *president.*

How is language redefined? The steps are straightforward. You nail down the exact new definition. You publish it with confidence, using clever associations that capture and hold attention. You use your redefined word in context repeatedly. Lastly, you put aside concerns about how far out into the world your altered language may spread. Iteration on a wide scale may or may not be in your power. Instead, focus on the world you can change. For most of us, that is our immediate and personal world.

Words are also redefined by creating new word combinations that create or reinforce new meanings. This too is being done in this book. Examples are: *nonordinary energy, instinct entitlement, Tame Attraction,* and *gender essence*. But don't just use mine. To really change yourself, invent a few of your own.

And now to the last of the three methods. If you are really daring, you can create entirely new words using new combinations of sounds. Word creation is not just the province of astronomers who are officially granted the right to name new stars and comets, or scientists authoring technical articles, who are expected to coin new terms. You don't need a license to create new language or anyone's permission. As with redefining existing language, the new language should be defined carefully, explained fully during early use, and repeated until it becomes familiar and accepted. This process requires confidence and a dedicated force of presence. New word creation also calls for having an ear for sounds that resonate. The word *Senté* is a rendering of the English language phrase, "the hand that becomes one with what it touches." It was created as the name for my body of work—although it also turns out to be (without the accent mark) the name for the strongest move in the game of Go.

The whole world doesn't have to use your new language element for your life to be changed by this process. New language can impact you hugely even if it exists only in your own head and the heads of those immediately around you.

If you doubt this, I suggest that you ask a friend or colleague to adopt and use a fabricated word for a week around your home and office. Casually monitor the flow of your own thoughts when this word comes up, looking for subtle changes in your capacity to pay attention and to think in fresher, more creative terms in the immediate aftermath of the new word's use. Ask yourself whether the use of a new word by just a single person does or doesn't have an impact on your attention. Obviously, I think you will find that most of the time it does.

As to the broader issue of how changing our language changes ourselves, see an excellent book by George Lakoff titled *Don't Think of an Elephant*. Its premise is that whoever controls the basic terms—the linguistic "frame"—relating to a social issue controls public perception of that issue and the choices made in relation to it.

It is time to reframe the role and nature of female people.

Both men and women need new language for talking about the feminine, and both need to stop using some of the existing language. It is obviously time to stop calling a woman "honey," "little," or "girl," for example, or addressing a woman by her first name in professional situations where a man is always addressed by his last.

New words are also needed for discussing relationship and sexuality. Wild Attraction is offering fresh vocabulary, but more important, it is offering a model for creating new words—for taking existing language, looking carefully at our actual experience of love and romance, and modifying that language to say something really worthwhile about sex and attraction (and potentially about everything else in our lives).

The current descriptive language for all things feminine is in general not sympathetic to women, or at least to women as I perceive them. We cannot afford to propagate that worldview. To illustrate this major failure in the structure of our language, I would like to examine a specific case.

If there is not a word for something, it is hard to pass along models of that thing. One word that our culture presently doesn't have is a gender-specific term for female nobility of character.

Is there, in fact, a uniquely feminine quality, or array of qualities, that could be considered the equivalent of the qualities we call "gallantry" and "chivalry" in men? My answer to that question is yes. If I am right and women in fact do display a feminine version of *gallantry* and *chivalry*, then where are our words for it? Have the terms *gallantry* and *chivalry* been culturally tagged to exclude applicability to female people because of cultural bias?

Remember the men who, in the middle of the night, gathered at the high-centered Volkswagen of my two overcoated female friends and collectively lifted the car off a bit of cement curbing? That was an act of chivalry within the common frame of reference. Those men were gallant. *Chivalry* and *gallantry* were among the first words the two women used once their Volkswagen was on the street again. But what would two men have said if they had been rescued by twenty women? I can guarantee that they wouldn't have had the needed words.

For that matter, what words would my stranded female friends have used if their rescuers had been women?

Gallant is a male-specific word. One dictionary definition reads (with italics added for emphasis): "Courteous, and thoughtful, *especially to women*. Brave, spirited, and honorable. Grand and majestic. Stylish or showy in dress. *Male courtesy to women*."

Chivalry is defined as the combination of qualities expected of a medieval knight, especially courage, honor, loyalty, and consideration for others—again, especially women.

The two genders emphasize somewhat different mixes of noble qualities—and so in fact do individuals. Both *gallantry* and *chivalry* refer to an array of qualities rather than to a single, easily perceived characteristic, and both of them, while still used occasionally, have strong anachronistic overtones. They are, therefore, ideal vehicles for exploring the issues of the celebration of noble character in men and women today.

It was somewhat remarkable to hear my two female friends use the terms *gallantry* and *chivalry* after the repair of their Volkswagen. For all their flaws, they remain perhaps the principle words available to us for acknowledging great character.

What word would *you* use if a heroic or remarkable woman had done something equivalent to saving you when your car was high-centered and you wanted to describe her to others afterward? Do you find it harder to find the right term than if a man had done the same deed? Most people do.

If you don't even have a term for the quality you saw in her, your encounter with her might be more difficult to remember, harder to frame internally, and more challenging to describe usefully to others. While talking, your focus might slip away from what is relevant—her character—to the fact of her gender, to her appearance, and perhaps to her possible sexual choices. The behavior that you saw her produce may thus never become a generic model that can be easily passed along.

The issue of the availability of words—specifically, defining terms—is of huge importance to our individual story of all things. As we saw earlier, each person's story of all things is his or her guess as to what is actually going on in reality on both the largest and the most personal scales. Your story of all things is the deepest answer you can come up with to the questions: What has led me to this moment? Where will this moment lead me next? Why is this so?

Your individual cosmology is something to polish up carefully and link directly to your sex life by asking yourself why males and females exist on the planet, where gender might really come from, and what it might truly offer. Your story of all things depends on words. And if you lack important words for framing the nature and role of women in reality, you are likely to find yourself underestimating the importance of women in the context of your entire experience.

All the way around, whether we consider the absolute number of defining negative terms or the ratio of negative to positive word use for each gender, women lose out when it comes to positive, defining language.

I mean, they *really* lose out. My search for definitions of chivalry or gallantry that apply specifically to women has so far come up with nothing. Consider the terms *honor*, *steadfastness*, and *valor*. Though not overtly gender-specific, they are male-tilted by broad context and long-established patterns of use. And these words, even though they can be applied to women, don't imply what *gallantry* and *chivalry* imply, which is a mixture of kindness, confidence, and power as specifically linked to one gender.

Even wonderful Internet resources, sites that are ideal for evaluating the male-female language problems prevalent today, such as the Center for Media Literacy, seem to overlook the lack of positive generic terms for female nobility of character.

Most sites that do offer descriptive words fall short. For example, I found the following list, assembled for romance writers, of terms for female characters: *Ladybirds (light or lewd women), shrew, vulgar tongue, scraggy, harlot, bawd, worn-out jade, wench, prime article, devilish good piece, hell of a goer, procuress, prostitute, innocent heroine, naughty heroine, abyss, bawd, demimondaine (a woman on the fringe of respectable society)*, and *courtesan, doxy, bluestocking, Cyprian (prostitute)*, and finally, *broad*. Admittedly, as words for the production of romance novels these are tilted toward the "saucy" side. But these are books about women characters with whom female readers will presumably identify.

Also listed on many sites as descriptive terms for female characters are words such as *dame, babe, chick,* and *bird.*

On the (relatively) positive side is *damsel* (a woman or girl; a maiden, often in distress; a lady's maid). I appreciate the word *mademoiselle,* the French equivalent of the English *miss,* referring to a young single woman. It sounds good, but it still doesn't specify a particular noble quality. We can also use *lass, maid, maiden,* and *princess.* Like *chivalry* and *gallantry*, these words tend toward the Victorian.

Lastly, of course, I must comment on the feminine version of the word *hero,* which of course is *heroine.* This term describes a woman's role in a story but does not specifically refer to character or nobility. *Heroine* is probably the most frequently used positive word for a woman in common vocabulary, but almost nobody I know would use it to describe a real, ordinary person.

By our language's glaring lack of gender-specific terms for female nobility of character, and the ongoing presence of specialized male terms such as *gallantry*, we can infer that a bias against celebrating the feminine exists in Western culture much as it does in places like New Guinea, even if it takes a less physically brutal form.

This language anomaly in no way reflects the actual nature of women as I have experienced them. Many women I know have shown chivalry equal to a man's in harrowing circumstances, including, in Patty's case, a brush with war in the jungles of New Guinea and making life-or-death decisions as a nurse-midwife at the bedsides of hundreds of women in labor. The emotional heroism of women, in my opinion, far surpasses that of men, on a daily basis. By *emotional heroism* I mean the complex choices women often make, setting aside their own needs or suppressing strong feelings, in the service of a greater good.

I have from time to time heard even very intelligent, educated, and cultured men state in completely matter-of-fact tones that women are inferior, less capable, or honorable. I have noticed that they seldom say these things in front of women, especially their wives, who I know as remarkably capable and high-functioning women. This, on its face, is difficult to explain. How can their perception of reality differ so incredibly from the obviously obvious fact that women play valuable roles in every aspect of life?

The complex issue of misogyny requires a lengthy interdisciplinary discussion well beyond the scope of this book. However, we can still make significant inroads by changing our language.

Energetic Fact of Life #37:

Many men think that women are less powerful and effective than males, and many women are conditioned to think that this can't change. The opposite is true. Women perform in life as well or better than men, and real change in the way females are being perceived can happen, starting in your own life. Your best response: Speak up for women. Cite feminine productive achievements in detail in order to highlight obvious absurdities relating to the denial of female accomplishment. If you are a woman, don't associate closely or develop romantic relationships with men who condescend to women. Watch for dismissive or demeaning energetic environments in which misogyny is present but unspoken, and leave them whenever possible. If some men think women are somehow less, then let them do without.

In general, the aware males in our culture share a low tolerance for letting hobbled males or unsafe males speak for them or set the cultural tone, because selfish aggression and oily codependence are inherently distasteful to high-functioning men. Aware males are able to see the roles of men and women more clearly than the other two types of males. They have a lot of positive things to say about women, and because they are beholden to no one and unafraid of censure, they are quite willing to speak up. If they have not done as good a job as was needed up to now, it is partially because they have not had the right tools, by which I mean an adequate supply of appropriate words and models.

What would the world be like if aware males were suddenly given the right words?

Chapter 16
Modern Courtly Love and Galadriel

Energetic Fact of Life #38:
People think they love and need the male or the female. This is wrong. In reality you need what the male and female together create: a blended "supergender." This intelligent energetic force is greater than the sum of its parts and is capable of endowing its human allies with unselfish wisdom and profundity. What to do: Pay far more attention to the room around you in the aftermath of great sex than you have ever done before, and ask yourself if any new perspective or state of being suffuses that moment. Is it possible that something other than you and your partner has suddenly been called into the room? Look for this same feeling around successful couples out in the world. Try to create this sensation with your mate in simple acts, such as when you are holding hands in a crowded environment. Use other simple physically entwining actions in daily life to promote an ongoing nonordinary blending with your lover, and then watch your state of mind to see what happens. Make this a daily practice for the rest of your life.

As the previous chapter reveals, I have long been looking for a term for chivalry without sexism, one that describes a different-but-equal feminine version of chivalry and gallantry. This word would convey a mixture of kindness, confidence, inclusiveness, style, insight, subtlety, and power, and it would apply especially to women. Many females carry these qualities, and remarkable characterizations of noble women exist in art and entertainment. One extraordinary example is the character Galadriel in *The Lord of the Rings*. That book is literally filled with depictions of both male and female chivalry, and some of their images are important for reasons that are to be touched upon shortly.

The search to describe real women who display qualities such as those ascribed to the Galadriel has led me into the past, and to an imperfect but useful medieval model that is thought of today as courtly love.

Courtly love is a literary tradition from medieval Europe, believed to have started around 1050 in France. (It had to be French.) Here is the Wikipedia entry for this subject: "In essence, courtly love was a contradictory experience between erotic desire and spiritual attainment, 'a love at once illicit and morally elevating, passionate and disciplined, humiliating and exalting, human and transcendent.'"

In its modernized, Wild Attraction version, courtly love can be redefined to describe the dance between two human beings who form a single unit. Together they accomplish an extraordinary feat and create an astonishingly beautiful work of art. In its redefined version, courtly love is about the creation of what I have earlier called a *supergender*, brought about by two people bearing merged male and female essences linked together in a single energetic unit. The supergender combination, when human beings create it, forms a field that changes human perspective and response. It fosters life responses that are powerfully compassionate, and that are selfless and conceptually very broad. The formation of this phenomenon is an actual event, one that trained observers can see, literally and directly. The supergender is not a metaphor; it exists in energy.

Furthermore, the process of supergender creation is happening all the time, unnamed and out of consciousness.

You may have subconsciously experienced the influence of supergender when you have been in the presence of one of those relatively rare couples in which the partners are perfectly merged and free of the remotest negative attitude toward gender in one another. A sense of miracle, of Mysterium Tremendum, arises when you find yourself within the zone of an extraordinary relationship. This zone is a great asset; it creates a powerful field of Energy within which to nurture new human life and build community.

Contrary to universal belief, people don't actually need the male and female; they need the thing that the male and female together create.

Wild Attraction as a system for pursuing extraordinary relationship can be thought of as a *modern courtly love*. The original system, at its heart, contained something instantly recognizable as valid and important to a practitioner of Wild Attraction, even though it was laden with romantic and patriarchal overtones that would, in practice, have prevented the merging of the genders and the creation of supergender as part of a couple's ongoing and attainable lifestyle.

The Wild Attraction version of this ideal thus represents a major upgrade over its precursor. Modern courtly love is not a distant literary ideal. It asks three vital questions that courtly love did not:

First: How should men and women best treat each other privately?

Second: How should lovers best treat other people around them when they are physically together in the daily world?

Third: How should lovers in extraordinary relationships best treat other people around them when they are moving as separate individuals, not physically together, in the world?

Modern courtly love, in other words, is about the blending of power, compassion, and gender in today's society. It incorporates and acknowledges both the "wild" and the spiritually sublime in male-female union. The model requires profound acceptance of individual personal power on the part of both partners. The benefits of modern courtly love vanish when either lover exhibits sexism or deep insecurity.

Modern courtly love requires a new definition of chivalry, a modern version that encompasses both male and female, which, in the new tradition of romantic language creation I hereby dub *energetic chivalry*. This term strips chivalry of its sexist baggage (much as *modern courtly love* does with *courtly love*) and adds to it the context of energetic gender essence needs and the ultimate goal of blending gender essences within a safe and mutually available couple. The male-female dance of polarized gender roles leading to merging becomes a single integrated power ritual in which everything that the man and woman do, both separately and together, represents the unit they form together on a gender basis. Energetic chivalry thus requires men and women to spend time exploring their power to create, move, and communicate in the world, and evaluating the use of these forces soberly.

Those interested in finding a model embodying the qualities under discussion here would do well to read J. R. R. Tolkien's *The Lord of the Rings* or view the justifiably famous film.

Galadriel wields a secret ring of power and is responsible for the creation and sustenance of an advanced and beautiful realm. She gives up the possibility of obtaining even greater power over others in a process that reveals both her potential ferocity and her great depth.

As a romanticized imaginary character, Galadriel is a useful device for making visible certain female qualities that tend to exist in the hearts and minds of millions of women but languish all but unseen amid the unglamorous demands of real life. She demonstrates selflessness, courage, wisdom, vision, creativity, sexualized and polarized feminine personal style, ritualized treatment of males, great abandon, a sophisticated relationship with emotions, and subtle use of power. Possibly no better example of female gallantry and energetic chivalry is available in literature.

The existence of the character Galadriel implies two questions: What kinds of power are you interested in seeking, and what are you being asked to do with your power, really, in the time you are given?

Chapter 17
At the Center of the Universe

Energetic Fact of Life #39:
People think they can get away with selecting lovers who are not their first choice, or with failing to assure their mate that she or he always was their first choice. Not so. It is essential to see your mate as your first choice in all the world, to place her or him at the center of your universe, and to express this in word or gesture on an ongoing basis. Your best action: Look at your mate every day and focus carefully on the qualities that you would most miss if she or he were to pass away. Articulate these qualities to yourself and contemplate their irreplaceability, laying any petty irritations or foibles aside as you do this. Write these qualities on a card, combine it with flowers or some other gift, and hand these to your mate while speaking the words on the card out loud. Create variations of this action. Remind yourself that there is an energetic element to "first choice" and "center of the universe," and ask your energetic system to mimic and support your physical disclosures.
Do this frequently in private and occasionally in the presence of close friends.

At the Center of the Universe

*P*atty and I had a delightful dinner last night with a couple we have known for a decade. When we first met them they were clients, and they have long since become close friends. Over dinner they recalled for us a three-hour coaching session they had scheduled in our private practice at the very beginning of our acquaintance. During that session we had explained and modeled various Wild Attraction ideas for enhancing their relationship. This was not relationship counseling; it involved sharing the Wild Attraction model as tailored for their specific circumstances and personal profiles.

They reminded us during dinner that the circumstances surrounding that first session had been troubled; they were coping with the immediate aftermath of a life-threatening illness and were dealing with issues relating to blending their extended families. Both partners at that moment had felt that their relationship was teetering on the brink of failure.

The husband emphasized, with an upraised professorial finger, that just one specific concept had saved their marriage. What follows is that one idea.

When you are chosen as a mate, it is extremely important to be chosen in a particular way. Your lover and mate must affirm that you are their first choice in the entire world. Being first choice is an energetic state, not just a concept or affirmation. The two partners may be many miles apart at times, but if both have this idea firmly on board, each of them will radiate a constant sense of first choice so strong that it crosses the distance between them by means of a subtle energetic transmission. This transmission states that no previous or future lover, or offspring or parent or movie star, could ever take precedence.

First choice as a relationship stance produces another very important motion; it places you squarely in the center of your beloved's universe.

As in first choice, a subtle energetic mechanism comes into play with this energetic ritual I am calling *center of the universe*. It is possible for you, with no more skill in nonordinary Energy than you already possess, to position the energy field of another human being right down on the patch of nonordinary firmament that is the zero-zero-zero spatial coordinate from which you measure the distance and direction to all else in your life. One way to do this is through a simple daily meditation. Picture an enormous black three-dimensional space. Imagine a signpost in the exact center of this immense space—perhaps at the intersection point of three huge geometrical grids that demarcate the x, y, and z axes, if you like to visualize this way. Imagine your signpost with many arrows bristling out, pointing in all directions, exactly like the signs at tourist sites around the world: 8800 miles to New York, 1700 miles to Tokyo, 5200 miles to Madrid. The energetic ground zero of your universe is exactly that sort of place.

Next, create a mental image of your mate and place that image right on the spot below the sign. Ponder this imagery for a moment each day, and think about what it tells you.

Every time you have to choose among conflicting demands on your time and attention, every time you feel pressure about your priorities and interests, take a look at the center of the universe and see whose eyes are gazing back at you.

Draw this space on a piece of paper, very simply. Then find a physical token that represents your mate and place it on the exact place on the paper that represents the center of the universe for you.

This simple visualization and accompanying simple physical action can work very well. It can change your behavior. It can help to snap you out of the dream that anything else could or should be more significant to you. Your mate is the most important person in your life. More important than your kids. Tell your lover that this is so, frequently.

You can also affirm and strengthen the energetic adoption of your mate as the center of your universe through telling him or her regularly, and in as many ways as you can think of: you are the most important person, experience, and thing in my life.

Patty advises our audiences frequently about the importance of personal confidence and freedom from psychological dependency when it comes to Wild Attraction's energetic rituals. Affirmations of *first choice* and *center of the universe* when performed as needy or clingy attempts to ingratiate or entangle a partner are highly distasteful. Like so many elements of Wild Attraction, these affirming messages depend on nuance. When performed, for instance, by an aware male who knows his own value and power and is confident (with the right nuance of healthy non-codependence) that he can get another partner at any time, these affirmations are vital and empowering.

For any woman, receiving the message that she is such a man's first choice and feeling herself to be the center of his universe can be overwhelmingly positive and transforming. Many find a deep relaxation and joy in being energetically claimed in this way. The inverse, of course, is also true; men feel the same as recipients of these gestures.

It is important to reinforce a point that was said earlier: The model elaborated in this book entails some risk for those whose psychological work is in the early stages, because it baldly holds out a dance of power as the primary way humans ritually bring about the merging of the male and female essences. Also, this model challenges fundamental aspects of ego and personality, and it urges the dismantling of aspects of the surface self that are sure to resist their own dissolution. People must be able to relate successfully to their individual power—to acknowledge it, develop it, and wield it not for personal gain but as creative self-expression—before they can relate to Wild Attraction and to another human being as an extraordinary lover. A person cannot actively play with power as a love ritual, as extraordinary relationship requires, until he or she has moved well past any lingering childhood or adolescent insecurity, pattern of rebellion from perceived authority, or need to resolve past struggles with people who were controlling or otherwise injurious.

Experiencing insecurity, discomfort, anger, self-doubt, and other signs of internal stress and resistance is natural, and almost everyone does. Wild Attraction is an invitation to move healing processes along as the first steps to better relationship, hopefully with the help of a skilled therapist.

Wild Attraction does not ask the impossible of you. It *does* ask that you make an effort to bring your best to relationship, not your average or your worst.

If you do not already have a mate and are searching for one, I urge you to search with the idea of *first choice* in mind. Accept no runners-up. The person you pick should, by force of will, be your first choice. This intent is not just a feeling. It carries a certain ruthlessness. It is a dedicated act of choice to get behind completely and radiate in thought, word, and action. Patty estimates that as many as ninety percent of women may not feel as deeply claimed or chosen as they would like. The feminine gender essence in even the most independent woman yearns for an act of merging that is only possible when she is claimed in a healthy way. This can happen best when she is paired with her first choice and her partner regards her as his first choice.

The woman who is still madly in love with her first boyfriend, the one she had back when she was sixteen, needs to snap out of it and get herself back onto planet Earth. The man who has a secret inner altar to Angelina Jolie and cares to burn those candles indefinitely is not a candidate for Wild Attraction. She can be a fantasy figure but not the center of his universe, nor an energetic competitor for the role properly occupied by his mate.

If you were extremely lucky, you received a center of the universe message from at least one of your parents when you were very young. (Good parents sometimes have the knack of letting their kids feel that they are the center of that parent's universe without actually displacing their mate from the central slot.) Even if you did, you still need the sensation of being regarded as the center of someone's universe as an adult in order to fulfill your highest potential. So does your mate. We can do this for each other in love and sex.

On the other hand, you might be among the many of us who were less lucky in childhood. If you feel that you never received such a message, now is the time to move toward being able to receive, and give, this amazing affirmation. Start by looking around at your life and wondering just who or what is, at this moment, the center of your universe. It could be anything, and nothing could be wrong or off limits. Ponder this, assign some person, place, or thing to this role as a placeholder, and start to visualize the human being that might eventually and appropriately reside in this most valued central square in your existence.

Give this message to your dog, your car, your child, and finally, when it is real, to your mate when that person appears. Search among your mentors and benefactors and look for signs that your presence, achievements, and contributions delight them so much that you might occupy the center of their universe, if only for a moment.

What do you do if your mate doesn't radiate the message that you are the center of his or her universe, or if your mate doesn't even conceive of it? What do you do if he or she demands it of you and you are not prepared to offer it? Or, what do you do if your mate offers this message and you don't know how to take it in?

Chapter 18
The Aware Female

Energetic Fact of Life #40:
The more the electronic media elevates celebrities, the more removed from greatness the average individual feels. This trend destructively inverts two important truths: everyone has equal access to human greatness, and there is always room at the top. Extraordinary relationships demand extraordinary mates; never lose faith that you can become one and that others exist. Your to-do list: Study relationship with at least the degree of fervor that you bring to bear on football, interior decorating, or child raising. Discuss great relationship with your mate on an ongoing basis. Ask questions of those whose relationships you admire. Demand more-than-average effort of yourself and your mate, and keep demanding it. Last and most important, name the greatness in yourself and your mate.

Every person who contemplates Wild Attraction and its specific models must come to terms with his or her beliefs about human greatness. Wild Attraction is about seeking a sexual relationship so great that it has the capacity to confer extraordinary qualities directly onto those who experience it. Therefore everyone who engages with it must eventually ask themselves what they think greatness is and whether or not they presently see themselves as a great person, or could ever do so. You are no exception.

You must be willing to consider yourself at least potentially a great individual and to put forth a level of effort and attention that is beyond the norm to manifest and enhance personal excellence. Wild Attraction is a call to action, but more than that, it is a call to greatness.

What definition of greatness is operative here? Consider both a standard and a specialized definition of this pivotal word. The standard definition of greatness, pulled directly from my office dictionary, reads as follows: *The quality of being great, distinguished, or imminent. Great. Of an extent, amount, or intensity considerably above the norm or average.*

My specialized definition of greatness is quite different: *Greatness is any quality of presence or performance that is irresistibly attractive to those who possess advanced consciousness and extraordinary powers of attention.*

Greatness is important not because of personal exultation, status, or power but because it is a language through which each of us can ask for concentrated, loving attention from minds more advanced and powerful than our own. Greatness irresistibly attracts such attention, and it is precisely this kind of elevated attention that changes us. The Wild Attraction creature is one (but not the only) source of this incredibly nurturing sunshine. It is the attention of more advanced minds onto developing minds that truly changes people, *not* our own attention, despite what contemporary culture would have us believe. No matter how much you pay attention to yourself, or to anything or anyone, your attention cannot change you. It can, however, change others. Your individual attention is given to you as a gift not for yourself but for those coming up the ladder behind you.

Wild Attraction is about attracting attention of the very best kind.

Allying with Wild Attraction is a matter of recognizing that the combined gender essences possess a quality of attention superior to our own and embracing the idea that this attention can change us profoundly. How do you become interesting to a superior intelligence? How do you learn to bask in the attention of a consciousness that few of us can see directly?

This is the point at which personal greatness comes into play. Greatness involves seeing what others don't see and doing what others won't do. The earnest and non-self-centered pursuit of extraordinary qualities is inherently *interesting*.

People commonly feel discouraged when comparing their personal attainments to the often-amazing achievements of people the media holds up as special. Greatness, as envisioned here, comes in more varieties than our culture celebrates. It is not measured against the output of others. It is a comparison between what you actually express and all that could be expressed in a given moment, or in your life. Many people are great or extraordinary in ways that neither they nor others ever understand. For this reason, it would be a mistake to interpret the Wild Attraction call to greatness through a narrow and conventional lens; greatness is a wide-open arc, and each person's possibilities are enormous—doing the best you can do in life is not just a hobby for the most competitive among us. Greatness as coined have is more than action and attainment; it also takes in a person's presence. By this I mean his or her qualities of beauty, character, and grace that can be seen in silence and stillness. Great presence is the equal of great performance in Wild Attraction—both reveal the individual's essence.

Any person can do himself or herself a favor by getting off the meaningless scale of "better" and "worse." Greatness is an aesthetic pursuit not a value. All people are equally precious, regardless of their apparent effort or manifest talent. Interestingly, those who understand this and can embrace individual greatness without getting tangled up in "better" and "worse," tend to be demanding in a positive way. They expect to give their best, and expect their mates to do the same.

The *aware female*, directly equivalent to the aware male, is Wild Attraction's model of the successful female candidate. She demands "center of the universe" and "first choice" messages from her mate. She will naturally not remain in a relationship if the kids are more central to her partner than she is, or if she finds herself overshadowed by his love of football or the job.

If you are a male and your mate demands first choice status from you, or offers it to you, your job is to get behind it, get with the program, suck it up, and learn to produce this vital gesture on an ongoing basis. Accomplishing this is mainly a matter of the way you pay attention and express yourself. You need to make the effort to pay attention to her as though she is great and you are great also.

Why will you do this? Because if you don't, you will lose your aware female mate—or never acquire her in the first place. You will be relegated, at best, to the mediocre in relationship. That would be a personal disaster.

Consider another scenario. What if you offer "first choice" and "center of the universe" status to your feminine mate and she can't or won't gracefully receive these messages? One answer is to give her this book. Another is to consider open and loving discussion, and offer to participate in joint relationship counseling. In the world of Wild Attraction, the ability to understand and accept those two messages is important.

The term *aware female* refers to a woman who intuitively grasps the energetic mechanics of gender and engages in ritualized gender play, while maintaining a positive stance toward personal power. She is comfortable pursuing and revealing personal greatness, and she encourages greatness in others, especially her mate. She is geared to make a powerful attention choice: she allows the best of what she sees in any person, place, or thing to be the defining quality of that element. She is gifted at displaying an art that is imperfectly described here as female gallantry.

The profound elements of personal character embodied

within the typical aware female enable her to move purposefully on a path toward feminine greatness, a path that demands courage, prowess and keen personal insight. These virtues typify aware women, and are obviously the same attributes that appear in aware men. Aware women and men are also similar in that both utilize their highest and best qualities to create sexual signals. Every aware woman displays her signature strengths through formalized noble acts—elaborate gestures of courtesy and selflessness that usually mirror the "nobility displays" offered by her male partner. The two forms of display are incredibly similar: The equivalent of gallantry in aware women often takes the form of rituals to be observed and appreciated by men, while men's gallantry is frequently practiced to capture feminine attention and provoke response.

As similar as they are, nobility in aware women and nobility in aware men differ significantly—feminine strengths are often more sophisticated and multilayered than those of males. And an aware female probably doesn't perceive greatness of character in quite the same way as her male counterpart. Patty prefers the term *female nobility* to describe the feminine equivalent of gallantry and chivalry. Significantly, the word *nobility* implies qualities of being, while the standard male terms—*gallantry* and *chivalry*—tend to evoke action. In her choice, Patty may be pointing to an actual distinction between female and male gallantry: the feminine version seems to be intrinsically more "being"-oriented than the male.

We can say that an aware woman is someone who is fully cognizant of female nobility and speaks fluently in a language comprised of noble acts. But this is a description and not a name. Fully comprehending the nature of an aware woman requires awareness of an X factor that has to be perceived directly, much as the flavor of chocolate (even in simple comparison to vanilla) must sooner or later be tasted in order to be known. An aware woman may not need a term for her own nature;

she grasps it directly. But the rest of us—the males who want to raise empowered daughters and relate to high-functioning mates, and the females who would aspire to real relationship functionality—*we* need a specific name or we will seldom see the actuality.

What if the world produced such a noun? Patty and I have experimented with the coined word *cetseva* (pronounced "set-see-vuh") and use it in Wild Attraction lectures to label and discuss the particular array of qualities, including the essential X factor, that are unique to aware women. If a man is gallant, the equivalent aware woman is *cetsevant*, which we pronounce as the word "savant" with "set" in front of it. Cetseva is a female nobility of character, an art form emphasizing strength, endurance, intricate persistence, inclusiveness, fluidity, lack of critical judgment, emotional intelligence, sacrifice, nuance, and grace. Ritually displayed within a relationship, it expresses a fierce and intelligent female sexuality that will provoke and inspire an aware male.

To pull the language elements of "aware female–ness" together, imagine a huge globe drawn on a blackboard, representing the ordinary daily world. Picture, within this chalk circle, two much smaller circles representing an aware male and aware female, placed separately, one to the right and the other to the left, and as far apart as possible. Finally, visualize a simple stick figure bed at the very top of the globe.

The driving concept within this illustration is that each individual can escape the ordinary worldspace and enter a much bigger one. To accomplish this, the aware man and aware woman develop extraordinary personal qualities and forge a great relationship. In the process, they have to move toward each other, undertaking power rituals and gender play that promote the merging of gender essences, thus bringing about transformation. Something new, at this point, enters the circle of the ordinary world—this new force is the supergender, the sentient force of Wild Attraction.

The qualities required to complete this process are gallantry/chivalry for aware men, and cetseva for aware women. These similar but sexually distinct arts are blended within an elegant dance of power rituals that has already been characterized here as modern courtly love. Gallantry, cetseva, and modern courtly love, working together, encourage the appearance of supergender, which levitates the couple to the bedroom and out the top of the globe of ordinary life, into something undefined and huge.

The cetseva of an aware female in daily life manifests as a presence or set of actions that multiply force. Its male counterpart, chivalry, is about generating force. To understand this, think of the difference between a single fighter and an army. A person who acts alone can get something done. A person who cues many others to act will get many things done. Chivalry will give you a fighter. Cetseva will give you a whole army.

An aware woman can command power of that magnitude. As imagined in the Wild Attraction model, she is definitely not a damsel in distress, although she can ritually feign that role. She makes sophisticated, multileveled observations more readily then men, and can discern what I call the issue of the moment and, more broadly, the main issues of a lifetime and even of our times. She can put aside distractions, including personal preferences, and do what is needed for the greater good. Unlike even aware males, she is working not for power over others but for functionality and the preservation and quality of life. She has an eye for what works.

An aware woman will unabashedly own her sexuality and can wield its healthy power to inspire and motivate, and even manipulate if needed. She does not internalize others' negative sexual behavior or views about either gender. She accepts the wildness of attraction and sex, and is the keeper of her own sexual reality. She does not let others define her as a woman, but she readily accepts the signals sent by her aware male counterparts about the incalculable value and overwhelming desirability of what she embodies in the world.

Aware females may enjoy male decisiveness within attraction rituals, but they are also decisive themselves and capable of acting ruthlessly with directness under pressure. Yet an aware woman is equally comfortable using indirect power to motivate another person (presumably male) to undertake deeds to impress her, or out of love and appreciation of her. This is the power to inspire.

Many aware women are trained in high-level personal arts. They move with remarkable grace, announcing themselves as beautiful, powerful, and intelligent. They know that women can be great, and that they as individuals have access to this greatness.

Aware females are not the least bit inhibited about displaying deep appreciation for gallant aware males, though without feeling obliged to indulge them.

Energetic Fact of Life #41:

Women are often encouraged to indulge the foibles, idiosyncrasies, insecurities, and follies of their men. Males do not need to be indulged by women, and generally should not be. Rather, it is important for males to frequently indulge (in the highest sense of the word) the aesthetic interests and personal wishes of their women as a way of displaying love, appreciation, and respect. Suggested actions: If you are a man, watch for cues as to what your mate really enjoys in terms of recreational time spent together. Look for activities that she may love but has never asked for specifically and surprise her by making them happen.

Another term that needs redefinition is *indulgence*. In the minds of many, the word carries a negative overtone: if we have to indulge someone, perhaps they are diminished or insufficient. Subconsciously we may frame indulgence as an act that the great bestow upon the not-great, or the not-yet-great. For example, we often indulge children. However, indulgence between gender-linked equals is not a diminishing act but a cherishing one. *Adult indulgence* is an indulgence that the great bestow upon each other and upon the world.

When women receive this kind of indulgence, which is neither diminishing nor disempowering, it becomes a primary binding force in relationship. A man identifies his mate's sometimes whimsical, often small-scale desires and fulfills them simply because the feminine thrives on loving attention; it is a woman's primary food. Adult indulgence is defined here to suggest a specific category of male action—small gifts and gestures and day-to-day acts of kindness, such as heading off occasionally to the mini-mart at midnight to get a pint of pistachio mint ice cream because your female mate has gone to the freezer and found it empty.

The term implies that an impulse from a female mate does not have to be practical, or logical, to be worth satisfying. If a powerful, independent man provides a gift that delights a woman for no other reason than that she wishes it so, that message of cherishment persuasively acknowledges her intrinsic value. It does nothing to disempower her.

If, on the other hand, a weak or psychologically damaged man's fawning servitude is disguised as loving generosity, the same trip to the mini-mart can be diminishing to both parties. Again, Wild Attraction's power rituals depend on the confidence, independence, and nuanced relationship skills of both the man and the woman.

In relationships where the male partner shows these small ritual courtesies frequently to his mate, the couple appears energetically closely bonded and both lovers are obviously highly satisfied. By comparison, couples in which the female indulges her male partner often look noticeably different. The partners' energy fields appear much less merged, the nonordinary communication is less frequent and less intense, they appear less satisfied, and they tend to be energetically available to third parties to an unhealthy degree.

Women thrive on nonentangled loving adult indulgence, which Patty—once again contributing a feminine version in the search for new language—prefers to think of as a special kind of cherishment that perhaps should be called *empowered cherishment*. Women do not thrive when they are expected to show this kind of indulgence to men. And aware men, frankly, don't want or need it.

Men thrive on appreciation for their *doing*. A daily dose of "Good job" is enough for the aware male. Aware women easily give themselves over to *being* as a respite from the daily demands of doing and providing. Receiving loving care does not diminish them but rather nourishes them.

This detailed rendering of the aware female is an attempt to cast serious attention onto the neglected topic of female greatness, as well to paint a portrait of what works best in the Wild Attraction model of extraordinary relationship. Women manifesting such traits—not perfect, idealized creatures but real-world women with quirks and foibles—have a competitive advantage and are likely to be able to carry out the kind of dance an aware male is interested in experiencing.

No feminine person has to conform to any man's idea of female greatness, including mine, in order to be a worthwhile and lovable person. But this description hopefully captures a spirit that exists abundantly out in the world. A high percentage of women are bringing this spirit to their mates, their families, and their communities right now. They are great. It is time for people to start talking seriously about it, with much better linguistic tools, because this is what *works*.

Chapter 19
The Nature and Inherent Needs of Humans

Energetic Fact of Life #42:
We are trained to think that giving positive messages to one another is optional or not needed, or that the same kinds of positive messages work for both genders. We also tend to believe that we have the option to remain silent when positive messages are obviously called for. These assumptions contribute hugely to human suffering. Everyone needs a daily diet of positive messages, and you can't opt out of this need no matter your degree of awakening or strength of will. Withholding a needed positive message from your mate is no different from sending a crushingly negative one, and negative messages destroy relationships. Your job: Ask for and offer five basic messages freely and ongoingly. Tell other people and especially your mate: "I see you," "I regret your pain and suffering," "You are loved and a part of the pack," "I appreciate your contributions and achievements," and "You are safe with me and from me." Add to these the vital gender-specific messages suggested in the Wild Attraction model.

Everybody needs positive messages, and no living creature possessing a personality can escape this fact any more than a sentient being living in a human body can deny that body's need for physical food. Equally important, negative messages are poison to the personality; they starve and deform it. It is therefore the business of all sentient creatures to avoid both internalizing negative messages themselves and offering a negative message as sustenance to any other person.

Each person must receive at least five key kinds of positive messages every day. In addition, the gender essences have their own set of message requirements, of which *center of the universe* and *first choice* are but two examples. As important as is our need for positive messages, (they are, in fact, vital to the creation of powerful intimacy), our requirement for specific signals is just one of many vastly underestimated stumbling blocks relating to need on the path to great intimacy. We must look at them all.

We humans are physical, imaginary, energetic, and spiritual creatures, and can be said to reside at once in all four corresponding realms. The fourth, spirituality, is an ineffable Allness of which we are a part and in which no need exists. But as creatures of the other three realms, we humans have needs. We can define a human need as an element the lack of which will either kill a person or destroy his or her quality of life and thus indirectly bring about death. The physical needs are food, drink, air, warmth, among others. The imaginary or psychological aspect of a person, as just mentioned, needs certain positive messages on an ongoing basis. The energetic needs are three: to gather Energy, to release content, and to live free of the Intent of others.

Finally, we must consider the issue of need as a special element in romantic relationships.

The profundity of the union between two sexually connected people makes them the primary message sources for each other. They are capable of delivering positive messages to one another at a depth possible for no one else (though as popular culture reminds us, they are also capable of delivering devastating negative messages whose impact can be so incandescent that recovery may never occur).

Gender relationships are thus the primary vehicles for meeting the human need for both male-female-specific signals ("Good job," "You are lovely and you are enough," "You are my first choice," and "You are the center of my universe" are examples) and basic positive messages. Yet paradoxically, no gender relationship can become extraordinary if it exists mainly as a machine whose job is to meet the needs of either partner. The best way to resolve this tension is to remain attentive to meeting mutual message needs, while never allowing need itself to become the driving force in the relationship—this is done by focusing on the relationship as an unselfish celebration of love. Extraordinary relationships must in the end exist to affirm that love exists, rather than to serve the false god of need.

Other ways are available to you to meet the life necessities of your partner (and expect your partner to meet yours) without letting the fact of need dominate your relationship. You can spread your dependency for messages and assistance fairly widely among a healthy community of friends. This obviously keeps each member of a couple from depending solely on the other.

Another important way to dodge the gray bullet of need is for each partner to develop a reasonable confidence that he or she can easily find a new mate if the present relationship fails. This kind of confidence, well exemplified by Rhett Butler in *Gone with the Wind* and discussed in more detail in chapter 21, does not have to diminish or challenge your mate, or undermine your mutual love and devotion. Rather, it frees your mate from the burden of obligation to you, allowing him or her to feel wanted more than needed. This can be an incredibly fulfilling relationship experience.

The real secret to avoiding need-based relationships is to choose a partner who is not inherently a needy or need-based person, and avoid entering into an intimate relationship as a need-based person yourself.

Having examined need itself, and the gender specific signals that we all must receive, we come at last to the five messages introduced at the beginning of this chapter as the primary needs of your personality. For years, Patty and I used to guest lecture at high school and university psychology classes. A description of the five messages was always our landing point, and we have been pleased at how many students have sent us appreciative letters over the years. We used to tell them this: No one is exempt from nature's mandate to be both a sender and a receiver of positive messages. As I continue to point out, silence is not good enough. The absence of a positive message is the equivalent of a negative one, and negative messages do not build healthy individuals or relationships. To fail to be an active positive message sender is to doom oneself to a life of limited or zero intimacy and message starvation, in which major aspects of the human composite remain unhonored.

You ... need ... to ... know ... this. You.

Despite the fact that these messages are obviously and desperately needed by everyone, our culture at present shows little consciousness of this basic fact of human life, and most people deliver only a fraction of the number of messages truly called for. We would do well to be sending positive messages to everyone around us, and especially to our mates, whenever such messages are true.

I am not encouraging you to believe that you are your own thoughts or personality. The Wild Attraction model is based on the idea that you are something more, and that, spiritually, we probably need nothing.

If you accept the premise that you are not your personality, it becomes possible to view the need for messages in a soft and gentle way. Sending and receiving positive messages is simply a way of treating your personality as lovingly and thoughtfully as you would treat your pet or take care of your car. Give it what it needs for love's sake, and it will serve you well. Do the same for the personality of your lover.

The necessary five messages are given here. They tend to build on one another in a hierarchical way—for example, most people need to feel seen before they can really hear an apology. That said, each message is a stand-alone, and all are equally important.

I see you. Tell your lover, and everyone else in your life, that you see them fully and completely. Then tell them exactly what you really do see. Let them know that you really are seeing them by paying careful attention and delving into detail beyond what they might expect. Tell them your impression of their hopes and fears, their special talents, and, when appropriate, their deeper feelings.

I regret your pain and suffering. Next, express regret. Tell your lover, and anyone else you care about, that you regret their misfortunes and sufferings. Feel free to apologize for the pain life itself may have caused them, if it seems appropriate. You can apologize for anyone, for anything, without taking the guilt or blame on yourself, and your apology will have value. Think of apology as the expression of regret rather than acceptance of blame. Remember that only about one out of every thousand needed apologies is ever conveyed in our world.

You are loved and a part of the pack. The third message to give freely to everyone is the message of unconditional love. I always think of this message in concrete terms. I want people to know that if I were the helmsman of a crowded lifeboat in frothy green stormy seas, and if they were to fall over board, I would go back for them. This third message is, therefore, a lifeboat message for me, rather than a syrupy declaration of emotion. The message you give your lover is an ultimate version of this message; it is both beyond gender and highly sexualized, and the pack is the couple itself. When expressed to the rest of the world, the message is free of gender context, and the pack is the fellowship of human beings everywhere.

I appreciate your contributions and achievements. People need to hear that they are appreciated for their contributions, achievements, and victories. Here too, people rarely receive the messages that they have earned. Moreover, most of the incredible feats achieved by human beings are internal. People suffer in silence, they struggle internally, they face demons and dig deep inside for hidden resources, and it is almost all hidden from view. Great things happen inside the human heart. Look there and don't hold back when you perceive something wonderful or amazing in your fellow creatures.

You are safe with me and from me. Finally, people need to hear that they are safe, really safe. Watch over them, and tell them that you are doing so. Incredibly, many people I meet have never been effectively told that safety exists. Most people believe only in degrees of jeopardy and live in degrees of greater or lesser anxiety, but never in true relaxation. The assurance of safety is a vital and wonderful resource that we need to share with one another.

It is the business of a seer to also share the observation that a great many contentious behaviors in the world are attempts to compensate for the lack of needed messages. People ask for raises because they haven't been told they are appreciated. People sue other people because they haven't received an apology. They destroy and even murder because they have never felt seen and it seems as though any attention is better than none.

Knowledge of the messages and their role in human life is one of the simplest and most precious things to have come my way in a lifetime on this path. It is the most needed idea about need. I hope it gets passed along.

Part IV

Love Is a Wheel

Chapter 20
The Ultimate Bicycle Built for Two

Energetic Fact of Life #43:
Despite the normalization of ordinary relationship perpetuated by our culture and by the force of denial, and the relative hopelessness or indifference with which many people regard relationship, extraordinary love is actually within the grasp of many, possibly most, people. Your best course: Do the necessary rituals whether you understand or like them or not, and snap out of the culturally induced dream that would have you wait forever for your instincts to change.

This chapter is a significant border in the study of Wild Attraction. Whereas the preceding chapters presented the what, where, and why of extraordinary relationship, the chapters that immediately follow are devoted to the how—the actions you can take to effectively pursue great love as envisioned within the Wild Attraction model. The three prime building blocks of Wild Attraction practice take the form of three lists: the *six stages of relationship*, the *five steps to candidacy*, and *the power rituals required for extraordinary love.*

These are lists of indispensable actions that work.

Experiencing extraordinary relationship is a matter of keeping reasonably good track of where you are on each of these lists and knowing how to move through them by undertaking the specific actions they call for. While this may sound mechanical, simplistic, and downright unromantic, the addition of these simple actions to a love life provides a strong, relaxed framework within which love can bloom.

I remember about five years ago trying to explain about the stages, steps, and rituals to a man I will call Alan. He was a handsome brown-haired professional in his early forties who had a history of failed long-term relationships. I watched him interact with his girlfriend at the time, Maxine, who was perceptive and obviously high-functioning but lacking in realistic models for intimacy. Energetically speaking, Alan was inappropriately forward. Maxine seemed to be honestly trying to figure out how to sustain a relationship with this attractive but problematic lover.

Alan could get women but he never kept them. He admitted that he tended to lose interest in them over time and was often frustrated by their insistence on fidelity, the need for which he found hard to understand. Yet he didn't like being alone, and was concerned that he had not yet put in place a long-term relationship that could last into his old age.

Alan's remarks indicated that he was nonfunctional with respect to the stages, steps, and rituals. In terms of the six stages of relationship, he was stuck in the fifth stage, seduction. The stages, arranged in sequence, are:

1. Friendship
2. General attraction
3. Contact
4. Courtship
5. Seduction
6. Sustained relationship

Wild Attraction is about moving from stage to stage, using the appropriate energetic power rituals for each stage, in the same way that human beings move through various life stages, from infancy to old age. Different rituals are required at different stages in the ongoing recurring cycles of male-female love. Unlike human life cycles, however, all relationships rotate through the stages again and again, each time in a new and different way. Once a couple moves to the level of sustained relationship, those lovers return intelligently to the earlier stages in a process that maintains sexual charge and honors the needs of the gender essences as the union develops. The sixth stage encompasses all those that came before. The list of the six stages of relationship is therefore a navigation tool that tells you where you are in the relationship process.

For instance, if you have a good circle of friends and have not been focusing on sexual relationship, you are in the friendship stage. Friendship is the first and most important of all the stages, because it sets the tone and the interpretive framework for all others. While in that stage, you practice the energetic rituals of friendship, which include mild, safe flirting and occasional engagement of gender essence, but nothing so overtly sexual as to trigger courtship. Once you start to actively search for love, but before you find Mr. or Mrs. Great Mate, you are in the general attraction stage, moving among your friends but using more overt rituals that announce your interest and candidacy.

The moment when you ask someone out, or someone asks you out, and a romantic date is green-lighted, you have reached the contact stage. You move to a new set of rituals and tasks, including such things as polarized gender essence engagement and telepathic relationship negotiation, which are described earlier in this book. From the contact stage, you enter the courtship stage, which has its own specific energetic rituals. Only then, after a period of getting to know the other person, do you reach the seduction stage.

If you use the rituals associated with one stage when your relationship is actually at another stage, as Alan seemed to be doing, you derail the process of merging the gender essences. The reason: Couples face a long, gradual road that begins with first contact and extends through various phases all the way to merging and the creation of supergender. Each step is dependent on successful completion of the one before. This is, in part, a clockwork energetic process that cannot happen if people mix up the stages. Another deal-breaking disadvantage of mixing them up is that in doing so you end up screening out any real candidates for love you might encounter.

The six stages of extraordinary relationship run along in parallel with the five steps to candidacy and the energetic rituals. To navigate in the Wild Attraction world, you move through all three lists at once. So, what are the other two lists about? The five steps to candidacy are, in order:

1. Becoming a candidate
2. Identifying other candidates
3. Attracting other candidates
4. Seducing a candidate
5. Binding (or keeping) a candidate

This list is the backbone of Wild Attraction, because success with this model is literally built around the issue of candidacy.

It is impossible to form an extraordinary relationship with someone who is not a candidate. Your challenge, then, in relationship is to find and bind the best mate you possibly can from the available pool of candidates. This may sound crass, but it isn't meant to be. It is real and it works. Deep down, everyone knows this. But many won't voice it to themselves in the mistaken belief that it devalues the importance of love in choosing a partner.

Most people focus the bulk of their attention and effort on the profiles of prospective mates and on trying to change other people in order to make relationships work. Attention tends to be lavished on the possibility of catching lovers who are rich, nice, good-looking, responsible, or in possession of some other desired quality.

People who are schooled in the Wild Attraction model think entirely differently; they tend to focus on refining their own capacity for great relationship and making this capacity evident to those around them in ways that automatically draw suitable candidates. Great candidates are normally psychologically aware, and they are able to demonstrate personal power or skill that is pronounced and beautiful, such as dancing or martial arts. In other words, relationship candidates speak a Technicolor language of action to reveal themselves to other candidates, rather than relying on words or on appearance alone.

The third list introduces nineteen power rituals required for extraordinary love—specific, nonpractical ceremonial gestures that are needed at the various stages and steps. In other words, you move from step to step, and simultaneously from stage to stage, by performing the appropriate power rituals. A person becomes a candidate through two parallel processes: One is the deliberate cultivation of ongoing change in a person that gives him or her a progressively greater depth, more insight, and greater psychological and energetic wakefulness. The other is the gradual acquisition of the knowledge and skills relating to the five steps to candidacy themselves. Ideally, great couples become better and better candidates in tandem: the longer they are together, the more skilled they become in the dance of extraordinary partnership.

Most rituals are remarkably easy to understand, remember, and perform. Some are overtly energetic, and some are simple physical gestures. All were derived from nonordinary viewing, observing what humans are actually doing subconsciously every day. Often, like Alan, they are performing the wrong rituals at the wrong times. You as a practitioner of Wild Attraction can choose and combine the gestures appropriate at each stage in many ways. Your particular choices can become a kind of personal signature.

Hundreds of other energetic mating rituals exist besides the ones presented in this book, but most of them require more advanced energetic training or are difficult to convey in written form. The rituals on this list are all you need to begin to explore extraordinary relationship (six of these were introduced in earlier chapters):

1. Indirect and direct power rituals
2. Whole-body or provocative body part illumination
3. Providing admiring, undemanding attention
4. Projecting consciousness of a wide field of available partners
5. Building charge
6. Matching identities
7. Welcoming eyes
8. Promising in Energy what you will actually do
9. Giving him a job / doing a job for her
10. Overlapping and merging energy fields
11. Energetic completion—emptying or filling docks
12. Apparent accidental nudity
13. Energetic claiming
14. First choice
15. Center of the universe
16. Full gender essence engagement
17. Using gender-specific language
18. Sending the five basic messages
19. Extending and retracting feminine gender essence

Here is what I told Alan and Maxine. Alan was, according to my model, enamored with just one stage of relationship, the seduction stage, and was ignoring or perhaps incapable of embracing the other stages. In terms of the five steps to candidacy, Alan was likewise focusing only on the fourth step: seducing a candidate. In terms of the power rituals, he was naturally using only the ones appropriate for seduction and was ignoring the rest. He seemed to me to be repeating that single stage and step, seduction, and never mastering it. His seduction skills were considerable, but because he was lacking other skills he was geared up only to seduce noncandidates—and noncandidates were the only kind of women who were ever seriously attracted to him. Maxine was a noncandidate, if only because of her attempt to relate to him. A qualified candidate would never do so.

I explained to Alan and Maxine that being stuck at a certain stage or step is relatively common. I had seen, for instance, people who only offered the rituals associated with sustained relationship, even if they were meeting a new potential love. The rituals they offered to lovers at the contact, courtship, and seduction stages were as comfortable and secure as an old bathrobe and a favorite green sofa. Relaxation and familiarity were always assumed. But sustained relationship rituals don't work well on first dates or in the bedroom when a potential partner is waiting to be seduced. Charge and romance are needed. As a consequence, these people languished in relationships that were devoid of "wild" and eventually lost the very mates that were worth keeping.

For Alan, it didn't matter whether he was with one of his three ex-wives, a new girlfriend, or a checkout clerk. He liked to energetically illuminate his shoulders in the presence of almost any woman, packing them with Energy to send sexualized signals. He also matched his gender essence ratio to that of the woman of the moment, as we saw the young man doing in

Lithia Park, and he sent provocative sexual messages in Energy. These are all energetic seduction rituals.

Alan used his seduction behaviors not only in the friendship stage but even when a relationship had developed past the stage of seduction. Not only was he offering the wrong rituals at the wrong times, he also wasn't performing the right ones when they were needed. For this reason, Alan had never been able to maintain a committed relationship for any period of time. He also tended toward superficial friendships. He never knew where he was at any given time with respect to the three lists. Therefore he was incapable of real motion on a relationship timeline. Alan had no idea what the gender essences actually needed from him.

Maxine could see wonderful qualities in Alan, and they kept her hooked. She yearned to find the formula that would move Alan past the seduction stage at which he was stuck. She alternated between joining him in his seduction model and backing away, signaling him to move on to rituals that were more appropriate to sustained relationship. Alan would placate her for short times and then revert, occasionally bringing up his frustration with her monogamy expectations. This cycle left Maxine confused, devalued, angry, and sad.

Alan and Maxine, genuinely curious, asked me what I would do in their shoes.

I hesitated. These two people were in the very early stages of forming a relationship; they were not committed and had no mutual investment to preserve. And both were insisting they really wanted extraordinary relationship. Considering this, I advised Maxine to ask herself why she was trying to create a relationship with someone who was at that point not a candidate for real intimacy and to start thinking in terms of becoming a candidate herself.

I told Alan that if I were in his position, I would probably drop out of the relationship with Maxine and spend a year alone. He was in midlife, he had followed a prevailing model of relationship that celebrated the male as a stud, and this had taken him nowhere. If he was interested in benefiting from the Wild Attraction model, he would need to completely re-educate and retrain himself, reframing his approach to adult relationship.

Not being a therapist, I did not attempt to deal with the psychological issues that might have surrounded Alan's choices, or Maxine's attraction to him. Instead, I advised them to seek psychological counseling in conjunction with their exploration of the Wild Attraction model. Then I went on to give them a mini Wild Attraction course, taking them through the rituals appropriate to the real stage of their relationship, which was sustained relationship.

Both were amazed at what was possible between them when Alan adopted behaviors more suited to general attraction, contact, and courtship, behaviors that reflected the real (or skipped) levels of their relationship, and Maxine could finally respond in a genuine way. The dynamic between them, during the role-playing and experimenting process, became mutually nourishing and poignant.

Alan, as far as I know, never took my advice to heart. I recently heard that he is still out there, cycling through female partners, five years later. Maxine, on the other hand, snapped out of her attraction to Alan shortly after our session. She is now a good candidate for extraordinary relationship. In fact, she has been married to another good candidate for years, and she occasionally writes to thank me for exposing her to a model that, for her, has really worked.

At the time, I came up with a metaphor for how the stages, steps, and rituals work together, and I know from speaking with Maxine over the years that this image helped her to keep the concept alive.

I advised Maxine and Alan to think of extraordinary relationship as a bicycle built for two. The six stages of relationship and the five steps to candidacy are the wheels of the bike. Rotating through these two lists, in tandem, evokes the sensation of two bike wheels going around and around. And as in biking, you are changed with each revolution of the two wheels. You move forward. You move through time and through the ongoing process of relationship.

The two bike wheels are bound together by the bike frame and handlebars, which symbolize the power rituals for extraordinary love. You move forward, with your partner, by balancing on the bike's two wheels and causing them to rotate by means of your combined physical pedaling motion.

If you don't have a partner yet, you ride your bicycle built for two with one empty seat, while employing the power rituals that are appropriate for friendship and general attraction and for identifying and attracting a candidate and becoming a candidate yourself.

In either case, you are always moving, always rotating those wheels and working that handlebar, always steering by means of the particular choices of power rituals that you make.

Once you get that bike up to speed, as Maxine did, you will be amazed at the places you can go.

Chapter 21
The Handlebars: Romantic Power Rituals for Extraordinary Relationship

Energetic Fact of Life #44:
Most people regard the capacity to pair up as a matter of communication skills and psychological understanding. In fact, from a gender energetics perspective, creating and maintaining a successful relationship is a matter of physical and energetic rituals that facilitate bonding, blending, and merging. These rituals always involve personal power. What you can do: Memorize a short list of vital rituals, discuss them with your mate (if you are in relationship), and make sure you perform them on a daily, weekly, and monthly basis.

Consider this website posting on the mating of birds from a site called "Paul and Bernice Noll's Window on the World":

> The potential pair ... engage(s) in a series of displays by one or both birds over the next several hours, days, or weeks, to initiate and strengthen a bond between them. The early displays may be subtle, or they may be quite apparent. Rufous-sided Towhees of both sexes briefly spread their wings or tails, revealing white spots; a Scarlet Tanager

male may drop its wings to expose its red back while a female perches in front of its mate, while Herring Gulls toss and turn their heads and provide choking or pecking displays.

Mating displays can also be quite spectacular, as in the sky dance of the Northern Harrier. Over fields or marshes across North America in April you may see this usually low-flying hawk climbing skyward on powerful wing strokes, and then plunging toward the ground while uttering a faint chipping call. The dive is usually repeated in a continuous series by the male, who traces a deep U-shaped pattern of cartwheels in the sky.

Like birds and a huge percentage of animal life on the planet, human beings are naturally driven to engage in mating rituals. Despite this, quite a number of people doggedly resist ritual behavior, some for psychological reasons: they feel that using ritual to encourage relationship and sex will deprive them of the deep sense of being unconditionally loved that arises from having to do nothing at all to get love. Some ritual dodges are not so love-oriented: some people routinely ignore the requirements of ritual out of laziness or contempt or a compulsion to short-circuit any process that would empower themselves or their mates.

Yet even opting out is a ritual statement, one that attracts certain kinds of mates (the wrong kinds). No one can escape the fact that most male-female pairing behaviors are reflexive and programmed. We all engage in them. There is only one question, then: Will we perform these rituals consciously, elegantly, and in ways that work, or will we let them be garbled, mangled, and out of order?

Most people are not opposed to mating rituals but don't engage in them simply because our culture doesn't encourage it.

The Handlebars: Romantic Power Rituals

I wish human cultures were telling all of us, and young adults especially, three things about mating ritual behavior:

First, the most significant mating rituals are energetic in nature, not biologically driven. Second, these rituals do not have to make sense in order to work; the specific actions are as meaningless as a male bird taking a twig in its beak, circling a perched female three times counterclockwise, and laying the twig at her claws. Lastly, the most important human mating rituals are about revealing power, symbolizing individual power, and providing a mock struggle in which the male and female pretend to battle for supremacy but end up realizing their equality.

In accord with these principles, the rituals in Wild Attraction are energetically based, are fundamentally impractical though vitally necessary, and celebrate gender power. Relationship power rituals are sets of counterbalancing gestures in which individual power is taken up and ceremonially laid down, with power being passed back and forth between the lovers. Performing them well requires confidence, careful observation, responsiveness, timing, and creativity.

Here is an example of the successful use of power rituals by skilled adults: A woman devastates a man using one of the rituals, *apparent accidental nudity*. She leans forward and allows her blouse to fall slightly away from her breasts, exposing flesh while pretending to be unaware of this indiscretion. The man recovers from the considerable impact of this exposure, and as a return display of subtle power over his own impulses, he ignores the exposed flesh and pays appreciative attention at eye level to the woman. She gets up and moves toward the door, hesitating. He smoothly gets to the door first, without appearing to rush, and opens it for her.

The man then suggests a future meeting, and the woman (adjusting her glasses in order to get her hands above collarbone level and thus activate feminine gender essence) expresses doubt that it will work out.

The man confidently assures her that it *can* be worked out. He gently but firmly takes the woman's heavy shopping bag out of her hands, helping her toward her car. His hands stay low and in front of his body, and his walk is in a straight line that follows his line of gaze—behaviors that activate and engage his male gender essence. His shoulders and butt are subtly illuminated. He moves slightly ahead of her (so she has to notice) but maintains a smooth presence that does not reveal that this is conscious.

Approaching the car, the woman moves in slight curves, her hips rotating forward and back, escalating the battle of gender essence engagement and forcing the man to pay attention to her as a sexual being. She tells the man, in confident and nonchalant terms, that she appreciates his offer to get together but isn't entirely sure of him. She pauses slightly at her car door.

He opens the door for her, and she slides into the car showing a calculated bit of leg, which he glances at appreciatively for just an instant, long enough for her to know that he has received her signal. As he hands her the shopping bag, a flood of energetic sexual imagery passes between them. She accepts the bag slowly, her gender essence extending toward the man with the outward movement of her hand and then retracting back seductively into her energy field as her hand gracefully pulls the bag into the car.

The man stands still, his field contained. He is again demonstrating his power by resisting a subconscious, nearly overwhelming impulse to extend his energy field into hers in pursuit. She puts the bag on the seat beside her with exaggerated care, appearing for a moment to forget that the man is present.

After a few seconds have passed, during which time each has carefully forced the other to wait for a response, the man bends down so that he is eye to eye with the woman and leans slightly closer. In a carefully cultivated, confident voice, he mentions a time and date and tells her he will be dropping by and picking her up.

She says, "You are pretty confident, aren't you? I like that."

The last thing he says to her is, "We'll have a great time. I'll see to it."

The twist to this vignette is that, although you might think this couple is in the early stages of a developing relationship, in fact this is a true account of an interaction between two people who have been married for more than a decade. This ritual, and others like it, are part of the reason that they are still married. And their level of conscious, committed skill is part of the reason that their relationship is extraordinary.

Perhaps the best cinematic depictions of power rituals between two members of an extraordinary couple are found in the work of Humphrey Bogart and Lauren Bacall, especially the film *To Have and Have Not*, which is highly recommended as an adjunct to the material presented in *Wild Attraction*. By many accounts, the onscreen magic was not staged but actual. Theirs was, very probably, an extraordinary relationship in accord with the Energetic Facts of Life laid down in this book.

Energetic Fact of Life #45:

Most people see power as the force used to bring about motion or change, or as a form of relationship that involves making commands and then being obeyed. This is not the case. Power is promise and fulfillment. Power can use any force or take any form; its nature is entirely elusive. The hallmark of power is the capacity in those who wield it to specify a change and then bring it about, by whatever

> means. Great power is fulfillment of promise beyond any reasonable expectation. If you can promise and fulfill something, you have power. Your suggested course:
> Begin a daily practice of making three oral or written promises and fulfilling them to the best of your ability at any reasonable cost.

Few things are as important in considering issues of power as reflecting on the nature of power itself. In nonordinary terms, personal power is not the force used to accomplish a task. Power is the mating of two elements: promise and fulfillment. Promise is the feminine aspect of power, the analog of feminine gender essence. Fulfillment is the analog of male gender essence. Just as supergender is summoned when male and female gender essences merge (which is, after all, a main point of human relationship), power is created when promise and fulfillment merge. In the nonordinary world, promise and fulfillment are not ideas; they are actualities with tangible substance. They may as well be two crystals in a sci-fi movie which, when brought together, radiate intense energy.

Our culture has greatly disempowered its citizens by destroying the concept of giving and keeping your word. People in general are trained to fulfill or to promise but almost never both. Although most systems of law are founded on the notion of specific promise, the rising fear of litigation alone has done unintended damage to promise and fulfillment because of the legal risk involved in specifying an intent before engaging in action and then failing to accomplish what was promised. Modern politics, in which promises are almost always empty, has further eroded what was once a point of honor. So has advertising. Neither promise nor fulfillment alone constitutes real power. Neither one without the other brings about real change.

You can snap out of this destructive sleepwalk through life. In love, especially, you can tell yourself and others in advance what you are going to do and then make sure you do it. The degree to which you can voice a specific promise and then bring it into fulfillment is the degree to which you are powerful.

Energetic Fact of Life #46:
Modern society tries hard to sell the idea that human beings should seek success entirely through relational power, our ability to affect our environment by influencing the actions of other people. But this notion is false. Relational power is useless unless it is grounded in concrete power, which is the ability to perform a high-level action involving promise and fulfillment unilaterally, using only your physical body and tools that it can directly engage. Your best course: Learn to perform at least one signature act of personal power, one that can be presented within an afternoon right in front of other human beings. Examples are: play guitar and sing, paint, draw, write, sculpt, or sketch, perform a martial arts kata or a profoundly beautiful dance, water ski like a professional. State exactly what you are preparing to do and exactly how well you are going to do it prior to any demonstration. Do this in front of your mate or prospective mate. Do it often.

Henry Kissinger was right: power is the ultimate aphrodisiac. Once Richard Nixon's secretary of state, he was a master of what might be called *relational power*. But if this was the only form of power he understood, he probably never would have had access to extraordinary relationship.

Human beings can harness two radically different kinds of personal power: concrete and relational. *Concrete power* is wielded independently of any other human being. Relational power depends on the perceptions and responses of others. Politics, military organizations, corporations, and many other institutions run on relational power. To wield it calls for a pragmatic understanding of human behavior and the ability to send signals that tilt the choices and actions of other people.

Both forms of power are needed in life, a fact which modern society seems hell-bent on obscuring. In the modern world, nearly every person suffers from some sort of power disorder, which come in three kinds: tendency toward relational power only; tendency toward concrete power only; or avoidance of either form. Hobbled males, for example, often rely only on relational power—they will converse and emote but may never take a unilateral step and file a lawsuit. Unsafe males, and other disgruntled people, can be seen to abandon relationship power altogether and rely on concrete power alone—they will punch you out rather than argue or debate with you. These "one-form-only" approaches lead to reduction of the capability to bring about real change; to disempowerment.

Of the two, relational power is overwhelmingly more common in today's world and is becoming more dominant all the time as technology reduces the demand for concrete power. But it is concrete power that is most often needed in interactions with nonhuman elements, as takes place in processes like farming, fishing, health care, and forestry.

Of the two, relational power is the more dangerous power to pursue exclusively, for reasons outside the scope of this book. And, although the modern world seems entirely oblivious of this fact, relational power works best when utilized on a firm base of a related concrete power that is regularly practiced and demonstrated.

When relational power fails three times in a row, or when you find yourself under attack by a person with superior relational power, turn instead to concrete power. Here is an example:

You are arguing with a male driver who has dented your exotic blue car while pulling into an space adjacent to where your car is parked. You witnessed the incident and are asking the driver for contact details, but he denies causing the damage and in anger refuses to cooperate.

You cue him to calm down, commenting that mistakes happen and surely insurance will cover the damage.

The driver calls you a rude name and gets out of his car.

In your third attempt to use relational power, you tell the man that you have had a hard day and hope to take care of this smoothly.

He sneers.

At this point, you stop talking to him. You walk around to a vantage point from which you can see the license plate of his car. You write it down. You take out your cell phone and snap a photo of the car.

You look around to see if other people witnessed the slight collision. If so, you get the needed details.

You file a police report, and probably a small claims court case as well, and if necessary an insurance claim. All of these actions are in your direct power to execute. You need no cooperation. If the degree of damage does not justify these acts, you walk away and deal with the repairs yourself, knowing that bad things occasionally happen. What you do not do is waste your time engaging with the other driver. Doing so would cost you on some level, needlessly.

If you are ever in conflict with a person who has no intention of engaging in a relational interaction, you will remain powerless as long as you reach for the tool of relational power. Until you convert to concrete power, the person with whom you are in conflict will prevail almost every time, and you will pay needlessly in attention, time, and Energy.

Extraordinary relationship and Wild Attraction involve a sophisticated blending of relational and concrete powers, but concrete power always comes first. This means, in practice, that you first display your capacity to accomplish something extraordinary using your mind, body, and Energy. Only then do you begin to send relational cues that prompt your partner's responses, which in turn will affect you.

Concrete and relational power are large-scale concepts. When they are applied to gender relationships, they take the form of *direct power* and *indirect power*, respectively. Because these specialized versions of concrete and relational power are perhaps the most important of the attraction rituals, I discuss them first.

Indirect and Direct Power Rituals

Women, as the carriers of primarily feminine essence, have their own brand of power that they not only prefer over its male counterpart but must wield on a daily basis. That power is indirect. It is the power to create an action gap that others around them are compelled to fill, regardless of their will or preference.

Indirect power is the power to open doors by walking up to them and stopping with graceful expectancy. Women need to be able to leave a bag of groceries on the seat of a car and have it magically carried into the kitchen. Patty and I call this "leaving gaps." Feminine essence requires women to practice the artful act of dropping a handkerchief in just such a manner as to ensure that a chivalrous male must retrieve it.

There is nothing trivial or trivializing about this power.

Women naturally seek subtlety and grace. Energy gives them indirect power as a way to communicate, and they are designed inherently to use it. They want to send out a subtle cue, to have it received, and to get a response back. The use of indirect power initiates a dance. It asks the male, "Are you out there? Can you listen to subtle cues and respond in graceful ways that honor me? Can you pay attention and appreciate?"

Although this fact is disguised in our culture, feminine power, the power to leave gaps that others are compelled to fill, is the power that runs the world. Corporate, military, and political power are actually feminine in nature. The power of those at the top is multiplied because of their ability to cue legions of others to make the leader's wishes real. That is what human organization is all about.

The male version of power, direct power, is limited to what a man can do with his own body, requiring no relationship or outside leverage. (Direct and indirect power are cross-gender—males and females have equal access to both—but they are not equally needed by the two genders.) Males need to experience and use direct power every day, and most of them need to risk their physical bodies from time to time in order to satisfy the innate need of the masculine gender essence to experience direct power. Men who wield direct power with abandon are not crazy; they need to take intelligent risks in order to be themselves.

Direct power is the ability to deliver a karate punch or to pick up a guitar and play a piece of music well. It is the capacity for acts that can be done right in front of another person, immediately, and that require no one else, and no outside agreement or permission to complete. The enduring symbol of direct power is the image of the blinded Samson pushing the pillars apart and bringing down the roof of the temple to which he has been brought for humiliation, thus killing his captors and, heroically, himself.

Male, direct power is important and equal and has its place. But, again, female power rules the world—co-opted, perhaps, by males who disguise it as the province of men and who also promote the dangerous Delilah myth (she cut off Samson's hair and took away his magical strength). This is a story, like that of Eve, that no one wishing to ally themselves with Wild Attraction should ever take to heart.

Women need to revel every day in the wielding of their signature power. Indirect power is most delicious when it is done in a dance with men who understand and appreciate this most fundamental of human rituals. On the other hand, if a woman repeatedly leaves gaps for a male to fill and receives no response, she will probably be emotionally stung. This is a point neither men nor women should ignore.

I advise women to walk away from males who won't take a cue and fill a gap. Especially, avoid men who view the indirect power ritual as a struggle for control or an attempt to exploit or run a man. Instead, find men who intuitively fill gaps, men who find it fun. The luckiest women may be those who are able to identify, attract, and keep the aware male Samsons of the world, those men who are confident and open, who genuinely love women, and who know how to treat them.

There are two ways to wield indirect power. In the first the woman extends a bit of Energy from her field outward until it encompasses some object in the vicinity that she would like to have moved or changed. She almost immediately retracts this Energy back into her field. This energetic motion is usually accompanied by a physical act, such as moving toward a closed door and then stopping and physically pulling back. This is a signal to a male who witnesses her movement—a cue to take the desired action.

The second is to solicit male action using energetic telepathy. A woman can easily inspire herself to send out subconscious energetic signals through the use of movements of her physical body. For example, a woman may gracefully point at a thing that she wishes to see altered by someone else, and then turn away, while casually contemplating the action she would like to see performed. Or she may simply focus her attention on an object with which she wishes to see a man engage, and then deliberately pull her attention off of it, leaving a kind of attention gap.

In the use of indirect power, physical cues, in the form of actions, words, body language, and other gestures, play a secondary but major role. It is the Energy (or more properly the Intent) of the act that determines its meaning. In other words, a physical cue without an accompanying energetic cue may not be adequate.

Men need to know that women should be encouraged to use indirect power. They need to use it to be healthy and fulfilled. Also, the merging of the gender essences cannot occur unless indirect power rituals are being practiced as a couple.

Both sides also need to know that the dance of indirect and direct power is not about gaining control. It is the necessary equivalent of the bird with the twig in its beak flying three times counterclockwise around its partner. It is a mating ritual that can be exciting to a degree that is almost off the scale.

In brief, the common indirect power disabilities are the failure by women to leave gaps and the absence of the reflex in men to fill them spontaneously. Frequently, females are able to fill gaps for each other but cannot leave them for males. Or they may find themselves compulsively filling gaps that are left by others, even males—perhaps to avoid the anguish of giving indirect power cues and receiving no response from males. I restate for emphasis: the suffering experienced by women who leave gaps only to have them ignored can be extremely great.

Finally, both powers, when misused, can become destructive. Direct power becomes mindless aggression. Indirect power becomes passive aggression. Real aggression of either form can destroy the ability of men and women to engage in this most important of sexual rituals.

Whole-Body or Provocative Body Part Illumination

Energetic Fact of Life #47:
Much of the Western world celebrates the psychosexual symbolism of body parts, using camera framing to display bits of the human body out of their natural and real whole-body context, for maximum erotic impact. This is even more true in Energy, through which people can and do highlight body parts for psychosexual entanglement and provocation purposes. But sexualized energetic illumination is a tool to use in the context of a close, well-established relationship, not out in the general environment, and never to sell products. Your best move: Radiate equal energetic highlighting of your entire body except when you engage in seduction rituals with your committed mate. In that circumstance, use illumination ruthlessly and without limit to build sexual charge.

Illumination is the packing of Energy more densely in certain parts of the physical body than in others, such as breast, butt, shoulders, and other psychosexually active body zones. This dense Energy has the effect of highlighting these zones, causing them to stand out very strongly, even to people with no conscious sensitivity to nonordinary Energy. These illumination choices send out highly provocative signals. The use of illumination to fragment the human body, presenting only a face, breasts, backside, or other selected portions of anatomy is completely inappropriate in the early stages of relationship: friendship and general attraction.

On the other hand, illumination is vital to courtship and to seduction. Many people in our society make extensive use of energetic illumination during the friendship and general attraction stages, and use it not at all during seduction. This is yet another inversion of what works, one that can have negative consequences in daily life. Think of your last visit to a typical high school, or the last time you worked your way through the channels on cable TV. Most of the females, and many of the males, were almost certainly inappropriately illuminating. You could tell that this was so if your eyes were automatically drawn to a particular part of the body and tended to linger there.

To accomplish energetic illumination, stand in front of a mirror and gaze carefully at sections of your body that you believe would be provocative to members of the opposite sex if they were somehow spotlighted.

Imagine the presence of a person you would like to bewitch through this illumination, and visualize them watching you appreciatively. Take a step toward the mirror and step away again, moving the body part you want to illuminate first, if you can, and with special emphasis. Pause and survey your body yet again, lavishing attention on the section or sections you want to highlight.

Lastly, look away from the mirror and then glance back, noticing which part of your body most catches your eye. Repeat these steps if necessary until you are reasonably confident that you have created the desired highlight. Then, of course, try this out on your intended recipient and watch for their response. Illumination is something everyone does subconsciously—conscious control develops quickly with practice.

Most of the time, energetic illumination is used for the most crass purposes: to fragment the human body and cause brainstem-level sexual attraction responses. This unhealthy habit energetically divides the mind and body into bits in the individual and collective subconscious. It also fragments human awareness and changes the way human beings perceive themselves and others. Crass illumination is also detrimental to your physical health, since it tends to underenergize those parts of the body not being illuminated.

The alternative is whole-body (or uniform) illumination. This is the most empowering and most authentically attractive state you can achieve.

Whole-body illumination is rarely seen in the United States, but it is practiced widely on the streets of Paris, France. In the Senté school we offered a class that included, among many other Wild Attraction subjects, a comparison of lingerie advertising during the 1990s in Paris and in New York. Incredibly, Parisian lingerie models, photographed in the skimpiest and most provocative clothing imaginable, still managed to project themselves as physically and psychologically complete people whose breasts and backsides stood out in the frame no more strongly than their hands, feet, arms, and legs. This was and remains an impressive achievement in the eyes of a seer.

By contrast, no American model we surveyed exemplified whole-body illumination. All of the photography from New York may as well have featured sliced-up, discrete body parts. Huge concentrations of Energy were carried in busts, butts, and faces compared with the apparently less interesting body parts, such as shoulders and extremities.

How do you accomplish whole-body illumination?

Go back to the mirror. Take a deep breath, drawing Energy up through your feet and legs as you do so. Take a loving and appreciative look at every visible inch of your body. Take extra time with the least appreciated and emphasized parts, like forearms, earlobes, and shins. Move your eyes and attention up and down your body several times, gratefully, with the intention of unifying your perspective of yourself both physically and psychologically, as if by means of your gaze you were filling yourself with a uniform golden light.

When you think the light is equally distributed, look away from the mirror for a moment, and then quickly look back.

If your gaze is drawn to the center of your body and takes in your whole form, you have achieved whole-body illumination. You may have to try this multiple times before you achieve a dramatic effect, but the repeated efforts are worthwhile. It is difficult to imagine a more beneficial Energy-related capacity—those who walk around in this state project health, intelligence, and vibrancy. They tend to attract other healthy and empowered people.

You may be wondering at the relatively cavalier suggestion in this section that you have the capacity to control and perceive your own illumination standing in front of a mirror. You, along with everyone around you, are already highly skilled at all the energetic rituals described in Wild Attraction. They constitute a birthright. Once your attention is drawn to these processes, and you become curious enough about them, you have to experiment to become proficient. If you are already paired up, your mate is your lab partner as you conduct the needed exercises. If you are single the world is your lab, but you will have to exercise intelligence and discretion. Sexualized illumination is not as useful as you might think during the general attraction and courtship stages of sexual intimacy.

Provocative body part illumination (the opposite of whole-body illumination) is by far the most useful in the last two stages of relationship: seduction and established relationship. Those who can consciously manipulate their illumination patterns tend to be adept at seducing good candidates for intimacy. Provocative body part illumination is one of the best rituals to use during romantic play in long-term relationships—to keep passion alive. Unfortunately, its huge misuse in the friendship, general attraction, and contact stages of mating is objectifying women on a global scale and thus dragging down our entire culture.

Illumination patterns are different in men and women and they are usually unconscious. The first step to making them conscious is to decode them and map their meaning and significance in the gender language of ritual.

Female patterns of illumination, when women are presenting themselves to men, usually include the lighting up of face, breasts, hips and butt, thighs and legs. When they interact with other women, they normally illuminate only their faces. Yet apart from the occasion of one woman meeting another, facial illumination is a serious problem. People of both genders are cued to illuminate their faces as a way of emphasizing the false idea that we are centered in our faces and that speaking and listening from face to face (instead of a healthier center-to-center approach) is a preferred mode of human interaction. I strongly suggest resisting the temptation to default into facial illumination except as a brief flash during a female-to-female greeting.

Male illumination patterns, when men are trying to appeal sexually to women, often include lighting up the pelvis and buttocks. When males illuminate while coming into proximity with other men, it is usually the highlighting of shoulders and arms, conveying the message, "I can kick your ass." This is actually a reassuring signal for most men; they feel more comfortable knowing the other males around them can be relied on for an intelligent and effective aggressive response in the face of a serious life challenge.

Notably, illumination is often used in reverse to downplay sexuality. Underillumination of the breasts and vagina, or the crotch and penis of the male, can be disempowering. Some very mild genital illumination seems to be required for both males and females in the course of daily life, and when it is entirely absent, the overall effect is one of emasculation or defeminization.

Like most of the fundamental Wild Attraction tools, illumination can either hurt you or can provide astonishing fire and excitement in your life.

Providing Admiring, Undemanding Attention

Providing admiring, undemanding attention is an easy ritual, a "must-have" in any qualified candidate's energetic practice of love. Start by thinking of attention not as a direction or a point at which to focus but as a fluid field. To pay attention is to extend this gelatinous, fluid attention field out into space so it enfolds and encompasses your partner. Even if your eyes are not directed at him or her, you must still sense your lover in your attention field, exactly as you would sense another swimmer in a shimmering swimming pool while you are underwater.

Keep the bubble of your attention gently extended into the room around you even, for example, when you are preoccupied reading the evening paper. Allow yourself to sense your partner as he or she walks through the room on the way to the kitchen. Respond, appreciate, and admire your mate as he or she passes through this field. Even if you make no physical sign that you are paying attention, your mate will be nourished in the process. Both genders need to be observed in this way, but to be a recipient is of special and tremendous importance for women. As we have seen, females must experience daily doses of admiring, undemanding attention. Men who neglect to offer this do so at great risk to intimacy, sexuality, and the long-term health of both partners.

Note that once again a nuanced understanding of empowerment is important here. Tilt this attending behavior slightly too far, into emotional hypervigilance or possessive attention, and the observer ends up becoming a need-based partner with a fixation on his or her lover. If this person happens to be a man, he is signaling that he is either a hobbled or an unsafe male.

Projecting Consciousness of a Wide Field of Available Partners

Nothing else that you could radiate is more attractive to a potential or actual mate, one who is an empowered candidate for extraordinary relationship, than your confidence that you have a wide field of candidates to choose from. Offer this confidence along with ongoing cherishing attention to your mate and you have a formula for relationship excellence. This is one of Rhett Butler's secrets in *Gone with the Wind*. It is impossible to imagine him unable to replace Scarlet. He is therefore set up for extraordinary relationship, even though his fixation with this quintessential woman in a bottle is his eventual downfall.

To do as Rhett does, simply imagine the businesses, schools, homes, recreational venues, and other social spaces that you visit periodically and where you are known and welcome. Picture the potential relationship candidates you have met in these places. If you have had success in making friends and forming relationships over time and across a wide swatch of geography, reflect on this as well.

As you walk into a situation where there are potential mates, or when you interact with your mate, replay these reflections with the sense that people you are with can subliminally feel them even though you don't voice them aloud. You aren't projecting to your mate that you are currently looking for a partner; you are allowing people to sense your confidence and capacity to find one if and when you choose to.

This is an act of neither defiance nor threat. It is a subtle communication relaying your simple awareness that you are not dependent on any person as the sole source of sex, gender essence access, or messages. Rather, you know that you can always get another mate if, for any reason, an existing or potential relationship reaches its natural end. This message is only seldom projected by individuals in our society; most people have learned to glamorize need as a language of love and to feel it is unloving to telegraph to mates and potential mates that you aren't dependent on them.

Fortunately, Wild Attraction is not about choosing between independence and dependence. It is about being interdependent and doing it confidently.

Building Charge

Charge is the accumulation of polarized Energy in a person of one gender that is matched by an energetic vacuum in another. This causes a palpable electric tension between the two, a buildup of force that becomes geometrically more intense the closer they get to one another. This energetic sexual charge yearns to be discharged through contact and merging.

Charge is a by-product of raw attraction, the result of either superficial psychological magnetism or extreme and genuine compatibility. For this reason no one should trust charge alone as an indicator of love or the potential for healthy intimacy. Charge is most appropriately used to fan the flames of real, awakened sexual desire and to fully unleash a suitable candidate's urgency to merge. Intelligent use of charge is a way to put the wild into "wild in ways that work."

Although charge is one of the most important energetic elements in attraction, many people avoid it, deadening themselves only to wonder why they attract so little attention.

Creating charge is partly a function of natural energetic chemistries about which we have little or no choice. But it is also a matter of blocking flows of a certain type of Energy through your body, which is the process by which charge builds up. The latter is something about which we can exercise substantial conscious choice. The type of Energy that is active in building charge is alpha Energy (described in chapter 3), the Energy that was in the pencil and that flowed through your arm and hand.

In order to build charge, you have to interrupt the circuit-like flow of Energy that runs between yourself and the ground. You do this while in the proximity of someone or some thing with whom or which you share the capacity to build charge, and with full engagement of your primary gender essence. Place yourself within twenty feet of a person to whom you are strongly attracted. Next, find something that, for you, seems as though it could function as an energetic insulator—perhaps a brick, a matt, or a white piece of paper. Place one foot on this object and keep the other foot in direct contact with the ground or floor.

The imagined insulator is a prop that acts on your intent and breaks the circuit of nonordinary alpha Energy running from the ground up one leg, down the other, and back into the ground. Once the circuit is broken, Energy will link to your engaged gender essence and tend to build up in you, creating a charge. Once the charge is created, relax and move about normally while gently visualizing the continuation of the charged state.

Next, walk toward your lover or intended lover. While you are still building charge it is better to avoid touch if you can. Use physical closeness, broken contact with the ground, sexual imagery, and other power rituals to keep the gender essences activated and engaged, and let time work its magic. Charge will probably build up. You can then discharge the Energy with a single touch, or with an orgasm.

Discharging Energy that is linked to sexual attraction multiplies power, though for very short periods of time, allowing you to reach heights of insight, perception, sensation, and personal change that are never possible with ambient Energy flows. For this reason, building charge and triggering creative discharge are more important than they may seem. Use charge frequently. It works.

Matching Identities

Energetic Fact of Life #48:
Most people think of their identities—the roles they play in life or the work they do—as integral parts of themselves. This is not the case. Identities are the equivalent of computer programs carried in energetic memory and can be turned on and turned off. Energetic role identities are created for every distinct role that humans play in life, but they are only useful in two conditions: learning to play a part on a team, and coordinating people in a team effort who do not know each other well. What you can do: Assign your clothing and accessories to roles you play frequently in your life and which seem to stick to you. Wear the assigned clothing or accessory when you play one of these roles, and afterward take it off. Taking it off is the important thing: this cues you to energetically remove the identity.

Identities—the programmed attitudes and interpretive frameworks designed to help a person live out life roles, like father or mother, daughter, fighter pilot, or business executive—are like invisible clothing that you and others often energetically "wear." They look, to a seer, like thin, pale blue onionskin layers of energetic gel overlaid on a person's field edge. Imagine your energy body as an egg-shaped field, translucent and fluid. Now picture the upper right front quadrant of this field. This zone is where energetic identity layers are most often installed. They remind me of the colored gels that theater lighting technicians slide onto the front of spotlights to create different hues of stage lighting.

People tend to put on energetic identities and leave them on for life. They end up burdened with layer upon layer, like a person wearing twelve sets of clothing at once, starting with a bathing suit and ending with a giant woolly-mammoth-thick gray overcoat.

These layers obscure a person's genuine responses to life, which makes dating, mating, and intimacy much less satisfying, thus hugely reducing what either gender can offer.

When people burdened with energetic identities get close to one another, their identities interlock to create weird attractions. Familiar examples are: the mother-teacher woman pairing up with the son-student man, and the daddy-boss engaging with the daughter-employee. Needless to say, these are dysfunctional attractions based on psychosexual issues, and they lead to awful entanglements. This, in fact, is one of the classic ways in which the Wild Attraction intelligence, when neglected, messes with your love life.

The problem of interlocking multiple identities is serious. Although energetic identities are very seldom needed, most people are conditioned to use them whenever they take on a role in life. Good relationship candidates learn to minimize reliance on them—identities are like workout shirts: they should be taken off immediately after use. Putting on a particular energetic identity helps when you are learning a new skill, because it contains response patterns that otherwise have to be painfully learned piece by piece. Role identities are also valuable when you are engaged in a team function with other people whom you don't know or with whom you haven't trained. Members of fire departments, for instance, can work effectively with other fire teams because the energetic identity of "fireman" carries with it a universal language, rhythm, and worldview that allows for instant cooperation.

If you are not learning or are not on a team, it's best not to allow yourself to carry energetic identities, which probably means breaking a lifelong habit. Get rid of them by assigning clothing to them and intentionally removing the clothing after each use.

Like many other energetic practices, putting on identities is dysfunctional in many situations. But the practice does have a part to play (so to speak) in extraordinary intimacy. They can be put "on" for the purpose of acting out fantasies within a well-established relationship. Interlocking energetic identities are extremely exciting ways to build seduction and charge. But one must understand the rules of identity before they can be broken safely.

Welcoming Eyes

The eyes and, surprisingly, the forehead, are the best points on the body from which to express a vital attitude toward life in general that I call *yes to the mystery*. This capacity to welcome all experiences, both positive and negative, and to exclude nothing from your world that arrives with the next moment is reflected in a look that I call *welcoming eyes*. Its opposite, *sorting eyes*, is the energy signature that radiates from the eyes of people whose attention is bent to the task of deciding what to accept and what to reject in life.

Perhaps the best way to explore welcoming eyes is to view two particular movies. One is the 1960s film *Camelot*, starring Richard Harris. As you watch the film, notice the degree to which Harris makes expressive use of his forehead. The forehead is the energetic center for expressing compassion.

The other movie is the third film in the *Lord of the Rings* series. In the scene near the end in which Frodo takes final leave of his companions and sails into the west, take a good look at the moment when he boards the ship and turns for one last gaze at his friends. This is a perfect depiction of welcoming eyes. It is actually easy to adopt the expressive power of these two remarkable actors by simply putting yourself in front of a mirror and experimenting until you produce something similar. Although I am giving it only a few paragraphs, this one idea encompasses every principle presented in this book and more.

The act of looking at your partner with welcoming eyes both nourishes him or her and changes you. Suddenly any previously intrusive negatives become uninteresting, while the beauty and grace of your mate can become delightful and relaxing even in difficult times.

Promising in Energy What You Will Actually Do

All of us use unconscious energetic telepathy to make promises to others. Unfortunately, most people who make promises today do not intend to keep them. Promises have developed to a point at which they are mainly offered to others in order to serve trivial purposes, such as gaining entrance into a desired social circle. Sometimes promises convey empty threats.

In attraction terms this represents a sad loss, because promise and fulfillment is one of the main signals that true relationship candidates are sensitized to look for.

Consider Raphael, a good candidate for extraordinary relationship. He is at a party surrounded by a number of attractive women, many of whom find him interesting.

Raphael is unusual because he has conscious perception of the energetic telepathy that is flashing around the room, as was depicted in the cocktail scene in chapter 3. The first woman he meets is Dorothy, a redhead, who introduces herself as a marketing executive for Microsoft. She makes use of buzzwords and an enthusiastic, staccato style of speech to convey to Raphael that she is an aggressive executive who gets things done.

He can see that she wants to be exotic and rebellious, but by reading her energetic telepathy he can also tell that she is burdened with fear and is in reality not a rebel at all. She is sexually insecure. The stream of images radiating from Dorothy to Raphael include an X-rated pirate-and-maiden-in-distress sexual fantasy scene that could have been culled from a romance novel. If he listened only to this part of her energetic communication, he would assume that she was sexually sophisticated and capable of fairly edgy sexual behaviors.

But Raphael knows, by studying her entire message, that she is promising behavior she would never undertake. She is presenting a fantasy woman to potential lovers that she is not emotionally prepared to deliver.

Raphael appreciates Dorothy's many good qualities but he eventually says a polite good-bye and moves on. In his eyes, she is not a candidate.

He meets two other women who transmit no sexual imagery or promises at all. This, in itself, is a kind of promise, one that keeps him from developing more than surface interest in either one.

Later in the evening, Raphael meets Tanya. Tanya is relaxed, confident, understated. She works as a physician at a small town medical center. Tanya shows only moderate interest in Raphael—after all, she doesn't know him—but she responds openly to questions about her life and job, and proves to be a pleasant and unentangled conversationalist.

After over an hour of polite discussion, an understated flow of sexual images pass from Tanya to Raphael. The imagery is realistic and explorative but not tinged with imagined sexual qualities that she does not in fact possess.

Raphael finds this communication far more attractive than Dorothy's because this woman is clearly making promises to him, sexually, about who she is and what she will actually do—promises that she will keep. She is a candidate for extraordinary relationship. Raphael makes sure to answer in kind.

After spending most of the rest of the evening in conversation with this interesting prospect, Raphael asks Tanya for her phone number, fully intending to call her the next day and ask her out.

How do you project sexual promises that you will keep? You do it consciously. You store up sexual imagery that reflects who you really are and what you will really offer to the right person. Consciously run this internal DVD right in the middle of conversations in which sexuality could even remotely be an issue. This is not ill-mannered unless you bombard people who cannot or should not be exposed to sexual scenes, like children or people with whom you are in a strictly formal relationship.

It is essential to "own" your sexuality and communicate its nature to others. Why would you not? Energetic telepathy is an appropriate channel for such communications. They are not an intrusion, and you will not be judged. You can use small, carefully chosen occasional verbal sexual disclosures, always in good taste and often under the guise of humor, to telegraph sexual aliveness and to physically cue the transmission of your more explicit internal erotic imagery. This imagery, which accurately reflects your sexual nature, is also part of the energetic "business card" you "hand out" to serious relationship candidates. Your suitability as a candidate is evaluated long before you get to the point of being asked, or asking for, a first date, and long before you end up in bed. It is a sign of command of relationship skills to tell the people around you what you are promising to your lover from early in the initial contact.

If you are not doing this, or if you make promises you won't actually keep, the Raphaels and Tanyas of the world will move right on by.

Giving Him a Job / Doing a Job for Her

Continuing with the example of Raphael and Tanya, embedded in Tanya's erotic promises was the message that there is sexual territory into which she has not yet ventured, and that a job opening exists for someone powerful enough to take her there. This concept—of a job that a male lover could do—is a vital ritual of its own. It doesn't have to be a sexual job, but sex is an ideal zone in which to offer a potential lover a task.

Few things are more irresistible to an aware male than an

aware female who is receptive to some form of further sexual expansion or exploration, especially if it has a spiritual or elevated connotation. Like so much in Wild Attraction, success with this concept depends on a nuanced understanding of its meaning and performance. We are not suggesting that women sexualize themselves in destructive ways or engage in inappropriate disclosures or offer themselves as though they require further sexual education from men. The unfortunate pressure on women to adopt promiscuous or trivializing sexual stances in everyday situations is an obvious and huge problem in today's culture. Nevertheless, a nuanced and intelligently wild bit of sexual disclosure, especially the hint that there is sexual territory yet to be explored, is vital. Aware males will move on fairly quickly in the absence of a signal, because they thrive on having something to contribute, someplace to go, and something to do.

Whatever the job is, it has to be real; it cannot be a series of meaningless tasks. But it can be creatively contrived as enticing and binding. And to work this way it doesn't have to be in the realm of sex. An aware female named Christine, having spotted an aware male to whom she had been introduced earlier in the day, took the chain off her expensive ruby red mountain bike and put a few gearshift parts wildly out of adjustment shortly before she walked past him on the sidewalk. She paused by him, using indirect power cues, and within a few moments he was down on one knee, working on her bike.

One thing led to another, and the two are still together. I see them riding in the park almost every weekend.

The complement of this ritual is, of course, men offering to do jobs for women. Both are enjoyable as love practices out in the human relationship jungle—even more so when both parties, under the pretense of need and courtesy, know full well what is going on and carry out their roles like actors in a play.

Overlapping and Merging Energy Fields

Overlapping and its close cousin, merging, involve blending the energy fields of two safe and committed lovers. These are two different rituals appropriate at different stages of relationship—merging being an act of high intimacy that should ideally take place only after safety and availability have been extremely well established. To understand these two related rituals, think of two balloons or giant bubbles able to cross into each other and eventually become one. This is actually easy to accomplish by linking (through visualization) the behavior of the fields to physical gestures such as hand-holding, hugging, sitting side by side, and eventually, sex. Quite often the real challenge is holding back from merging and overlapping until the appropriate stage of relationship (courtship and beyond for overlapping, and sustained relationship for merging).

On the other hand, some lovers may face the opposite challenge. One or both may experience difficulty engaging in merging or overlapping, perhaps because of negative past experiences involving intrusive or abusive people. Both partners must feel safe with each other, and available to each other, or field blending (and ultimately, gender essence merging) is unlikely to occur. Anything less than the merging of fields, once the couple is far into the relationship and has established safety and availability, is a form of destructively holding back.

Extraordinary relationship is about intelligently transcending the need for boundaries, not about learning to sustain them better. When it is time to overlap and merge, the process can be among the most satisfying energetic experiences in a human life. But these are not behaviors for the first stages of relationship. Overlapping is a stepping stone: reasonable latitude exists for the use of this ritual in courtship and beyond. But merging with people you don't know well offers much less room for error: it can result in a variety of serious but often hidden injuries.

Energetic Completion—Emptying or Filling Docks

Energetic Fact of Life #49:

Many people remain energetically connected to old lovers, imaginary lovers, parents, children, and other significant people in their lives, even if these are people with whom neither safety and availability nor relationship chemistry exists. This is a tragic illusion. In the same way that a small dinghy tied up at the dock of the Queen Mary can keep that huge ship from steaming into its home, old or unrealistic loves, even imaginary ones, can occupy your energy field and lock out new, vibrant, and real ones. What you can do: Let go of or recontextualize old loves and other relationships that can never be real or extraordinary. Throw out old love letters, take down posters of movie stars on whom you nurse crushes, or take your pet's framed photo off the nightstand where the photo of a lover should be.

Energetic completion, or *energetic mating* as Patty and I sometimes call it, is one of the most useful practices in the Wild Attraction system and possibly the single best defense against unwanted attraction and infidelity, whether your own or on the part of your mate.

The basic idea of energetic completion is this: When you are in relationship, your partner's energy should permeate certain gaps in your energy field that are designed to be filled in by a mate, once you get one. As long as *only* your mate fills these spaces, you will radiate a look of matedness that discourages unwanted attraction. If people or things other than your mate fill up these gaps, or *docks*, you will have trouble feeling connected to your lover and the relationship will likely erode. If the docks are not filled at all, you will find yourself with unwanted and unnecessary third-party attractions on your hands.

Picture a situation in which you are married or in another form of committed relationship and you find yourself in the grip of an almost overwhelming mutual attraction with a third party. Or, alternatively, picture your partner in exactly the same situation.

Wouldn't it be wonderful if you had the power to reduce that attraction?

You do.

To understand this nearly miraculous mechanism, picture your energy field once again, focusing particularly on the top one-fourth of the field edge as it wraps around the front, sides, and rear of the energy field, like a ski cap. In this zone you can find palm-sized, roughly hemispherical indentations that function as energetic docks, places where palm-sized pieces of Energy from the energy field of your mated partner can plug into your system. Resting alongside the dozens of docks in your field are similar detachable hemispherical patches of your own Energy.

These fluid, flexible receptacles and plugs, looking somewhat like blood corpuscles, are the equivalent of energetic sexual organs. When you are energetically mated with a lover, and when safety and availability truly exist, each person transfers the half-globe patches of Energy from their field into the matching docks in their partner's field.

Unlike physical sex, which of course happens within discrete and relatively short time periods, this form of sexuality can be an ongoing exchange, in effect becoming a lifestyle choice.

What happens when these energetic components are exchanged between two people? Since part of each partner's energetic structure is now integrated into the other partner's field, the transfer of vital messages is hugely enhanced. Each can feel the core messages sent by the other with heightened acuity. They can profoundly sense each other's presence, and the state of being of one lover directly influences the state of being of the other.

The deep satisfaction and pleasure of this union, which I call *energetic completion*, is spread across broad swatches of time. Most people are not consciously aware of it. But physical sex is often made great because, in parallel with physical intercourse, the partners unplug these half-globes of Energy and ritually replace them, a process that hugely heightens physical sexual pleasure and impact.

Energetic completion, or docking, has a vital effect on your attractiveness, and that of your lover, to third parties. When a couple has exchanged all the energetic half-globes in their fields, or "filled their docks," they appear sexual and attractive but completely off the market. There is no dynamic charge external to the couple, no place for other people to attach to, and nothing is out of balance. Consequently, external attraction forces are, almost unbelievably, muted or shut off entirely.

This mechanism has tremendous power. If I look at a married couple and see that their docks are not full, I can predict with some accuracy that they are experiencing third-party attractions and that one of them is likely to have an affair. On the other hand, completely full docks are a sure sign of a healthy and nearly bulletproof relationship. Obviously, then, figuring out how to keep your own docks and those of your partner full, as well as how to ritually empty and fill them in the early stages of sex, is hugely in your interest.

Moreover, it is critical, if you are single and seeking relationship, to walk around with empty docks in order to invite interest from other available single people—not docks full of bits and pieces of Energy from old or imaginary lovers, or from people you are close to who will never be lovers.

The tools Patty and I recommend to learn these tasks are humble Post-its, the little yellow sticky-edged notes you probably keep in your office drawer.

Start by sticking about a dozen of them to your upper body—on your chest, forehead, face, ears, shoulders, and behind your head. If you are in a relationship and your partner is willing to engage in such a strange ritual, ask her or him to do this with you, preferably with another block of Post-its of the same size but a different color, perhaps pink.

The first step is to remove the Energy of old partners from your docks. Take a look at yourself plastered with these squares in a mirror, and in the most nonchalant manner affirm in your mind that these bits of paper represent real things present in your energy field related to your gender essence and to partners past and present.

Unless you are a rare exception, your docks contain Energy from a mixed bag of sources. Humans these days are not trained to manage energetic completion with intelligence, so most men and women have Energy from many different people cluttering up their docks, even if they are in good relationships.

Clear your docks by ritually taking all the bits of paper off one by one and dropping them on the floor. Leave them there for at least three hours before you throw them away to give your system time to energetically disconnect from them. Otherwise you might reacquire the Energy they represent during the cleanup process.

If you are single, take a fresh block of Post-its and put it in your pocket as a reminder that when you are well into a high-functioning relationship, you will fill your partner's docks and ask her or him to fill yours. For now, take a good look at yourself in the mirror. You may be seeing yourself truly energetically available for the first time in your adult life.

At this point, you can walk away. You are done. Go out into the world this way and see what happens.

If you are in a relationship and your partner is with you, each of you can take a fresh pair of Post-it blocks and simultaneously put new paper squares from your own block onto your partner's chest, shoulders, face, forehead, and back of the neck. Intend this as an analogy for transferring Energy from your field edge into your partner's docks. This association requires little effort; it will happen at the barest suggestion within your imagination.

When you are done, stand side by side and look at yourselves in the mirror. You will probably never have looked more mated than you do at this moment.

Energetic completion that happens spontaneously and without special attention is a long slow process that can take up to two years to complete. And it rarely begins until two people have been together for many months as lovers. Initiating energetic completion consciously, especially with physical props such as Post-its, hugely accelerates the natural process.

Be sure that you and your partner are safe and available with respect to one another before you undertake this ritual blending of Energy, and avoid doing it with people to whom you aren't deeply committed.

Every time you have sex within the context of a serious relationship, include this process of emptying and refilling docks, using Post-its until you don't need them anymore, and see what it does to your sexuality. That feeling after having sex of languor and blissful drifting partially results from the natural energetic completion that even mediocre sex often provides. When you include energetic completion consciously, the post-sex sensations can be greatly heightened.

What do you do if you find yourself feeling an unwanted attraction for a third party and you are far away from your lover? Patty and I have a red phone hotline idea to offer. Here's what to do: Look up over your right shoulder at the sky or ceiling at a forty-five-degree angle. Imagine a red phone in front of you that you can pick up and speak into, giving you an instant hot line to your mate. Inside your head, ask your mate to refill your docks while you reach out at that forty-five-degree angle and refill his or hers. This energetic action alone may give rise to the creation of the supergender, in addition to other benefits, and can change your state of being dramatically.

As a final comment on energetic completion, think back to the beginning of chapter 5, where Patty and I asked two male-female pairs to come up beside us at a lecture. One of the couples was strongly mated, the other was composed of strangers. Remember when I snapped my fingers and instantly changed the apparent matedness of the two pairs? This is what I was doing: clearing the docks of the married couple and filling the docks of the two strangers.

Apparent Accidental Nudity

This next ritual was described at the beginning of this chapter, but it is worth another word or two. Apparent accidental nudity is the artful revealing of sexualized flesh—usually by a woman but occasionally by a man—without appearing to do so on purpose, exclusively for the eyes of a relationship candidate or partner whom you wish to attract or seduce. Those willing to employ this tremendously powerful ritual deliberately and with intelligence often do very well as candidates, because it indicates that they relate effectively to their personal power as a female or male.

Naturally enough, many women are reluctant to consider apparent accidental nudity for a variety of reasons. At the same time, a huge number of women are much too willing to use this device and overdo it, exposing flesh to any and all so that the art and charge associated with this intentional indiscretion ceases to have power. Although attitudes towards it vary, when practiced intelligently, apparent accidental nudity works.

Energetic Claiming

Energetic claiming is a mating ritual that, as we saw in chapter 8, must be done within a committed couple on a recurring basis. Women languish when they don't experience being claimed. In fact, Patty reports that women commonly complain that they don't feel adequately claimed by their mates, and those who have engaged in this power ritual feel strongly about its importance.

This ritual is not about subjugation. It is about commitment and the interplay of direct and indirect power. In energetic claiming, the man expresses a strong willingness to act in order to enforce a contract in which the woman is available to him and to no one else. Implicitly, he is similarly bound to her and is further bound to protect and nurture her. This signal of claiming her is directed as much to other people as to the woman, and it changes the Energy signature of the woman so that she identifies herself as claimed even when she is not in her mate's presence. Interestingly, and perhaps obviously, women cannot claim themselves. And, vitally, *energetic claiming has nothing to do with forcing the woman to do any specific thing against her will.*

Claiming should be backed up with action whenever the male's exclusive hold on the female is threatened from outside the relationship.

Conversely, women can and should regularly claim their male partners. This is especially significant with respect to other females in the environment, but unlike a male claiming a female, it is not a required mating ritual. Males do not languish when not claimed. (When a female claims a male partner, she should have her male gender essence at her center midline and her female gender essence tucked under her left armpit so that her male essence is engaged.)

It is in fact the woman who initiates the process of claiming by signaling energetically that she wants to be claimed. The male should never claim her in the absence of this unmistakable signal. Her energetic signal may be accompanied by a strong show of physical independence or willfulness, or of extreme softness and receptivity. Any time after this signal is sent the male may energetically claim her in a four-step process:

First, while physically a short distance from the woman, the man makes the statement "You are mine" in both Energy and words, conveying exclusivity, protection, cherishment, and certainty. His male essence should be strongly engaged. Ideally, the man is not hyperattentive to her response; rather, his message is confident and self-assured as he views the woman through a lens of heart-based awareness in addition to male direct power.

Second, he focuses his attention on her field edge, a few feet out from her skin, and he imagines that he is grasping her energy body with his own. Nothing physical or energetic is actually changed or moved during this process—he is simply holding her field with wisps of his own, as one would place a hand on another person's forearm without shifting that arm. After several moments, he releases this energetic claim.

Third, he approaches her, takes her in his arms and holds her, saying in soft words that he loves and cherishes her, and that in his mind she is his and his alone.

Finally, he sends this same message, that he claims this woman, to anyone else in the environment in body language, Energy, and if possible in spoken words.

Like the other Wild Attraction rituals, claiming should be powerful and fun, and it yields tremendous closeness and relaxation if done on a regular basis.

First Choice

As was discussed in chapter 17, everyone in a committed relationship, but males in particular, would do well to generate the energetic signals of *first choice* and send them to their partner in words, in the language of gifts, and in Energy. Every person needs to have this experience of hearing themselves honestly described as another person's first choice out of all the world's millions.

Center of the Universe

Perhaps the most powerful message one human being can receive from another is that he or she is the absolutely most cherished being in that person's life, placed at the zero-zero-zero reference point from which all distances in life are measured. Like *first choice*, this ritual was discussed in detail in chapter 17. The potent message "You are the center of my universe" is vitally needed by each person in order to construct a healthy personality, and it cannot be faked.

If we are lucky, we get this message as children. Normally, having received it and heard it even once as a child, we can usually attract it again at different points in our life. But if we do not receive it in childhood, we search for it, usually unsuccessfully, for the rest of our lives.

Never hold back delivering this message if it is a genuine truth.

When you perform the necessary inward reflection to realize that your partner is the center of your universe, and if you then voice this feeling in words, your energy field will convey this message to your partner via Energy in powerful ways. Voice it frequently and remember it always.

Full Gender Essence Engagement

See chapter 5 on using physical gestures to move and engage a person's dominant gender essence (for a male: hands at the belt buckle, eyes and body facing directly forward, both heels down; for a female: hands above the collarbone, eyes and body out of line with each other, one heel raised).

Using Gender-Specific Language

See chapter 8 on "Good job" for males and messages of appreciation for the presence and loveliness of women.

Sending the Five Basic Messages

See chapter 19 on the five basic human message needs.

Extending and Retracting Feminine Gender Essence

The opening section of this chapter briefly depicts the energetic ritual of extending feminine essence and retracting it to initiate courtship or seduction. This ritual is superficially similar to the indirect power ritual also described earlier in this chapter, in that both involve extension and retraction of Energy. But that ritual involves an object—the woman extends and retracts her attention and energy to an object she wishes to see moved, leaving a vacuum that a mate will hopefully fill by carrying out a desired action.

A woman performing the ritual of extending and retracting feminine gender essence begins by walking to within twelve to twenty feet of her male target, and turning her body slightly at an angle so her left side faces toward the man. She then inclines her body center slightly in his direction, left side first, by moving her hips toward him without moving her feet. At the same time, she casually imagines her feminine essence extending outward and crossing the space into the man's energy field. As her hips rock back into normal alignment, she visualizes her essence slowly and enticingly retracting back into her field. For a moment she remains in position, not looking intently at the man but unobtrusively watching for his response.

Under ideal circumstances, the man reacts to this cue by walking over to her, stopping at a respectful distance, and engaging in conversation as the first step in the physical process of contact. Any man in this situation would be well advised to avoid responding with his energy field or intruding in any way into the field of the woman except via the conversation itself.

These rituals, when offered in the right contexts and the necessary order, can do more than merely change your love life. If they were to come to be widely and correctly practiced, the world itself might change.

The selection of specific rituals I have provided here is designed to provide you with a starter set—just enough to get going. They are like basic colors of paint on the mixing palate of an artist—you can use them to create an infinite number of colors. These and others like them are the keys to incredible human possibilities, and they promise wonders.

The time has come to look at the wheels of our bicycle built for two.

Chapter 22
The Front Wheel: The Six Stages of Relationship

Energetic Fact of Life #50:
Most people seek competency in relationship skills that are relevant to a single stage of relationship only and then get stuck in that stage. But relationships, like life itself, progress through stages. Each stage requires different energetic power rituals, mindsets, and models. What you can do: Learn to think in terms of these stages, know which one you are in at any given time, and understand and physically practice the rituals appropriate to your present stage, while avoiding those that are not.

The six stages of relationship are: friendship, general attraction, contact, courtship, seduction, and sustained relationship. Each stage is associated with specific Energy rituals (described in chapter 21) appropriate to that stage. Certain rituals are also particularly to be avoided in each stage.

Some of the questions most often asked about the stages of relationship are these: If the cycle of stages is continuous and rotational, like a bicycle wheel, just how do the earlier stages get recycled during the later ones? Once you are in sustained relationship, do you go back to the beginning again and pretend to repeat the process? Or is sustained relationship a destination that, once reached, ends the cycle?

To explore these questions, separate the first five stages, friendship through seduction, from the last stage, sustained relationship. Think of the first five as the process of climbing onto the relationship bike, balancing on two wheels, and getting up to speed. Think of sustained relationship as a category of its own.

The deeper benefits and greatest potential for travel are found in sustained relationship, which is when you are pedaling the bike at a continuous speed, steering it, and taking a journey. It is here that the merging of gender essence can occur and change can unfold in the most stunning ways. The demarcation between sustained relationship and all the other stages is thus of outsized importance. The first five stages as a unified block have two purposes: to get you to sustained relationship with a real candidate, and, once there, to help you maximize that relationship over its lifetime.

The first five stages as described in this book have of necessity been tilted toward the first purpose. They are needed by single people in order to successfully reach sustained relationship with a real candidate. Because of limitations to the size and scope of this introductory book, the second purpose, to maximize sustained relationship, is only hinted at.

So what can we say here about the second role of the first five stages: helping to maximize the vibrancy of sustained relationship and preserve it? Once you reach sustained relationship, intimacy and sex might be seen as two entwined movements: awakening and reawakening. Within the Wild Attraction story of all things, sex itself is about these two motions. We awaken things within ourselves and within our partners through sexual intercourse and through all the attendant intimacies that accompany lovers on their journey through life. And because they fade in the course of time, they must be periodically reawakened and remembered.

Thus as awakening progresses, sexual relationship offers its second gift: the power to help lovers reawaken themselves, to remember their greatness, the extent of their journey, and the incredible aspects and insights that have come forth in them. This second gift is especially important, given the fact that the human mind immediately sets about trivializing and normalizing every extraordinary experience. Without an extraordinary way to remember and rekindle as we age, we can lose the wonders we are granted.

Lovers in the sustained relationship stage thus dip into the rituals associated with the earlier stages in personalized, sophisticated patterns that can't be placed into a simple, universally applicable list yet are not random. They re-experience first contact or seduction or courtship, choosing on a given day whichever one seems to reawaken those aspects of memories that seem most at risk of slipping out of vivid recall.

When the couple is strained, they re-explore the rituals of friendship, where most human resilience resides. When the distractions of daily life become intense and charge is lost, they return to seduction.

A very great deal can be said about this art, and hopefully it will be said in the future.

Stage 1: Friendship

The friendship stage is about relating to people in your friendship circle with whom you share trust and confidence without necessarily inviting sexual relationship. Friends treat each other as equals, with gentle acknowledgment of each others' gender status. Friends may engage in safe, mild gender play, and may send approving respectful messages to each other about gender—this is the stage for sharpening your relationship skills and improving your understanding of the other gender. General intimacy needs are met, and a pool of potential relationship candidates is established and reinforced. People get to know each other without the pressure of dating and courtship. They relate on the basis of common interests and mutual enjoyment. The health of individuals or of established couples can be measured by the richness of their friendships and the vibrancy of the circle of people with whom they live out their lives. Within a couple, the degree of intimacy is determined by the power of their friendship—it is the foundation of all else.

The energetic power rituals appropriate to this stage include mild but daily use of indirect and direct power rituals, welcoming eyes, occasional full gender essence engagement, and the deliberate use of gender-specific verbal language ("Good job" for males; "You are lovely and it's great to be with you" for females).

To this can be added the general practices of sending the five basic messages and paying admiring, undemanding attention.

Stage 2: General Attraction

In the general attraction stage you are moving in a field of close friends and associates while actively interested in attracting a mate, exploring sexuality, and searching for extraordinary relationship. You are switched on but still single.

The energetic power rituals appropriate to this stage include whole-body illumination, the giving of admiring, undemanding attention (placing any potential partner in the center of your field of attention), and projecting consciousness of a wide field of available partners. In the general attraction stage, interdependence is a lovely personal presence choice. People who seem to do best at attracting good candidates are effective at dealing with their individual needs but also relaxed about belonging to and being helped by a circle of friends. They project neither dependence nor excessive independence.

This is a good time to regularly use your Post-its to empty your docks and keep them that way as a default. It is also an excellent time to engage in direct and indirect power rituals, adding the occasional use of physical props, such as keys or pens, to enhance the engagement of your dominant gender essence. Make sure at this stage that you are capable of building and feeling strong gender-based energetic charge. People who lack the capacity to build up sexual charge rarely move beyond general attraction to the later stages of relationship.

In this stage it is best to avoid overly specialized illumination of provocative body parts. Males should take care to be energetically reserved, and women should avoid the ritual of extending their feminine essence forward and retracting it at this point. Both genders are wise to avoid overlapping and merging their energy field with other people; premature merging is a sign of dysfunction that will discourage good relationship candidates from exploring you as a potential partner. They will walk away.

Stage 3: Contact

At the contact stage, you have identified someone as a potential candidate and you want to change the way he or she perceives you, shifting from being a friend or acquaintance to a love prospect. This extremely brief stage takes place in that moment when you approach someone and invite him or her to take the first step in the courtship process, usually by asking for a date.

The energetic power rituals appropriate to this moment are the matching of gender essence ratios, as described in chapter 7, and massive, overt direct and indirect power rituals of all sorts. This is also a good time for a woman to use the ritual of extending and retracting her feminine gender essence, as well as for momentary locking of gaze with sexual overtones.

Your docks should be unfilled, and you are well advised during this stage to be in full gender essence engagement, with none of your secondary gender essence in an active state.

Have fun and be daring. Offer your potential mate a job, or offer to do a job for her. Experiment with whole-body illumination, with flashes of illumination of provocative body parts. Also, this is a good time to make sexual promises of things you would actually do, using energetic telepathy. Finally, make good use of the time you spent in front of the mirror practicing welcoming eyes.

During this moment, the temptation is particularly strong to move all your Energy into your head, thus becoming energetically a face on a stick, and being hugely disempowered. Energetic faciality will turn off a real candidate for extraordinary love. To avoid this, speak and move from your body center while maintaining whole-body illumination.

Stage 4: Courtship

Courtship is a stage of discovery naturally designed for the exploration of mutual safety and availability. Normally, this is a dating period that starts out casually and gradually becomes more serious as the relationship becomes exclusive. Traditionally, it precedes sexual intercourse, but today many (if not most) people have transposed seduction and sex onto the beginning of courtship, and even contact. Courtship, ideally, is the period in which people work out whether or not it is safe and appropriate to have sex with a potential partner. The energetic power rituals especially appropriate to this stage are apparent accidental nudity, overlapping—but not merging—of energy fields, and occasional specialized illumination of psychosexually active body parts (you know the ones I mean) directed at your prospective mate (for instance, walk by your partner and illuminate your rear end).

This is also a great moment to check to see that your docks are clear.

During this phase, you would do well to avoid energetic and physical behaviors that would telegraph to others that you tend to see a lover as a brother or sister, friend, community member, or colleague. Many people unwittingly announce to the world that their models of sexual relationship are family-and-friendship-based rather than lover models. Serious candidates for extraordinary love (and even most noncandidates) will walk right by these individuals. Patty and I call the specific Energy associated with these models *bluff Energy*.

Stage 5: Seduction

Seduction in Wild Attraction terms is the transition to committed relationship. Of seduction, little more need be said, as it is the most electric and best attended of all the stages. The energetic power rituals appropriate to this stage are overlapping and merging of energy fields, energetic claiming, full and strongly polarized (either undiluted male or female) gender essence engagement, and illumination as a language that tells your lover exactly what to touch next.

Seduction also demands massive direct and indirect power rituals, a bombardment of the full promise of what you will actually do transmitted via energetic telepathy, the emptying and filling of docks, and a ritual that is all but essential in this stage: apparent accidental nudity.

The more you add of these and other ritual tools, delivered wildly but in ways that work, the more exciting and rewarding the process of seduction becomes.

Stage 6: Sustained Relationship

Sustained relationship, which is in a category of its own in relation to the prior stages, is the period of maximum change and of maximum reward from the forces of Wild Attraction. Here the attainment of extraordinary relationship become possible. In sustained relationship, the couple cycles through all the stages of relationship over and over in a nuanced dance between the partners.

The energetic power rituals appropriate to this stage are: center of the universe attention, indirect and direct power rituals at least once a day, and extension of feminine essence followed by male response. This is the stage at which the creation of supergender can and should be ongoing. It is the stage at which the merging of the gender essences can totally change your life.

In sustained relationship, you are well advised to use props and physical motions to draw attention to gender essence, to keep the relationship from losing charge, and to keep up the practices relating to male and female language use, energetic claiming, and first choice.

Some Wild Attraction rituals are particularly useful when associated with sexual activity during this stage: emptying docks to build up charge before sex, then refilling them during sex, matching authentic gender essence ratios (for example, 80:20 and 20:80) and then playing as a twosome with various ratios for variety's sake (one lover shifts her or his gender essence engagement and challenges the other to match it), and transmitting sexual or gender-oriented imagery via telepathy.

On the other hand, it is particularly important in this stage to avoid engaging in certain rituals, particularly those that can cause jealousy. These include the practice, appropriate to general attraction, of walking around with your docks unfilled (except as part of the ongoing seduction process between you and your lover). Obviously, it is also highly counterproductive to send center of the universe messages to people other than your partner or engage in energetic mating rituals with them. The number of people who fail to avoid these and other obviously destructive behaviors remains a never-ending source of astonishment.

Our Wild Attraction students routinely boil this material down to personalized ritual checklists for each stage. They keep these lists on hand until they have internalized the practices and no longer needed written reminders.

Many have commented that they found it difficult, at first, to appreciate just how amazingly well this material works—a difficulty that vanished the moment they ventured out onto the complex waterways of love with their new and revolutionary charts.

CHAPTER 23

The Rear Wheel: The Five Steps to Extraordinary Relationship

Energetic Fact of Life #51:
Most people believe that they can acquire a high-functioning, empowered, and effective mate without first becoming such a person themselves. This is one of the most serious misconceptions in present-day society. You need to become a viable candidate for relationship yourself before you focus on finding a mate who is capable of extraordinary relationship. What you can do: Look back over your love life thoughtfully, making written notes that help you see your past patterns and comparing them with candidacy for extraordinary relationship as it is presented in this book. Acquire the skills needed to become a viable candidate and to create and maintain a relationship with another viable candidate. This takes work.

Candidacy is the last part of the bicycle built for two that we must explore before you take it out for a test ride. It is the rear wheel, the one that the pedals connect to directly by means of a chain; the issue of candidacy is what drives the bicycle. This means, in practice, that moving through the candidacy list is what you conceive yourself to be *doing* as you engage in relationship. I think of candidacy as the central issue in Wild Attraction, and I think of the candidacy list in this chapter as my main orientational resource: Am I a candidate?

Is this person a potential partner? If so, how do I attract, seduce, and, most important, keep her or him?

Finally, if I do my job well enough in relationship, my partner and I will become irresistibly attractive to other powerful people. What am I going to do about that?

The answer to the last question is this: seek a constantly greater mastery of the five steps presented here. Almost anyone can improve the odds of attaining extraordinary relationship by putting their attention on their own candidacy and the candidacy of prospective mates.

The five steps concerning candidacy are the pathway to extraordinary relationship, and you can't skip a step, or add one, and expect to complete the journey. Identifying, attracting, seducing, and binding noncandidates are almost entirely different from doing the same with candidates for extraordinary relationship. And almost everyone in the Western world is a graduate of what could be called the Media School for Sexual Relationships with Noncandidates.

It is time to tear up your diploma.

Step 1: Becoming a Candidate

Energetic Fact of Life #52:
Most people are conditioned to believe that only two power and self-sufficiency choices are open to humans: dependence on someone else or complete independence. This is yet another tragic inversion. Becoming a candidate for extraordinary relationship requires stepping beyond being dependent or independent and embrace interdependence. This means learning to form relationships based on love, not need. The burden of individual need can be spread out among one's circle of friends and supporters, not placed on the shoulders of a mate. Your best response: Maintain a

> vibrant base of healthy friends, pursue long-term personal interests, maintain your psychological resources, safeguard your physical health, and show a reasonable capacity for basic financial success. Also, acquire a thorough understanding of the mechanics of romantic relationship and develop all the needed skills.

Not just anyone can be part of a truly great thing. To join the Beatles, for instance, called for the capacity to play music extremely well. Similarly, becoming part of a great relationship requires the burnishing of a certain fundamental greatness within yourself.

When I affirm that latent greatness is present in most people and that we are all far more than we realize, I also know it sometimes pushes buttons. Many people respond that they have trouble seeing or admitting to greatness in themselves or others. Others have spoken out that striving for greatness seems like an outlandish effort that may be okay for others but will never pay off for them.

Undeniably, considerable work is needed to develop great qualities, and I sympathize with people in busy lives who don't see the need. But my answer is always that finding a spark of greatness within yourself is a necessity that will reward you beyond your wildest dreams.

The difference between traveling through life in a great relationship, as compared to an ordinary one, is like the difference between flying in an airliner and walking. From a vantage point in a figurative passenger jet, most people on the ground look weighed down by a lifetime of conditioning. They have been told that the price of an air ticket, paid for in the coin of personal greatness, might not be worth it. The effort may not be fruitful or even required. The truth is just the opposite. Exploring your greatness is essential and, far more than most people may realize, is likely to bear fruit. A flight toward the triple star of greatness, candidacy, and profound intimacy is well worth the work involved in cutting old baggage away. It is worth overcoming any apprehension about flying that might linger in your psyche.

The ability to envision oneself as in some way extraordinary, as possessing a precious nugget of greatness, is the first needed quality in every candidate.

For this reason, a candidate places a strong emphasis on action over thought: he or she learns what works and then does it. He or she also studies in detail the worldview, motivation, mechanics, philosophical approach, rituals, and techniques required to take the next four steps. In real terms, this means experimenting with the action suggestions outlined in this book, learning from your mistakes, and constantly developing your skills. Pick one chapter a month and work three things from that chapter. Do this for as long as it takes for your patterns to change.

Changing your patterns includes releasing any entrenched negative attitudes toward your own and the complementary gender essence, and cultivating a positive view of both men and women. You will also want to know how to be safe and available to others. If you are not already skilled in these areas, you may want to work with a therapist to explore safety, availability, and attitudes toward the opposite gender from a psychological perspective.

Being a candidate also means mastering a few simple energetic perceptual acts and movements. Learn to pay attention to subtle signals and to make educated guesses about what is being said energetically by you and to you. This takes time, attention, and a relaxed mindset in which you never believe you know what is going on, but you form and test working models.

To become a candidate, develop personal power and fascinating skills through which to reveal yourself to other candidates—perhaps painting, musical performance, or another art, or a physical movement capability like dance or a martial art. This is where personal greatness comes in. Greatness attracts the attention of those whose attention is most valuable. Attention is the coin of the realm in Wild Attraction; you will benefit if you explore the prospect of paying attention to attention itself.

Imagine yourself as the best possible candidate you can be, someone capable of attracting and relating successfully to the best candidate you can conceive of. What would you be like?

For one thing, you would not be like anyone else. You would not be Brad Pitt or Angelina Jolie. You would be you. You would have created your own effective personal relationship style. You would have identified your weaknesses and blind spots, your misconceptions and other personal barriers to relationship success. You would have connected with many high-functioning friends and would celebrate your own amazing gifts, qualities that you had painstakingly developed and could now offer to others and thus reveal yourself.

Most important, you would be positive, yes-based, embracing all experience in conjunction with developing the look of welcoming eyes. You would know your strong points, your own highest and best. And the highest and best of those around you would be your focus much of the time.

Why imagine yourself as a candidate? Because the most important quality of a candidate for extraordinary relationship is the capacity to imagine yourself as one.

Step 2: Identifying Other Candidates

Energetic Fact of Life #53:
Most people are problem-and-solution oriented and navigate through relationship (and life) by avoiding negative outcomes, eliminating negative conditions, and sustaining a fundamentally fear-based perspective on life and love. This is not a useful approach for relating to the supergender. It is best to cultivate a "yes"-based, self-expressive approach to life in which all experience is welcomed and included, and "no" is rarely needed and never central to your field of view. What you can do: Cultivate "welcoming eyes" which is a look that compassionately welcomes all experience into your life. The best way to do this is to develop the expressive muscles in your forehead and consciously use them to convey to other people your state of being and response to the moment.

By this point in the book, the importance of choosing well when it comes to selecting a mate is clear. The core of this huge topic is simple and can be expressed in one sentence: The best way to identify other candidates is to take your time, maintain high standards for a mate for yourself, and watch for and pay attention to warning signs. You must somehow maintain this realistic outlook without losing the sense of welcome and inclusion that is essential to being a good candidate yourself. Hence this book's emphasis on welcoming eyes.

There are, of course, many other considerations in the all-important process of selecting a mate. One is the simple matter of selfishness. People who are not self-referencing—who are, instead, attuned to the needs of others and to fun and to social responsibility—are obviously better candidates for extraordinary relationships than are those who think and communicate about their own needs first, or who never address their own needs at all. Patty reports that one of the most common complaints among women is about men who talk only about their own lives, interests, and needs. A high percentage of men in the course of an entire evening will never ask a single question about the woman in their presence. This astonishing yet common manifestation of self-centeredness is a deal-breaker for anyone seeking extraordinary relationship.

Another deal-breaker is low expectation. Many people are geared to seek matches that don't work and then spend the rest of their lives compensating for their poor choice. The culture's almost obsessive search for relationship skills marks the pervasiveness of this problem. The truth is that relationship skills, however much we all may scrabble for them when the going gets rough, are needed more for dealing with lovers who are poor candidates than for managing great relationships. If you choose well, you hardly need relationship skills. What you need in great relationships are good friendship skills. For this reason, the Wild Attraction skill set is not a compendium of relationship skills but rather rituals that need to be present in any relationship that works. In your search for a candidate, look for people who put friendship skills ahead of relationship skills, and for those who practice being available.

Search, also, for men or women who can offer a high level of safety to others, and who have developed strong message sending and receiving skills—which involve, among other things, speaking verbally, energetically, and with physical gestures all at the same time (for instance, as from a male perspective in a prior chapter, saying "I love you" with words, flowers, handholding, and eye contact).

Yet another useful indicator of candidacy involves expectations regarding the length of courtship periods. People who put scant emphasis on courtship may not be ideal candidates.

Courtship must be long in order for any person to truly get to know potential relationship candidates, and to arrive at authentic responses to them.

Apply this to yourself as you undertake your search. Take the pressure off. Date frequently, for its own enjoyment, without the pressure of actively yearning for Mr. or Mrs. Right.

A dear friend and long-time associate who worked for years at the Senté Center is a human resources specialist who has honed her skills in some of the world's most dynamic corporations, including Intel. Her name is Pauline. Patty and I always loved to sit in on job interviews that Pauline conducted because she is a genius at making hiring choices. Pauline always took care to write down, in advance, a clear description of the role for which she was choosing someone and the qualities essential in a person filling that role, as well as a list of attributes that could be deadly.

Pauline was also great at putting people at ease and prompting them to talk about themselves, their job histories, and their attitudes and skill sets. She assumed that the most important things to find out about potential employees were more evident in body language and the way they spoke than in what they said. She drew the most insightful conclusions about people from the smallest clues.

For instance, one person who was applying for a job at the Senté Center presented herself confidently. Based on outward appearances she seemed to be a terrific choice. Patty and I came away impressed. But the day after the interview, Pauline sat down with us with a gleam in her eye. "Did you notice that little slip-up from our front-runner candidate yesterday?" she asked us.

"Notice what?"

Pauline smiled and handed us a couple of pieces of paper. "When I asked her about her last job and why she left, she hesitated for half a second. She recovered well, but I could tell something was there, something I should pay attention to. I called her back today and asked her more questions. I also phoned a couple of her references again and made some careful small talk. It turns out our leading candidate felt discriminated against in her last job and took the company to court."

"Was it a legitimate grievance?" Patty asked.

"Maybe," Pauline told her. "But that's not the point. What caught my attention was the language she used during the phone call. She said, 'They owed me. And not only that, my boss in the job before that owed me too.' There was something in the way she said it." Pauline shook her head. "In my experience, it is best to stay away from people who think that other people owe them something."

We did hire somebody else, just because of this small slip. And about a year later we heard that the woman had been hired by another company in town and ended up taking them, too, to court. We were delighted to have passed on hiring her.

Pauline's process, in this case, is clearly akin to the processes that candidates must use to assess other candidates successfully. Paying attention to small cues very early on is even more important in matters of love than it is in business: all of us are inclined to see what we want to see when gender and sex become issues.

Here are a few questions that Patty and I suggest you use whenever you find yourself assessing a potential relationship candidate: Does he or she emphasize action, not thought? (Watch what the person actually does.) Does the candidate move slowly and reasonably through the stages of intimacy? Does he or she intuitively understand healthy relationship rituals? What is her or his attitude toward the gender essences? Does her or his language reveal any "battle of the sexes"

assumptions? (oh, women! Or: oh, men!) Are there subtle signs of scorn in the candidate's body language?

If the answers to these are encouraging, you might search more deeply: Are you noticing any signs of issues with power and control?

Does the candidate show signs of isolation, unshared friends, or blank spots in your knowledge of how they spend their time? If the answer to this last question is yes, proceed with a great deal of caution until these blank spots are filled in.

Step 3: Attracting Other Candidates

Energetic Fact of Life #54:
Nearly all humans are conditioned to work on communication and political skills or status or authority as a means of fitting in and getting along with others. This is a misunderstanding of the essential nature of both relationship and power: relationship requires the healthy use of power as a binding force, and power is not about getting what you want, it is about relating to the universe and to other people. Your relationship to power governs your relationship to all things. What you can do: Stop understating or overstating your capacity to promise and fulfill. Also, own your greatest moments, skills, and achievements; tell others about them and listen to others making similar disclosures.

For me, this little section is one of the most interesting in the book, because it reveals something really new about how to attract lovers and how to make choices about the people you are attracted to.

Personal power, particularly the way you relate to it, is like a radio set with various channels. All of us send out and receive attraction signals. The stereotypical mousy housewife, through her powerlessness, is sending a signal. So is the demanding and obnoxious alpha male through his abuse of power. Victims and victimizers find each other across great distances as a result of these signals. So, too, do empowered men and women—they send out signals of their own through the healthy and confident use of power for self-expression. The housewife and the abusive male are not listening to the healthy power channel. Attraction to empowered lovers never happens for them.

The way you relate to human power in the world determines the channels on which you transmit and receive signals. (If you don't make this choice consciously, your subconscious will make it for you and the results might not be pretty. That is what is happening in most people's lives.) The power channel idea of attraction is not to be confused with earlier comments in this book about power concerning promise and fulfillment. This section is not about defining power; it is about explaining the role of power in attraction.

The phrase *relate to power* points to a combination of qualities. It refers to the way a person feels emotionally about his or her power—the mousy housewife is afraid of hers, the abusive alpha male is addicted to his. It also refers to a person's outward stance toward power, how they portray themselves to other people. The term *relate to power* also encompasses a man or woman's degree of aggressiveness in grasping power and ability to deploy it. Finally, it alludes to personal confidence and the willingness to be seen as powerful and to take responsibility for it.

Each person can consciously choose among eight ways of approaching his or her innate power, each of which is the exact equivalent of a two-way radio channel. Each channel allows you to communicate with and attract a different kind of person. These eight power relationship styles, like a list of Citizens

Band radio channels and presented in a progressive hierarchy, are as follows:

1. Powerlessness (has no power at all)
2. Latent power (has potential power that is not yet developed)
3. Power avoided (actively avoids power of any kind)
4. Power tolerated (accepts power in himself or herself and in others but only grudgingly)
5. Power sought/celebrated (seeks power for enjoyment and aggrandizement)
6. Power sought/denied (seeks power passive-aggressively, that is, while appearing to have none)
7. Power mastered/wild (has considerable power but uses it without restraint or compassion)
8. Power mastered/restrained (has even more power but uses it rarely and never for gain)

Each channel gives you access to people who have made the same power relationship choice as you. The following are some basic guidelines:

Anyone can transmit and receive on any of these channels at any time, and you can shift between them at any time. Your choice of channel not only influences the types of people you are attracted to, and who you attract, repel, and become entangled with, it also shapes your attitudes toward yourself and the attitudes of others toward you.

You dial up these channels through paying attention to your attitude toward power as expressed in your choices in daily life and the actions you take. For example, if I happened to observe a man walk into a department store and begin to berate a sales clerk and I decided to intervene, I could make a personal power choice. If I became aggressive myself and attempted to throw the man out of the store, I would be showing a power mastered/wild relationship to power. If a female customer who was inclined to choose wild solutions to ordinary problems was in the store and observed this, she (as a power mastered/wild person) would probably feel attracted to me.

If I were to take a power mastered/restrained approach, I would probably step in, divert the man's attention in a low-key manner, resist cues to escalate, and ease him away from the clerk. A different female witness, one who was herself inclined to power mastered/restrained choices, would probably notice my actions, remember them, and find herself attracted to me.

This concept, which may strike some as a clever gimmick, is in fact one of the most serious ideas presented in this book. Your choices about personal power run your life as much as any other single stance you take. If you are not making these choices consciously, they are being made for you and have become a habit.

The optimum progression in relating to personal power is to find a way to recognize and accept your latent power, which is where most of us start out, and then experiment with power until you can move through power sought/celebrated (which can be a necessary but brief stopover) to power mastered/restrained.

If you have power issues, I would say that it is essential to do whatever it takes to resolve them and to develop a positive attitude toward power, both your own and the personal power of others.

Power is ultimately a language of relationship, not a way to get what you want. People with real power who are genuine candidates for relationship use their power sparingly to reveal themselves to you honestly, and to encourage you to love and expand your own power as a means of self-expression and attaining deep change.

This idea alone is worthy of, and probably requires, an additional Wild Attraction volume of its own.

Another approach to attracting qualified mates is to advertise through your own behavior. Develop grooming and personal habits that telegraph interest, confidence, and consideration for the other gender. Speak and move in ways that communicate consciousness of, and confidence in, your own gender essence, telling others that you relish it. Avoid telegraphing that your gender essence, or that of another person, is a problem to be solved. Don't dilute your primary gender essence with your secondary one. In other words, don't mix your male and female gender essences to suit people who are uncomfortable with male or female power. You can't afford to miss the opportunity of a lifetime as the Rhett Butler or Galadriel of your life walks past, unimpressed.

Another way to advertise is to radiate enjoyment. Practice *enjoying* the opposite gender in others, on an aesthetic level, without any demand. Appreciate them. Avoid generalizing or projecting the behavior of one man or woman onto another. Remain open.

You can help yourself attract nonneedy mates by showing that you understand the dynamics of human need and can see to your own needs and smoothly meet the needs of a lover. This is another form of advertisement. Strip the glitz away and focus on human fundamentals. Human beings question members of the other gender only too rarely about what actually works, what is needed and wanted, and how the world looks from their perspective. Learn what the other gender essence actually craves from those of your own primary gender essence. To the extent that it is real and natural for you, be prepared to offer all of those things to a mate as an act of appreciation rather than as a bargain.

Remember, advertise.

You can let your actions as a relationship candidate become a powerful and attractive statement to the world. Show that you are willing to work at relationship and courtship. Put yourself in active situations, such as personal interest clubs, dance classes, and other co-ed adult activities where you can meet potential mates without the pressure of dating and sex. Size them up over time. Form friendships first. Date and socialize until you have the gut-level realization that you can identify suitable relationship candidates, and that you have the skill to attract a wide variety of potential mates. Being such a person, out in the world, is a form of advertising that an opening exists for another one.

Confidence, confidence, and more confidence. The common view of confidence is that it derives from knowing that you will not fail. But confidence stems from not caring whether you succeed or fail. This approach to confidence works very well in relationship; failure does not reflect badly on those who attempt great things. It is a natural and inevitable stepping-stone toward success. Confidence grounded in this attitude toward failure is almost as great an aphrodisiac as power.

Finally, and simply, silence is not an option, just as inattention is never an option. Never be energetically or physically silent for too long. Instead, be open and communicate freely about yourself in daily life.

Our recommended cheat sheet for attracting another candidate includes the following indispensable qualities to be looked for both in yourself and in your potential mate: He or she emphasizes action, not thought. A good candidate shows power, relates to it well, and does this in locations frequented by other potential candidates. You and the person you are looking for each make a point of practicing whole-person illumination and maintain this stance while dating a number of people on an ongoing basis until the courtship stage is reached.

Step 4: Seducing a Candidate

Energetic Fact of Life #55:
Although current models of relationship would have us believe that it is the male who initiates mating rituals, in fact the female initiates them energetically while her partner remains energetically reserved. The male's job is to pay carefully attention to her subtle energetic and physical cues and to physically enact the actions she suggests. Your course of action: Learn your role, whether male or female, and practice it in appropriate settings and through dating a variety of people, without expecting or promising that a date will lead to anything beyond a pleasant evening. If you practice your skills when you don't need them, they will be there for you when you really do.

There are vast differences between seducing a qualified candidate for extraordinary relationship and seducing someone who is not.

Noncandidates may respond to approaches that telegraph lack of safety (which in the extreme can include threats of abuse or other forms of diminishment) as a means of generating excitement. Candidates will not. Noncandidates respond to seduction techniques that do not require openness or availability on the part of the seducer. Candidates do not.

A noncandidate can be seduced by creating power conflicts and imbalances, skipping stages, and providing trivial triggers for superficial sexual attraction reflexes. Candidates cannot be seduced this way. Candidates can't be dazzled by shape, physical possession, status, fame, or other substitutes for real power.

Passive aggression won't seduce a candidate; she or he can't be conned into providing mercy or guilt sex. Qualified candidates can't be rushed.

The woman's role in seduction is to be energetically aggressive and physically subtle. To attract a person carrying male gender essence she uses the ritual of extending her feminine essence into his energy field and then drawing it back into her own field, bringing the male's attention with it.

A noncandidate can be seduced via this technique at any time. A candidate will respond to it only in a context and stage of relationship where it makes sense.

The man's role is to be energetically reserved and to wait for the woman's energetic cues. In response to her cues he then initiates key physical actions. He does the physical work of approaching her, chatting with her, and exploring possibilities. He takes on more of the physical risk of failure and rejection. He also offers decisiveness and confidence.

Noncandidates will fall for a man who is energetically forward and invades a woman's energetic field, an intrusion that is a deal-breaker even when done under a guise of politeness. No candidate would fall for such an approach.

Our cheat sheet for seducing a potential candidate would highlight the following key qualities in you: You at your seductive best emphasize action, not thought, while revealing in Energy exactly what you would actually do. The James Bond or femme fatale in you shows a ruthless commitment to what works in relationship, while taking intelligent but refreshingly wild risks. The exotic predator in you is creative when it comes to seduction and uses surprise in both large and small ways (and in a wide variety of moments) where others might do only the expected.

Step 5: Binding (or Keeping) a Candidate

A few ideas that were covered earlier in this book are worth restating. You are the person predominantly responsible for your mate's fidelity, and he or she for yours, and you can maintain it through engaging the specific energetic and physical practices that the gender essences demand.

Nature abhors energetic vacuums and will always fill them eventually. The better the job you do loving your mate, the more lovable your mate becomes to others. In simple terms, this means that your task is to leave no energetic or psychological gaps in Energy, no vacuums in your mate's field that another person might energetically fill. Keep your own and your partner's docks full. Stay on duty, and keep playing your role in ongoing rituals. Complacency is probably the most common cause of divorce. Almost every element mentioned in this book should be brought into play over time to help you keep your qualified candidate once you have found and formed a relationship with that person.

You hold your mate's comfort and commitment to you in your hands. If you carry predominantly feminine essence, you are responsible for maintaining the flame of sexuality for and with regard to your male counterpart. Carriers of male gender essence bind their mates through providing deeply committed, constant, and curious attention, in accord with the needs of the feminine gender essence.

Your success as an extraordinary mate can elevate your partner to higher levels of desirability. It is wise to remember the almost infinite field of other, fascinating candidates out in the world, some of whom may be more skilled or more supported by circumstance or other factors than you. You could lose your mate to forces of Wild Attraction that no one can resist.

Knowing this, you can do something that few people even consider. Early in your relationship you can ask, "What do I do, or should I do, that is irresistible to you and makes you content and happy to be with me?" What you hear may surprise you, because this question and its answers are rare in our culture—even though all too often we resent our lovers for not understanding the simple things that would make it impossible for us to leave them. Don't wait for your mate to ask. Ask him or her. And then tell your mate what it takes to keep you.

Another enormously helpful concept as your relationship extends over long periods of time is that of *energetic borders*.

In the middle of anything, for instance a song played on a guitar or a long interstate car trip, the energy associated with that thing tends to slump in the center. A graph of the energy curve of any process actually looks like the support cables of a suspension bridge, drooping in the middle. Marriages are long continuous states or acts. Lacking a clear definition of an ending or any natural fixed borders in the middle of a marriage, the Intent of marriages can be weak, and the available energy in a relationship can decline over time.

But you don't have to suffer from a drop in energy and Intent in the middle of a relationship. Energy gathers at all borders. It appears spontaneously at birth and death, at the beginning of a novel and at the end. It gathers at natural boundaries, such as the new moon and the first day of spring, and at human-made borders such as changes in presidential terms.

The way to keep the energy up in an open-ended process like a marriage or any other long-term relationship, then, is to create interesting and powerful internal borders at which significant things change.

One way to do this is to place a term limit on your marriage. Patty and I, half jokingly, created a one-year marriage with renewable options. Every year we re-decide whether we want to continue. Proposing again is fun. In addition to this annual re-upping, we rotate roles in many areas. We alternate with respect to which of us keeps the financial books, takes out the trash, and pays more attention to the children. We organize extraordinary events from time to time to establish fresh borders. Patty and I invest in remodels of our home or office space or change physical space in less dramatic ways, such as rethinking the use of rooms. Even if the new arrangements are less convenient, they pay off well in terms of keeping the Energy of the relationship from dropping.

These changes are intended as real borders, and we try to take in the Energy made available when they arrive. I am particularly fond of breaking weekly rhythms, such as occasionally inserting an activity on a weekday afternoon or ignoring our end-of-week fatigue and doing something dramatic and strenuous. I may surprise Patty at such a moment with flowers at the door or some other small gesture that she cannot plan for or expect. She will do the same for me. In this way, we create new borders and are able to maintain high Energy in the relationship, even though our love life has no clearly defined ending.

Again, although this idea is presented in only a few paragraphs in this book, they are important paragraphs. Creating energetic borders is an idea that works.

Patty's and my summary sheet for this relationship step is simple: Do every important thing in this book and you will keep your mate, if it is even remotely possible to do so.

As the jetliner at the beginning of this chapter finally turns into its final approach for landing, consider this: One of the most glaring errors an individual can make is to focus on what other people do or don't do while radically underfocusing on his or her own behavior. Becoming a candidate oneself is the first step to extraordinary relationship. The remaining steps—identifying a candidate, attracting a candidate, seducing a candidate, and binding one—are not separate from the first step, they are part of it. They are tasks for the candidate to complete, not merely understand. Some people diligently apply these ideas about candidacy to critiquing the actions of others, totally neglecting what is required of themselves. Obviously, I am suggesting the opposite approach.

The time has come to disembark from the plane and get onto the bike. Having combined the qualifications covered in the steps to candidacy with the relationship stages and power rituals, you have assembled your bicycle built for two and it is ready for you to ride.

At first, learning to ride may be a matter of trial and error, the wonderful feeling of balancing yourself on two rotating wheels and moving forward might elude you. If so, remember the steps to candidacy. They comprise the drive wheel at the back of the bike, the one connected to the pedals. The rituals are the handlebars by which you steer.

Fortunately, once you learn how to ride a two-wheeler, you never forget.

Part V

To Have and Have Not

Chapter 24
Taking Advantage

Energetic Fact of Life #56:
We are trained to fear, resist, and fixate upon external enemies and to see ourselves as our own most faithful and loyal friend. This is an inversion—most people never experience an external enemy that even begins to match the power of the opponent within. Although you may not know it, one of the greatest blessings that you can experience is a single moment of life in which you are not your own worst enemy. Seek such moments by exploring the possibility that you are, or can become, your own greatest advantage. Your best course: Reframe your concept of external advantage and learn instead to seek disadvantage, from which your hidden greatness can arise.

Think of the best thing that could happen to the human race, and imagine it is happening right now. You are present at a moment of "first contact" with a culture immeasurably more advanced than ours. Its representatives are offering you a gift of your choice—one that could be shared with all of humanity. What would be the biggest possible advantage a more advanced civilization could ever confer?

My wish would be that a superior culture would bestow upon each human being the capacity to benefit directly from the experiences of other people. With such a gift, raising children would be an entirely different process. Our children would finally be released from having to repeat their parents' mistakes in order to learn. Our exploration of reality would become exponentially more vivid and far reaching. Such a miraculous endowment would not exempt us from error, but it would free us to make new mistakes, more creative and daring mistakes, in place of the same old ones. Humanity as a group could access new experiences and see and feel things never encountered before.

A few humans walking the Earth today already possess the capability to profit directly from others' experiences. Those with even a drop of this capacity are the people best able to maximize their quality of life. Throughout history, members of this subculture have searched for ways to share their advantage with those who have yet to discover it. Wild Attraction aspires to membership in that movement.

Of all the things I learned from my martial arts mentors over the course of thirty-seven years of training, one of the best was a simple concept called *a secret of the masters*. This is an item commonly found in the bag of tricks of those who are trying to pass along the extraordinary experiences of great people who have walked remarkable paths.

A secret of the masters in fact isn't a secret kept by the masters; it's a secret that nonmasters—everyone but very accomplished adepts—unknowingly conspire to keep from themselves even though the secret is available in broad daylight. Denial plays a large part in this, giving rise to a process of normalization that takes extraordinary insights and converts them into ubiquitous clichés. Secrets of the masters usually sound simple, like platitudes, and usually you have to hear such secrets voiced hundreds of times before you really hear them.

Once revealed in the right way, a secret of the masters seldom makes things easier. Usually, it makes everything far more difficult for a while, because it forces the person who hears it to work differently, and to see differently. This can be an enormous challenge.

You need the equivalent of a secret of the masters if you are to benefit from Wild Attraction. Changing your relationship pattern is in fact tremendously hard. As you put the model presented in this book into practice, you will probably find yourself confronting a huge cultural and familial force.

The secret of the masters interwoven through all the observations in this book is this: *Physical acts cue energetic acts.* A gong should sound as you read this. As you already know, this phrase means: if you want your energy body to move, undertake a physical motion that suggests the energetic one. Simply visualizing an energetic movement and expecting it to occur is foolish and ineffectual; it almost certainly won't.

This apparently simple idea is the flying carpet that can give you reasonably quick access to Wild Attraction benefits that came to me only after a lifetime of intense training and effort.

Physical acts cue energetic acts is the main source of advantage presented in this book, but it's nearly useless unless advantage is understood from a seer's perspective.

In the minds of most people, to learn a secret of the masters is to be handed an advantage from outside ourselves. And an advantage provides us with an edge over all others who seek what we seek.

We learn these twin falsehoods in early childhood. Even in fairy tales, characters search for external advantages, including, notably, poisoned apples, pixie dust, and the sword in the stone. These advantages are, as often as not, ways to prevail over or get ahead of other people. They almost never lead us inward or teach us to mentally stay home inside our own minds and bodies. Rather, the more remarkable the advantage, the farther outside ourselves we are trained to look. In almost every film or book in which the heroine or hero must accomplish some impossible feat, she or he does so because of some extraordinary advantage obtained in an extraordinary way from an extraordinary source.

In children's films and stories this advantage is fanciful and magical, like Dumbo's feather. In fantasy and often in more serious literature it is the artifact, such as the One Ring. It is almost always imbued with an undefined but very nonordinary-ish power.

Location itself is an occasional advantage. The most famous example in the Western world is Superman. He comes from Krypton, with a red sun, and thus is far more powerful than we locals, upon whom a mere yellow orb shines.

The advantage of a seer, from the perspective of nonseers, is that he or she can see certain things that others can't. (Though take note: this is not exactly the way that seers conceive of their advantage.) The seer's or wizard's advantage is widely perceived as deriving from some form of exposure to secret knowledge or, as in the case of Luke Skywalker in *Star Wars*, to flow from something special in the bloodline. The latter kind of advantage is obviously not easily bestowed on others. Most people are thus safely locked out of bloodline advantages that could confer real responsibility or demand extraordinary effort—hence the widespread appeal of the prince or princess, for instance, in entertainment. People can contemplate and enjoy bloodline advantages from the safety and comfort of a theater seat.

In more conventional settings the advantage takes the form of a weapon. This can be the just-invented machine gun in World War I movies or Robin Hood's bow and arrow or the Lone Ranger's silver bullets. It is probably no accident that these and many other examples are blatantly phallic, given the power of adolescent male competitive fantasies and the link in the minds of men and boys between perceived advantage and their own sexual attractiveness.

While there is much crossover, men and women may have inherently different concepts of advantage. Women, whose advantage instincts are probably superior to those of the average man, tend to perceive advantage in relational terms, as in forming alliances, changing personal appearance to facilitate new forms of expression and attractiveness, or increasing communication skills and emotional intelligence. Men tend to perceive advantages in physical terms. Most recently, advancing technology itself has become the key physical advantage: the latest computer, the ultralightweight backpacking tent, the carbon fiber tennis racket, the newest high performance sports car.

In win-lose games, advantages over others often become the deciding factors. But win-lose advantages are not optimal in real life, because life is, in the end, not a zero-sum experience. There is always room at the top, and most of the time we gain and lose together, not at each other's expense.

The concept of external advantage will work against you in the creation of great relationships and extraordinary human beings. It will take you out of yourself, and it can falsely reduce your expectation of the level of personal effort needed to achieve your goals. The point of this chapter is thus to explode the myth that any object or condition outside yourself, or even any idea, can ever be an advantage to you. You have no advantage but yourself.

Consider instead, the possibility that external *disadvantage* has value, and think of the pains I have taken throughout this book to demonstrate that you are at a huge disadvantage in the face of the force of Wild Attraction and in the face of your own culture.

Few aspire to disadvantage, even though human greatness does not depend on advantages, and in fact many of the finest moments in human history have arisen out of terrible disadvantages. Think of a much-beleaguered and desperate George Washington crossing the Delaware with frozen, half-starved, poorly armed troops, or of Captain Cook's notoriously underequipped voyages of discovery. The disadvantages they faced were in fact the crucible for these men's greatest moments.

Great relationships, also, usually arise out of the seedbed of disadvantage. In the book *The Greatest Generation*, Tom Brokaw describes a number of marriages that were formed during World War II under conditions that presumably would yield mostly failure, including extremely rushed courtship, long periods of separation and uncertainty, the alienation and extreme duress of combat, the displacement of populations, and other terrible wartime stresses. These unions, both anecdotally and statistically, proved far more resilient than the marriages of the much more advantaged baby boom generation, with its notoriously high divorce rates.

Yet the huge majority of people persist in searching for advantages. And when it comes to love and sex, the advantages that men and women seem to covet the most take the form of "secrets of success," rather than secrets of the masters. These are two entirely different things.

If you Google "secrets of success" you will be directed to hundreds of titles, among which are: *21 Success Secrets of Self Made Millionaires, 10 Secrets of Success that Make People's Dreams Come True, 10 Secrets for Success and Inner Peace*, not to speak of *The 6 Secrets of a Lasting Relationship* and *100 Simple Secrets of Great Relationships*.

As you have undoubtedly noticed, numbers often accompany the word *secrets* in the titles of modern how-to books. One secret is seldom enough in the world of self-improvement. This is an important distinction: Secrets of success come in clusters, while secrets of the masters arrive, almost always, alone and unadorned. (This is not to say that the contents of "secrets of success" books are unworthy. Some fine works have been published using the device of "the secrets" in the title or structure.)

Secrets are also very much a part of the Wild Attraction model. After all, much of feminine allure is based on the careful presenting of partially revealed "secrets." And men are programmed to try and uncover them.

The problem with the concept of secrets is that, in the minds of many, a secret is regarded as a shortcut. The rules of mass marketing put a premium on secrets, presenting them as free advantages—advantages that don't involve personal work and engagement. Such secrets rarely create better people, although sometimes they do offer a legitimate way to win when winning is essential.

A secret of the masters, on the other hand, is something already in plain sight whose true value is revealed to a lucky few through effort and attention expended over time. A secret of the masters is therefore something you can't buy, and it offers a value that you have to seek and discover yourself.

Value of this kind, when it is revealed, is always the same. It is always you. As stated a moment ago, you are your own best advantage. The only way any external thing becomes a real advantage is when it awakens in you the capacity to comprehend something new about the universe around you and to grasp its mechanics. Moreover, once the advantage is present within you, it can be expressed through the use of almost any external object or skill.

The advantages of greatest value usually require considerable effort along some challenging path. If someone sells you an idea in a book, such as this one, that idea may seem to be an advantage in its own right. But in fact it can, at best, be only a source of advantage. It can benefit you only when it is combined with a serious effort on your part to learn from the experience of others.

The capacity to absorb the lessons of other people's lives is the factor that distinguishes a person who can be wild in ways that work in relationship from someone who cannot. Hence my fanciful request at the beginning of this chapter.

Until the advent of such an intervention, which is not expected anytime soon, humanity as a whole may continue to stumble, especially with regard to relationship. But individual men and women can keep working to uncover clues as to the nature and workings of gender. We can also ponder the expansion of our own minds. We can learn to *learn*, in the sense described in this chapter. We can also learn to *move*, in an expanded, nonordinary meaning of the word. Once these two capacities are united, we have the potential to travel to amazing places together.

Chapter 25
Best Friends

Energetic Fact of Life #57:
The cultural model for engaging spirituality and the nonordinary often involves a diminished, marginalized view of the physical body and the celebration of the imagination and personality. This is yet another inversion. Your energy body and your conscious imagination are barely on speaking terms. In the search for extraordinary relationship your physical body is the most effective conscious conduit to the energy body. Your finest course: Study a serious form of high-level physical motion and learn to move your body in ways that manifest grace, meet a difficult external standard of beauty and form, and require you to transcend your habitual, instinctive ideas of motion. Also, develop a set of movements to function solely as prompts for the motion of your own energy field. Learn to integrate them into your daily actions in ways that seem natural and draw no attention. Use this second layer of motion as much as you can, and then express yourself, interact with others, and reach out to the mystery through your own fluid and magnificent energy field.

Just as everyone, in the face of Wild Attraction, needs an advantage (remembering that advantage is ultimately internal), everyone also needs an ally, a powerful best friend. Your imagination can never be that ally. Although most people assume the contrary, in fact the imagination suffers from an utter lack of traction in energetic space. As has been pointed out, visualizing that you are centering yourself or communicating telepathically is little better than a waste of time. I love and respect the human imagination, and I don't want to see it burdened with uses for which it was evidently not designed. In terms of energetic power, the imagination is like a sleek blue sports car with tires that never touch the pavement; no matter how fast the tires spin, the energetic car never actually moves.

The imagination gains power in the energetic realm exactly the same way that it brings about change in the physical world: through your physical body. The antidote to trying to move your energy body through visualization is to adopt conscious movements of your physical body in ways that are energetically intelligent and suggest the energetic movements you want to make. In fact, this is the only reliable way to mindfully develop conscious influence over the actions of your energy field. *Physical acts cue energetic acts.* And *your physical body is your best ally.*

From the first day of my training as a seer, I was never allowed to visualize or imagine Energy. My trained engagement with Energy was entirely kinesthetic. I was schooled to move my physical body first, until the day I had direct contact with my energy field and could reliably and verifiably move it without attempting to visualize. For example, on day one, in the amazing open office that was my energetic gymnasium for six years (it had no furniture other than bean bag chairs and was surrounded outside by little brooks), the first thing I was ever taught was to create a tangible energy flow from me to my mentor across the room. She described the task. I began to imagine a flow of water rushing outward as though from a water hose.

She shook her head.

"No visualization," she said. "Feel the Energy as an actuality rather than making a picture of it in your head and then moving that picture around."

Many subsequent experiences have proved that she was right, and I am pleased to pass her advice on to you. Gently disregard the images generated in your head space and, instead, feel what is going on around you. Engage Energy directly or not at all. If you can't feel the Energy as though it were a body part, then use your extended hand to express the motion you want until the day you can feel energetic movement without trying to create a mental image.

Only after attaining a certain mastery was I able to seize my nonordinary birthright and live consciously through my energy body without using physical motion. Even today I will, out of love and the memory of my long road, use a motion of my hand or body to prompt some energetic expression, even though it is no longer needed.

My reverence for physical motion is deep, and my fervor in advocating it is correspondingly intense. Many of the most adept and healthy energy-oriented people I know are also extremely dedicated physical-body people.

I invite you to return to my energetic training gym. Imagine yourself as split into four parts, represented by four people standing in a tight square in the middle of the room, close enough to reach out and touch one another. These four people represent four aspects of your nature, and we will name them Conscious Mind, Subconscious Mind, Physical Body, and Energy Body.

These are really two teams, one composed of Physical Body and Conscious Mind and the other team made up of Energy Body and Subconscious Mind.

As they are arranged on the training floor, Conscious Mind is standing immediately behind Physical Body, and Subconscious Mind is standing directly in back of Energy Body. The two pairs are side by side, all eyes forward.

In this training example, Physical Body will do whatever, within reason, Conscious Mind asks. If Conscious Mind says "Kiss the girl," the girl will get kissed. Similarly, Energy Body will perform any motion conceived by Subconscious Mind. If Subconscious Mind says "Caress that woman's behind," the behind will be caressed with a wisp of Energy.

Even though all four are bound together in a single system, Conscious Mind and Subconscious Mind, being bound in separate teams, can't talk to each other and don't really know each other. They can't coordinate their senses or their motions. This is the normal human condition.

On the other hand, Physical Body and Energy Body, even though they are on separate teams, happen to be best friends. If asked politely, each will do exactly what the other does. They can communicate directly, in contrast to Conscious and Subconscious Mind.

A woman accepting a gift from a man she admires can use this principle to subtly convey her interest in him. She makes a small, simultaneous gesture with her left hand to cue her field to energetically support her right hand as it picks up the offered gift. When the physical and energetic bodies receive the present together, the giver feels far more admired and appreciated than when the acceptance is merely physical.

An accumulation of "both-body" signals of this kind can build up tremendous charge between a man and woman.

Let's say that your life depends on being able to consciously bring about a coordinated movement of Physical Body and Energy Body. How would you solve this problem?

The answer is simple. You, in the role of Conscious Mind, can use your imagination to ask Energy Body and Physical Body to link together and move as one. Note that this is not the same as moving an imaginary replica of your energy body inside your head and thinking you are moving the real thing. Linking the physical and energetic bodies together is one of the few powerful uses of the imagination in Wild Attraction. Once they are linked, any motion of your physical form will move both of them as a single unit.

You can experiment with this easily. In your mind's eye, visualize a blackboard. On that blackboard someone has scrawled a stick-figure drawing of your physical body. Beside it is another simple drawing, an egg-shaped circle representing your energy body, or energy field. With an imaginary hand and an imaginary piece of chalk, inscribe a large circle on the blackboard that encompasses the two drawings. Inside that circle write the words "Please act as one." This or any similar imaginary action is all that is needed. The imagination is perfectly adapted for this function. People unknowingly do this many times a day. Don't work hard at it; do it as casually as possible.

Within the blink of an eye, a link is established. After this imagined suggestion, every move that Conscious Mind makes is imitated immediately by Physical Body and mimicked almost simultaneously by Energy Body. These figures in the training space stand there moving in synch with each other—hands over mouths, hands on hips, hands waving, sticking out tongues.

Your unified aspects are capable of doing sophisticated things in this state. They play guitar, they drive racecars, and they make love. Acting together, they generate great power, great enough to change your life. This kind of motion makes for extremely profound sexual experience.

It is well within the power of any novice to link the physical and energy bodies together simply by voicing the request inside his or her head. Once this is done, that novice, or you, only has to learn the principles of energetic behavior and Wild Attraction and use physical motion to set about making any relationship more functional, or more extraordinary.

If you want to reach across the room to someone with Energy, you can simply stretch out to them in a casually disguised gesture with your hand. If you say something loving or sexy and want to transmit that same message in Energy, you can direct that Energy to them with an understated gesture of your arm. If you want to block unfriendly Energy you can hold up an outstretched palm.

All the physical cues to direct your energy body and its behaviors can be disguised as expressive gestures that almost never draw a comment.

During talks on Wild Attraction, I frequently explain simple energetic techniques such as *centering* and *grounding* and then ask the audience members to line up and practice them. Two things always happen: Everyone closes their eyes and concentrates in order to visualize, and everyone becomes as motionless as statues.

In short, people who are trying to influence their own Energy turn instinctively to their imaginations. Even if the group consists of a hundred people, I never see change in a single energy field as they first give this a try.

After the first attempt, I show them how to assess the extent to which they are centered and grounded by pressing the palm of one hand against the palm of a neighbor. Then I ask them to keep their eyes open, relax their minds, and center themselves again, this time linking it with the inward physical motion of their chest on each exhale, without thinking about the process at all.

Then, as they ground themselves, I ask them to grab the floor with their toes and heels, much as a cat would claw the fabric of a sofa, and to drop their tailbones about a half-inch downward, toward the center of the Earth. Usually, this is just a matter of softening the knees.

Within a few seconds, the entire group has performed an energetic adjustment at near mastery level; every one of them is almost as centered and grounded as an experienced adept.

Next, they assess the degree to which they are centered and grounded using the same exercise as before. This time they feel connected, resourced, and powerful in a way that is directly experienced and undeniable.

This is always a persuasive demonstration.

Even so, this idea needs to be repeated again and again in future meetings with the same group. The insight about the uselessness of visualization tends to slip away, and the old reliance on imagination resumes its dominance. Although this is a surprisingly difficult issue, the long-term success rate for people who have cultivated a physical approach to relationship energetics is high. You, too, can overcome the problem of "imagination addiction" by revisiting the issue periodically.

The advantage this book offers for exploring extraordinary relationship, *physical acts cue energetic acts*, functions best when it is paired with its nonidentical twin: *your physical body is your best ally*. Like the physical and energetic bodies—or, for that matter, like a man and a woman—the two together are exponentially more powerful than either one acting alone.

CHAPTER 26

Use It: A Call to Action

Energetic Fact of Life #58:
The widespread perception of relationship as a context for self-discovery and a crucible within which to work out our "stuff" is wildly off the mark. In fact, relationship is not meant as a place to struggle, work hard, find ourselves, or face our problems. Extraordinary relationship, despite the fact that it involves doing what actually works, is almost effortless. Discovering what works is a spiritual path. Your best approach: Watch for the voice in your head telling you that love requires you to work hard and that it is normal to suffer for love. When you hear it, ask yourself if you really believe this. Then, crucially, make sure that you yourself work, that you find a partner who works, and that neither of you normalizes to behaviors that cause relationship pain. This is the key to effortless love.

You have now been given a tour of fifty-eight instances in which modern culture promotes assumptions about male-female love that are the opposite of what actually works in an energetically literate relationship. In addition to these fifty-eight, which have been singled out as Energetic Facts of Life, over a hundred more such societal inversions have been presented and turned right side up within this text.

The audacious suggestion being made here is that ninety-six billion humans over a period of eleven million years have remained almost completely in the dark about the single most obsessively examined and universally shared of all primate experiences, sex. With exceptions that are mainly the province of Eastern thought, all of human culture is portrayed in these pages as having failed to see the true purpose of gender and failed also to divine its mechanics. Many people might intuitively respond that such could not possibly be the case.

But a quick look through a medical text from the seventeenth century would show that being wrong about anatomy and sexuality, among other things, has actually been the norm. Prior to the advent of microscopy, and later, advanced imaging systems such as X-ray and MRI technology, prevailing functional models of the human body's internal organs were as topsy-turvy as our culture's present model of love. For example, over a span of centuries experts believed that the seat of consciousness was the heart, not the brain. Human health was linked to four humors, which led to the widespread and often fatal practice of bloodletting. The fact that blood actually circulates in the body was not discovered until the sixteenth century. As for misunderstandings about human sexuality, in *The Technology of Orgasm* Rachel P. Maines discusses the centuries-old concept of female hysteria, an ailment once thought to afflict a large percentage of women. The cure for this perceived illness was the practice, by doctors, of manually massaging women to orgasm, a treatment that was apparently time-consuming and thus often delegated to midwives. Belief in hysteria as a disease can be traced back to the time of Hippocrates. It fit neatly into the four humors theory of health prevalent in the Middle Ages, and remained widely accepted until early in the twentieth century.

Anyone reading a four-hundred-year-old medical text might marvel at the anatomical ignorance of our forebears, but their ignorance was inevitable considering the primitive vision-enhancing technology that prevailed until the last few decades. They had only their unaided physical senses with which to observe the universe.

In the modern era, humans make stunningly powerful inferences into the nature of all things. But we do this only because of great leaps and precious visionary insights on the part of our ancestors, insights that were anything but obvious at the times they occurred. This is an important yet much overlooked aspect of our past. Those who came before us accomplished a great deal with few tools. Lacking advantages, they frequently operated at their communities' outer edge of human understanding, skill, and level of tool sophistication.

In 1976 I was fortunate to tour an exhibit of artifacts from the tomb of King Tut in the company of an ideal companion for this adventure—one of the most remarkable people I have ever known. He was a world-class martial arts master, a gifted and knowledgeable jeweler and goldsmith, and a brilliant artist. The items that touched our amazed eyes were striking in their male or female genderness, capturing and preserving the essence of a profound love between a young king and his now long-vanished girl queen. This obvious, deeply mated quality was so strongly present in their everyday possessions that I almost expected the man and woman to step into the room hand in hand. While examining a jade comb I found it effortless to visualize the queen tending to her lover's hair. It was impossible not to imagine the king placing a simple but stunning lapis lazuli necklace tenderly around his bride's graceful neck.

As my friend and I stepped from artifact to incredible artifact, he provided an ongoing evaluation of the methods that might have been used in the making of each one. Time and again he admitted with admiration that the skills necessary to produce a given object no longer exist in the world. Standing only a few feet away from the famous gold death mask of Tut, my companion explained that no one alive today could reproduce that artifact using the materials and technology that had been available when they were created, over thirty-three hundred years ago.

I recall being shocked to hear this, because his perspective contrasted so starkly with my assumptions about progress and advantage. It was my first exposure to the seer's concept of disempowerment, by which is meant the loss of the power within an individual to fulfill his or her full promise within each moment. The men and women who lived before us may have possessed far fewer technical resources, but this lack of resource was hugely empowering to at least some of them. Pointing at various features of the luminous golden and blue mask, my friend showed me how the Egyptians had been able to shape complex, symmetrical curves by hand, using primitive tools, without the higher mathematics or computer-controlled machinery that we rely on today.

Today, more than thirty years after that museum visit, I have come to feel that the issue of empowerment and disempowerment extends to every aspect of human endeavor, and that male-female love is our bellwether, our canary in the cave. When we lose empowerment in love, we are on the verge of losing it in all things.

What does it mean to lose empowerment? Since the presence of empowerment is normally invisible and unremarked, much like water to a fish, a drop in level can go unnoticed. But as empowerment diminishes, individual self-confidence diminishes also, as does the ability to stand up to authority, and the capacity to withstand pain or loss and still move forward.

Loss of empowerment is going on today because the average man or woman is increasingly unable to imagine what his or her tools make it possible to achieve. As a result we are shrinking as the ceiling defining our present capacity expands ever outward. In Frankensteinian fashion, the tools we created in the hope of finding a better life are turning on us. This movement is not happening overtly, as Mary Shelly envisioned in her masterpiece, but subtly.

I have used the words *empowerment*, *skill*, and *greatness* throughout this book in ways that have probably made them seem interchangeable. But they are not. Empowerment is a precursor to the development of skill. Advanced skill, combined with attention and effort, can lead to excellence, transformation, and eventually to greatness. An aware man or woman is someone who senses this movement and flows with it. Great relationship is thus both a means and an end within this spiral. Great human beings produce extraordinary relationship, and these relationships produce ever-greater humans. This book advocates greatness as almost a new human norm.

Greatness is that which irresistibly attracts the attention of loving, superior sentience. The presence of advanced attention is the only thing that really changes us, and the benefits of receiving it are always extraordinary. The best thing you can do for your children or your mate is to develop your capacity for extraordinary attention and lavish them with it.

No headline has yet been published, as far as I know, trumpeting the impending death of personal greatness. But sometimes the old and the experienced among us are willing to testify that individual greatness is in decline. I attended a talk given by a friend who lived through World War II in Denmark. He described the Nazi occupation and the heroism of the Danish king and many Danish people. During the discussion, a European woman in her eighties who had immigrated to America in the postwar period stood up and soberly declared that if the United States had to fight that same war today, we would lose. She asserted that people no longer have the spirit, capacity, or intent that seemed sewn into the fabric of society during the 1940s. Something nameless but important has been lost, she said, and along with it a basic respect for femininity. Profound courtesy once prevailed even amid widespread misogyny. Its loss was both important and disturbing. The other senior citizens in the room nodded quietly.

Part of the call to action embedded in this book is that you consider reframing your sex life in grand terms and put yourself right out there among those who are exploring greatness in the face of advanced technology as a new frontier of human experience and capacity. You are being asked to perceive your love life as a vital part of our large-scale struggle to survive and advance as a species. You are being offered the chance to express human experience at an entirely new level of beauty. You can do this by joining up with something that you may not be able to see but which you can safely accept as a hypothetical force that wants to change your life through gender's amazing attractive power.

This new perspective on sex and love, as a form of alliance, is free of any invitation to frame negative judgments about yourself or anyone else. If we as a species have not as yet discerned some vital principles of human sexuality after eleven million years, perhaps it is only because this task is monumentally difficult and we have lacked the collective senses that would have helped us to do any better than we have done up to now. To preserve a perspective, consider how much progress has been made in recent history in terms of the psychological and physiological aspects of love and sex. One example is the groundbreaking work of Masters and Johnson, who named and overturned their share of culturally inverted principles of relationship. Great minds are making revolutionary advances in our understanding of love and sex and thereby contributing enormously to our empowerment. Even though this has not been enough, it is a good start.

The "head over heels" condition that characterizes our culture's approach to love, despite the work of these and other brilliant human beings, probably has its roots in one of the deepest recesses of the collective human psyche. If you walk out far enough along the path of gender love, and if you include its intrinsic nonordinary aspects, you will eventually pass through an invisible, unsuspected portal. You will cease to be what you are and become something you are probably incapable of imagining prior to that transformation.

Passing through that portal is not a step-by-step process of growing and learning. You as you exist up to the point of change will be erased from the dark surface of the cosmic blackboard. A new, perhaps much vaster, you will be sketched in. This transformed you will see life in wildly new terms, will perhaps not identify with any concept of self at all, and will in all likelihood be on more intimate terms with Mysterium Tremendum.

No stranger looking at the new person who is suddenly standing in your shoes would be able to work backward, read through a batch of psychological profiles, and figure out which of a set of previously present human beings was the old you. Nor would any such observer be able to trace the intermediate steps between the old and the new.

The fact that change on this scale can happen, and that humans have within their grasp a set of actions that can tilt the odds in favor of such a change, is the buried treasure of Wild Attraction.

But radical change is a messy business. If this type of change ever happens to you, you might discover in its aftermath that everything you had previously taken to be bedrock has turned to mush. Your core assumptions, your choices of friends, your enjoyment of your job, your love of the place you live—all these and much more could be wiped away. The change that extraordinary relationship might bring could drain the chemistry out of almost every element of your prior life, even, at an extreme but conceivable edge, out of the extraordinary relationship itself.

Incredible risk and adaptive effort accompany real change. For this reason, almost all socialized human thought is dedicated to managing, limiting, preventing, or carefully controlling change, and our personalities are little more than machines designed to avoid it. (This is why your personality alone can never be allowed to choose your lover. Your core nature must have the deciding vote.)

The impulse to dodge change has been with humans for a long time. It runs deeper than the urge to reproduce and deeper, even, than the drive to survive. A great many people have chosen to die rather than open themselves to real change. How, then, can it be a surprise that the human mind will still huddle, as though in the glow of an ancient campfire, clinging to false assurances that the wild force of gender can be tamed or held at bay?

Change aversion is probably the most compelling explanation for the cultural inversions of the real facts of life—what really works when it comes to relationship—that I constantly observe. From this perspective, it is no mystery that every important tenet of energetically aware love has been systematically overturned in our culture. Denial would have it so.

Just as scientific insight grows, human advances in the capacity for healthy, functional perception of expanded reality can also leap forward. What was once denied by science or relegated to the worlds of religion or the supernatural does not have to remain so. Astonishing capacities for nonordinary experience arise in individuals from time to time, allowing various perceptual barriers to be pierced and new understandings to flow into our daily lives from somewhere outside the standard paradigms. The call to greatness presented in this book has arisen directly as a result of one such unusual series of events. Something ultimately inexplicable is happening to me, and to Patty. We have mapped the process through which this particular extraordinary relationship has come about, with the thought that others who are drawn in this direction might be able to experience at least some of it for themselves. The wave we caught is already carrying other people to unique vantage points.

One way for your subconscious mind to position you to miss this wave and block the benefits of exposure to the Wild Attraction model (or any other revolutionary idea) is to arrange for an inner voice to speak up and say, accurately enough: *There is no proof.* The mental act of focusing exclusively on the issue of truth or falsehood is a way to divert yourself from making decisive changes in your behavior that could improve your relationship or even save your life.

If you wait to act until a majority of people agrees on the certainty of any radical discovery, your stance is no different than the position of the Bush administration on the subject of global warming.

We live in the world of sophisticated body scanners, and we have achieved consensus on the existence of germs and gorillas. But widespread nonordinary perception at high levels of functional acuity is probably not going to arise anytime soon. Consequently, we as a race are not going to be able to sit down together, gaze at the mechanics I report here, and debate meaningfully about our mutual nonordinary experiences and interpretations. You as an individual may not have an energetic seer's constant daily reminders that physically invisible forces exist and can powerfully affect you.

To name the lack of these daily reminders in the lives of most people (like the act of listing the many obstacles to relationship) is to risk provoking negative feelings. But these disclosures are offered with positive intent. They are signposts revealing a path to extraordinary relationship, and not with the intent to discourage or disparage. In that spirit, Wild Attraction ends with a description of one last, particularly well-hidden relationship tar pit.

The easiest way to dodge the change bullet is simply and nondramatically to forget those key points that would affect you the most. Even if you have felt open and excited while reading this book, chances are that you have been subconsciously screening for the specific elements in this model that would deeply change your life. It is likely that these have been earmarked to be wiped from memory or otherwise set aside. The things you consciously found most interesting in these pages—which will be the easiest to remember—are probably the ones you don't need because they are not the ones that could further awaken you.

To at least partially overcome the denial that lies at the root of this forgetting, you can reread the Energetic Facts of Life scattered through this book from time to time and thus have them in mind when you are out in the world and under the pressure of Wild Attraction. You can also make an effort to remember the gorilla, and the cocktail party that featured you as an observing eye up on the ceiling, the prototypical lecture, Galadriel, and the bicycle built for two, with its spinning front wheel of relationship stages and its rear wheel of rotating elements of candidacy, both spiraling over and over as you pedal forward toward change.

Energetic Fact of Life #59:
Although humans purport to seek what will change them, and society pretends to encourage change, in fact nearly everyone finds and makes the life choices that are guaranteed not to change them. Extraordinary relationship is perhaps the most powerful transformative vehicle to come within the grasp of most people over their lifetime. Part of your task, if you wish to invert the social norms and do what actually works in love, is to overcome what may be a deeply buried driver for choosing safe nonchange. One way to do this is to stop seeking more and more choice in daily life, and to look instead for situations in which you have no choice but to do and to be changed. Your best response: As you put the basic Wild Attraction model into practice, ask yourself if the element you are choosing to leave out, skip over, repress, or dismiss, thinking it is not applicable, interesting, or necessary, might actually be the very ingredient that would catalyze real change in you, in your life, and in your world.

Having now read this book, you no longer lack access to basic information about the Energy and Intent that underlie gender dynamics. You now possess a different level of understanding about gender relationship than the vast majority of human beings on the planet. For everyone else, ignorance of an energetic view of love remains an excuse for ill-advised relationship behaviors, relationship mediocrity, and the squandering of one of the greatest gifts that humans as a group have yet been offered. It also remains a palliative for those with relatively healthy relationship patterns, who, thinking they have achieved all they could ask for, are not pushing the boundary further.

But you no longer have that excuse. You have, in effect, pressed your fingers into a Chinese finger trap from which there is no escape. The choice between relative sexual barbarity and extraordinary relationship has become a conscious one. From now on, if you are ever unhappy at love for an extended period, it will partially be a result of your own deliberate decisions.

On the other hand, if you find yourself in a relationship that surpasses any prior expectation, it may well have come to pass because your selection process relating to sex and attraction is daring and intelligent and you have chosen wisely.

You will have become wild in ways that work.

Afterword
by Patricia Richards

This is no ordinary book. It exists as a result of powerful nonordinary events. *Wild Attraction* points back, over and over, to a special time and place at which Paul and I stumbled into what could be among the most profound voyages of love that any human has ever experienced.

Wild Attraction is therefore a deeply personal story, one that has always been difficult to disclose. I feel that it has to be told, no matter how inconvenient it may be for some—or how unbelievable. The personal history revealed in this book highlights important human possibilities and inherent capacities that are too real to be denied or left unshared.

In 1993, my well-planned professional medical career and personal life were turned on end when Paul and I discovered that we shared the capacity to simultaneously experience prolonged out-of-body merging as well as mutual energetic travel and communication. These did not occur only when we were asleep and dreaming. They occurred volitionally, while wide awake and across town from one another, and even across the country from each other. We found we could repeat these coupled visits to completely nonordinary and unsurpassingly beautiful etheric environments at will, over and over again. It was astounding and awe inspiring. These visits, which continued for years and which recur to this day, remain by far the most deeply moving experiences of my life.

The indescribable grandeur of experiencing another person at this level is beyond any verbal description—the poet Rumi provides the only body of work I have seen that comes close to capturing it. The energy body is sensual, graceful, and beautiful. Deep telepathy from essence to essence occurs, time and space are fluid, and lovers experience the wonder of "two souls dancing" without gravity or effort. The touch and transmission of experience from one energy body to another is exquisite. Having been there, I can never see life or love or humans as ordinary again.

Within this grandeur, Paul and I had to work out a way to live together in "normal" reality while navigating our now constant sense of nonordinary openness and loving energetic connection. Our life together became unimaginable from within an ordinary framework—there were certainly no models or helpful tips for energetic merging in daily life. How was I to live with ongoing mutual telepathic communication that no longer allowed for being emotionally hidden? I learned that I simply had to let go. The resulting relaxation and joy of deep cherishment became and remains a profound treasure. Sexuality became startling and seemingly galactic in scale. Two humans with four bodies create nuance and beauty and sensation I had never imagined or dreamed was possible. Within it, a new sense of personal power emerged as I confronted both a calm, centered sense of singularity as a sentient being and a deep union with my lover and with all things.

Almost two decades later, Paul and I are at this moment finishing *Wild Attraction*. The manuscript goes to print in just a few hours, and I write these words with a strong sense that I may have no more important gift to offer to others than the keys contained within it.

As you close the covers of this book and begin the process of awakening the nonordinary lover in you, I offer a parting testimony: The experiences Paul has given voice to in this book are real. He lives the model he has outlined here, as do I. It works, beyond anyone's wildest dreams. I also offer a suggestion: If fantastic relationship happens to be your heart's desire, consider giving your full attention to the methods we have shared in these pages.

Attention can be put to no better use.

Acknowledgments

The fact that this book exists is remarkable. *Wild Attraction* was written in sixty-four grueling days and was edited and otherwise prepared for publication in a similar, very compressed span of time. It was all the time available: Patty and I realized that *Wild Attraction* would only come into the world as the result of an accelerated gestation, a brief and very intense labor, and a rushed delivery. And so it did.

The production of this healthy and happy book could not have happened without an astonishing and intrepid effort from my coauthor, Patty, whose insight and determination, and boundless enthusiasm for the subject, fueled our effort from the beginning. Her tireless advocacy for the reader amazed me, and her instinct for what works in an introductory Wild Attraction experience for newcomers became the spirit that suffuses this work. She has lived what we wrote, and her vast experience as a teacher of extraordinary relationship animates every page.

Our editor, Carolyn Bond, stepped into the fire of this challenging project and demonstrated amazing insight, determination, scholarly depth, and remarkable compassion as we all flew through a task that would have been a labor of love had it been undertaken at leisure, but was an endurance test and a daily challenge to our perspective because of the pace at which we worked. Carolyn challenged us in the most inspiring ways, she gave of herself far above and beyond what could ever have been expected, and she showed real greatness throughout the project. I have worked with many editors and she is by far the best in my experience. Any shortcomings in the book originated with me and only survived into the final draft because our team reached the limits of the available time.

The breathless pace of this project turned out to be a blessing because I was gifted to see many amazing new qualities in Patty and Carolyn. Brilliance, determination, creative vision, and tradecraft—these and more were showered on me by my two teammates.

To both of them I am extremely grateful.

Paul Richards
September 18, 2008

Other Wild Attraction Products and Services from the Senté Center

*I*f you enjoyed this book and would like to delve more deeply into the Wild Attraction world, you can order these and other audio products:

Wild Attraction: Unleashed

A two-CD set (or downloadable audio file) with a running time of 134 minutes

A lecture by Paul and Patty Richards, delivered in the period immediately after the creation of the book *Wild Attraction: The Energetic Facts of Life*

In this amazing lecture, Patty asks Paul to take off the gloves and deliver an unvarnished view of relationship in the Western world. She prods him to reveal personal truths about a seer's ideal of intimacy, his thoughts on the development of the Wild Attraction world, and what he would say candidly to anyone who has read the book and wants to move as far as possible toward extraordinary relationship. Patty's insightful and sometimes playfully provocative questions prompt one of the most remarkable lectures in the seventeen-year history of the Senté Center. This is a must-have for all who have read the book and emerged inspired and curious to know more.

> ### *Wild Attraction: Understanding the Hidden Energetic Attraction Forces that Powerfully Shape Your Love Life*
>
> *A two-CD set and booklet (or downloadable audio file) with a running time of 94 minutes*
>
> In this compelling original interview, the seer's view that humans inhabit a second body composed entirely of Energy, and that gender and intimacy are shaped as much by elements of Energy as by physical genetics, is examined in depth.
>
> *Paul and Patty Richards explore:*
>
> ❂ Practical methods for escaping the trap of psychologically based attraction and for identifying and building connection with truly suitable matches
>
> ❂ The very different needs, drives, and languages of the male and female gender essences, with details about their roles in mating and relationship
>
> ❂ The importance of expressing love, safety, regret, and sympathy between lovers
>
> ❂ Simple techniques that can be practiced daily in order to keep intimacy vibrant and alive over time

To order these products, or to enroll in Wild Attraction seminars or online webinars, go to: www.wildattraction.net or email: wildattraction@sentecenter.com.

Finally, check for the flagship Senté Center introductory product:

Through the Eyes of a Seer: Reawakening Personal Power in a World of Lost Vision

Through the Eyes of a Seer is a stunningly produced 12-hour audio course that vividly recreates the ethics and beauty of the seer's world. The presentation of this original worldview is interwoven with easy-to-follow, step-by-step labs and exercises designed to empower you and expand your capacity to understand your own perception.

This unique view of personal empowerment will continually surprise, challenge, and delight you. The program offers a distillation of material refined and proved during fifteen years of teaching energetics and intent by seers Paul and Patty Richards. The simple but astonishing new skills it offers, once integrated into your daily life, will leave you wondering how any person could move successfully in today's world without them. The course is a life-changing resource for those who would like to blend a professional, educated mindset with an intelligent and rigorous exploration of nonordinary Energy and Intent.

Through the Eyes of a Seer is available as a deliverable 11-CD set with a printed guidebook or as downloadable audio files plus a 72-page course guidebook.

These and other products and services, including online webinars, are available through the Senté Center, Inc. Email us at sente@sentecenter.com or visit our website at www.sentecenter.com.

Alternatively, send an inquiry by mail to:
> The Senté Center, Inc.
> P.O. Box 3308
> Ashland, OR 97520

There is no such thing as an ordinary human being.

Chelsion Press, the publishing arm of The Senté Center, Incorporated, is devoted to preserving and disseminating the work of authors and lecturers who are pioneers in the applied nonordinary sciences—people working to create ever more extraordinary human beings and advocating a new standard of attainable personal greatness in daily life. Chelsion Press encourages the development of new forms of advanced consciousness through increased understanding of Energy, attention, and Intent. We offer a wide variety of thoughtfully chosen titles, products, and services.

Please contact Chelsion Press via the worldwide web at www.chelsionpress.com or by email at chelsionpress@sente-center.com.